Seymour Dexter

Treatise on Co-Operative Savings and Loan Associations

Including building and loan associations, mutual savings and loan associations,

accumulating fund associations, co-operative banks etc.. With appendix containing

laws, precedents and forms

Seymour Dexter

Treatise on Co-Operative Savings and Loan Associations
Including building and loan associations, mutual savings and loan associations, accumulating fund associations, co-operative banks etc.. With appendix containing laws, precedents and forms

ISBN/EAN: 9783337312077

Printed in Europe, USA, Canada, Australia, Japan

Cover: Foto ©Suzi / pixelio.de

More available books at **www.hansebooks.com**

A TREATISE ON
CO-OPERATIVE SAVINGS AND
LOAN ASSOCIATIONS

INCLUDING
BUILDING AND LOAN ASSOCIATIONS
MUTUAL SAVINGS AND LOAN ASSOCIATIONS
ACCUMULATING FUND ASSOCIATIONS
CO-OPERATIVE BANKS, ETC.

*WITH APPENDIX CONTAINING LAWS, PRECEDENTS,
AND FORMS.*

BY
SEYMOUR DEXTER

NEW YORK
D. APPLETON AND COMPANY
1889

PREFACE.

No form of direct co-operation among men of limited means is attracting more attention at the present time than the class of associations which we have grouped under the name of Co-operative Savings and Loan Associations.

Professor F. B. Sanborn, Secretary of the American Social Science Association, at its annual meeting at Saratoga in September, 1888, in a report— the most complete ever made in this country relating to them—said very truthfully that " at the rate the building associations are now gaining, the time may come when their accumulated savings at any one time may exceed those of our saving-banks, and it is doubtful if any system of savings has been devised which has such a tendency to produce frugality among persons of small incomes as the building-association methods."

Their business methods have been little understood in the past outside of those engaged in conducting them.

From Philadelphia, as their "breeding-place," they have spread throughout the country, chiefly through the agency of persons, who, being interested in an association in one locality, have migrated to another and become the moving spirit and authority in organizing one where they were unknown before, each association becoming a new center from which knowledge concerning them has radiated to other localities.

In this manner faulty methods were copied and transmitted from one place to another as readily as good ones, and it has often occurred that the organizers of the new association but imperfectly comprehended the scheme which they were attempting to put into operation, and unwittingly modified it, while in other cases changes were made to secure some benefit to those managing it which the original plan did not contemplate. The legislation in nearly all the States has been crude and general in its provisions, thereby permitting speculative features to be added to the beneficial methods, by visionary men, as well as by those who were seeking solely their own advantage.

Information concerning these associations in books or current literature has not only been meager and fragmentary, but quite inaccessible to those wishing to learn their manner of conducting business, or to investigate the benefits accruing therefrom.

From these causes a great diversity in their methods has come to pass in different parts of the country, and many variations in the details of the same general method in the same locality. As found at the present time, they are a natural development in direct co-operation which has come to pass with but little guidance or supervision by the State. While the history of such development must record many failures, when considered as a whole they have been more uniformly successful and attained better economic results for those interested than any other form of direct co-operation undertaken in this country, and are now attracting widespread attention as "institutions for savings," their friends claiming for them advantages which the savings-bank does not possess.

Our aims in the preparation of this book have been—

1. To fill an apparent demand for information relating to this form of co-operation, and to place such information in a form accessible to all desiring it.

2. To explain the principles upon which the typical association is founded in such a manner that the reader who is seeking general information on the subject may readily understand.

3. To describe the important variations from the typical association now in operation, tracing their development and the causes which have induced them, and discussing briefly their respective merits.

4. To furnish a complete guide to all persons wishing to organize and conduct them upon methods that are safe, equitable, and uniformly successful when adhered to.

5. To correct certain false notions which are often entertained by those conducting these associations relating to the subject of premiums, and the benefits accruing to the borrowers therefrom, by reason of dividends added to the shares of stock upon which they have borrowed.

6. To print, in a convenient form for examination, the best statutes in this country authorizing their formation, and to recommend to those interested in legislation relating to these associations the New York act of 1887 and the laws of Massachusetts.

We are earnestly desirous of encouraging the growth of this form of co-operation upon simple, safe, and equitable methods, believing that when so conducted these associations are the most potent agency for stimulating steady savings, industry, home-owning, and good citizenship, yet devised and put into operation.

CONTENTS.

CO-OPERATIVE SAVINGS
AND LOAN ASSOCIATIONS.

CHAPTER I.

CO-OPERATION, INDIRECT AND DIRECT.

THE word co-operation is a generic term. There are many species of co-operation, and each species has many varieties. Some are direct, and others are indirect.

The earliest and most universal form of co-operation is government. This is one species. It has many varieties, and the greater number have been conducted in the interest of special classes. Reigning classes have considered the masses of the people unfit to have a voice in the control of the government, as fit only to be subjects, whose highest duty was to obey. They were zealously taught the "divine right of kings" to rule. With the reigning class there was a direct co-operation in government; with the masses only an indirect. While the latter loyally obeyed the laws and submitted to the commands of their rulers order and stability prevailed. Comparative security from foreign enemies and from personal violence within was thereby obtained. The preservation of the family and the possibility of peaceful living were better than anarchy, where none were safe from rapine and personal violence, where every man must stand guard over his own person, family, and property.

The struggles, the conflicts, and the failures have been manifold in the endeavors, by the masses, to secure a government which should be conducted for all classes alike. It is the pride of our country that direct governmental co-operation has been attained, a government by the people and for the people. The fame of its liberties has indeed encircled the globe. No more sacred duty calls upon us than to discharge to the best of our ability the obligations of our citizenship. Whoever proves himself unworthy of membership in this grand co-operation is unfit to become a member of any other direct co-operation. The American citizen that will sell his vote or betray a public trust, or seek to induce another to do so, deserves only to obey the mandates of a kingly power.

Religious organizations constitute another species of co-operation. With us, these organizations have no power of compulsion; they are voluntary. There is direct co-operation of all who unite to secure the ends for which the organizations exist. Divorced from the state, they stand upon their own merits. The good they accomplish is measured by the individual worthiness of their members. The church-member who proves himself unworthy to be a member in the direct co-operation of the church, proves himself unworthy to be a member of any other direct co-operation, the objects and aims of which are worthy.

Another species of co-operation has for its aim social enjoyment. The normal man hates solitude; he loves the society of his fellows, whether at work or play. The forms of direct co-operation for social enjoyment are various. Some are beneficent, others pernicious. Some lift men and women into higher planes of thought, arouse noble aspirations, and stir only pure desires; while in others, each helps to hurl down the manhood or the womanhood of the other; together, they stifle worthy aspirations and fan impure desires, and march down the broad avenues that lead to the bottomless pit.

Another species of co-operation has for its object education. It is one of the worthiest of our many co-operations. There are many varieties, but the most beneficent of them all are our free schools, which should be cherished by every friend of direct co-operation. We should study to improve them in their teachers and appliances and multiply their advantages. They are the stepping-stones to the attainment of mental training and knowledge by the masses of our people, such as shall make possible the successful development and conducting of direct co-operations in the struggle for food, clothing, shelter, and material prosperity.

Another species of co-operation has for its aim the material welfare of those associated therein. Here, as in the domain of government, the realm of religion, social enjoyment, and education, there are many varieties; some are direct and some are indirect. Next to government the most universal form of co-operation is that which results from the " division of labor," or, as it is called sometimes, " the organization of labor."

While we may count upon our fingers the grand divisions of labor—agriculture, mining, manufacturing, trade, transportation, professional and personal services, the various subdivisions of these divisions will number more than a thousand. We are too apt to overlook the great co-operation arising out of the organization of labor, and neglect to give just credit to the beneficent results arising therefrom.

The co-operation thus resulting is indirect. We call it indirect for the reason that the divisions of labor come to pass wholly from selfish motives, and to secure individual gain, regardless of its effects upon other men or classes of men ; nevertheless, the good results are manifold. The blacksmith learns and follows his trade solely for his individual gain; although wholly selfish in his motives and aims, he is not blameworthy. He comes to be an expert in his trade, and, by reason of that expertness, he can produce more that is beneficial to society, or, in other words, more of wealth, than he can by being a " Jack of all trades and master of none." He indirectly co-operates with the carpenter, the cabinet-maker, the farmer, the tailor, the merchant, and others.

While each of these, in his dealings with him, is ever seeking to obtain the product of his labor as cheap as he can, and obtain as high a price as he can for his own products that he sells to him, yet the blacksmith will secure the necessaries of life and many of its comforts in much greater quantity than he would if he attempted to build his own house, construct his own furniture, raise his own food, make his own clothes, and effect no exchanges with any of them. Meager, indeed, would be the quality and quantity of his food, clothing, and shelter, if he had to obtain them from nature, unaided by the indirect co-operation that results from the division of labor. What is true of the blacksmith is true of every one else.

The merchant, while he seeks to buy as cheaply as

he can and sell at as great an advance as he is able,
works out a most beneficent co-operation between those
of whom he buys and those to whom he sells. The
owners and managers of railroads build and conduct
them from the motive of personal gain, and quite regardless, as a rule, as to how their business enterprise
may effect the material prosperity of those with whom
they come in contact. They have in many instances
been able to amass with great rapidity fortunes of such
magnitude as to almost become a menace to our free
institutions; nevertheless, they have been the means
of an indirect co-operation, beneficent in as great a degree as the magnitude and success of their endeavors.

There are some classes in our community who are
wont to cry out in bitter terms against our whole industrial system, founded upon this division of labor,
and regard it solely as a mighty machine, whereby the
few despoil the many. That many evils have come to
pass must be conceded.

That many classes of laborers do not receive an
equivalent for the product of their labor can not be
truthfully denied; that some men amass fortunes they
have not earned, and that there is the possibility of a
great increase in results for good, must appear to
all who intelligently and candidly review the results
of our competitive industrial organization. But let us
not overlook the good that has come and is still flowing from it.

Let us keep clearly in mind that it is the highest
form of industrial co-operation that large masses of
society have yet been able to maintain successfully.

The day-laborer secures more of the necessaries of
life amid the grindings of industrial competition, al-

though the employer retains the lion's share of the results of his labor, than he could possibly secure if he was laboring alone in "the struggle for existence." Let us not tear down and destroy, and "fly to evils that we know not of"; but, as we attain wisdom and experience, modify and add to. We believe there is a better form of co-operation attainable, where each shall help the other to increase the result of his labor, and neither take from the other any part of that which his labor has produced.

It is toward co-operation as an ideal industrial sys-· tem that large masses of our people are moving. In theory it is enticing; in practice it is difficult to attain. The narrow selfishness of the average human activity thwarts the most generous labor of the unselfish, chills the enthusiasm and weakens the efforts of the philanthropic.

Let no man or class of men ever think that such a system of direct co-operation can be thought out and planned by the brain of man and put into successful operation in all industrial activities and among all classes, as a new scheme or creation, at any single epoch in a nation's history. If ever attained it must grow and develop—as men grow wise and self-restrained—through long periods of time, and be tried by innumerable failures and great adversities.

As in the years gone by, the pioneers, advancing westward, have here and there gone forth in the unbroken forest, felled the trees, built the hut, and through years that have lengthened into generations of father and son, the son taking up the work of the father, or a new comer occupying the abandoned beginning, gradually, with unremitting toil, widening the clearings, improving the land, until, by-and-by, clearings opened into clearings, and productive farms joined farm to farm, and the prosperous agricultural community came to pass; so must be the beginnings, the progress, and the attainment of that direct co-operation that relates to the material welfare of society as a whole.

Many pioneers have heretofore gone forth, many huts have been built, many small clearings have been made; some are widening; many are deserted; some have been re-occupied; but the great forest of selfish, grinding competition still remains unbroken.

Our political institutions, joined to the growing intelligence of the masses of our people, present opportunities and advantages for beginnings here and there in direct co-operation in matters relating to material welfare never before existing.

The spread of education and varied knowledge among the masses of men, and our modes of rapid transportation and communication, surpass, not only the ideals, but even the highest flights of the imagination of the centuries prior to our own.

While many failures are doubtless before us, we believe many grand social achievements are yet possible in the material welfare of men. Much has been already reached by means of co-operation. Yet all that has been accomplished is but the beginning of greater achievements to come.

The efforts in the special form of co-operation under consideration have been more uniformly successful than in any other. The associations formed for the purpose have various names. The most common name is Building and Loan Associations, but different names

are used in different localities, such as " Building Associations," " Mutual Savings and Loan Associations,"
" Homestead Aid Associations," " Co-operative Banks,"
etc. We prefer to class them under the name of " Co-
operative Savings and Loan Associations." This, to
our mind, describes them more accurately than any
other name by which they have been called.

CHAPTER II.

IN every business center of our land, whether a city or a village, there is a large class of the population that work for wages. Some are artisans, some are clerks. Their thrift and prosperity must always depend upon the amount they save.

It is not the amount of wages that the wage-worker earns and receives that makes him prosperous and ultimately independent, but the amount that he saves from his wages.

Habits of saving can be cultivated as well as habits of spending. With every person the temptations to spend money are manifold. The devices by which he is induced to part with his money are numerous and ingenious—from a church lottery to the dice in a beer saloon. Then the urgency of appetite and the allurements of social enjoyment, even when innocent and harmful, are seductive influences that lead to the parting with money in the face of resolutions to save it.

To encourage savings, it is important that there should be abundant opportunities for laying them by where they will be safe, and at the same time beyond immediate reach for the gratification of passing de-

2

sires. To secure this opportunity, there should be in every town savings institutions of some kind, where the wage-worker can deposit his savings at frequent intervals, and allow them to accumulate, and where interest or profits upon the accumulation shall be added to them from time to time.

The wage-earner will be more liable to withstand the temptation to spend his money if he has undertaken to save a definite sum each week or month, and deposit it at a given time, than he will if the amount and the time of depositing are left uncertain. Having undertaken by an agreement to save a fixed sum monthly or weekly, and deposit it at a certain time in the month or week, he will have a definite purpose in view, and will plan to carry it out. An act of this kind by one artisan or clerk tends to stimulate his associates to do the same, and the example of each will stimulate others in the good work.

Any one who steadily follows a course of saving forms a habit of great importance to his future career. A man with a definite object before him, and to secure which he is laboring, if it be a worthy one, will be a better man, and more successful in his undertakings, than if without a specific aim of the kind. He labors best who labors to attain some result beyond the wages he receives. If the clerk has made a firm resolve to save and accumulate his savings until they shall amount to one thousand dollars, he will be a better clerk by virtue of this resolution. His task will grow easy as he pursues his aim, the first hundred dollars saved being the hardest to secure.

All persons concerned in savings will take greater interest in their mutual endeavors if the savings institution in which they deposit is of their own forming and under their own management, provided, of course, that the system upon which it is organized and conducted insures the safety of their savings, and secures a satisfactory rate of interest or profits.

Among the many worthy objects which the wage-worker, whether artisan or clerk, may seek to attain pertaining to his material welfare, none will exceed in beneficial results the determination to own a home. A home of his own does much for the one who labors with brain or muscle. "Home, sweet home," even in song and melody, has softened many hearts and moistened many eyes. As an object in view for which to labor, it has warded off many shafts of temptation, lightened the fatigue of toil, and filled many of the hours of rest with pleasant day-dreams. A man who has earned, saved, and paid for a home will be a better man, a better artisan or clerk, a better husband and father, and a better citizen of the republic.

Every influence that encourages and stimulates home-building and home-owning works good to the individual and to society. In home-building, as in savings, the endeavor of one in that direction stimulates his friends and his neighbors. When several are working together, they become a center from which an influence radiates throughout the community. Whenever an individual has set a home, neat, comfortable, and paid for, before him as an object to strive for, and has steadily pursued his resolve to save his earnings that he may attain his purpose, he is well started toward success and material prosperity, according to the measure of his abilities. The greater the number of such persons in a society the greater will be its prosperity and the higher the tone of its morals. In the hands of citizens such as these the destinies of the republic will be safe.

The greater number of those who commence life without the aid of a patrimony do not fully appreciate the influence and importance of owning a home until they have married and are at the head of a family. Their home is a rented house, or rooms in a tenement. Rent-day comes as certain as the seasons. It does not stop when the mill or manufactory shuts down; it takes no account of sickness and doctors' bills, baby outfits or nurses; it does not adapt its exactions to the varying prices of meat or flour. If not paid the notice comes, "move out"; and if the tenant does not move or pay, the sheriff comes quickly to compel it.

There is no pride in caring for, improving, or beautifying a rented house—shall I say home? No, it is not a home; it is but a stopping-place, a structure to ward off the winds and the storms. No tendrils of heart affection cling to it. It is all the same to the tenant if he move to another house the next month, except for the expense.

How often such a family wish for a home of their own! But its attainment seems so impossible that no endeavor to secure it is aroused. There are many of these that would make the endeavor if a feasible way were pointed out. If by some means the sum they pay in rent could be applied in payment for a home, they would gladly avail themselves of the opportunity.

If, instead of making large payments, they could pay in monthly payments, and at the same time not pay more for the home than its fair value, the advantage would be greater, and increase the chances of ultimate success. All members of the family could unite in the good undertaking, and new hope and incentive to labor would lighten present toil, and make more easy self-denying frugality.

Just these advantages and opportunities for securing a home the institution for savings in every business center should afford. It may be asked : How can it give such opportunity if conducted upon business principles such as will make it a safe place for savings? Let us explain. The safest loan for a savings institution is a first mortgage upon real estate, provided the amount loaned does not exceed a certain percentage of the fair market price of the real estate loaned upon. What that percentage should be, to insure safety, depends upon several conditions, viz. : 1. Whether the real estate is principally land, or its principal value arises from the buildings upon it. 2. Whether, at the time of the loan, the land has an inflated or speculative market value, or is depressed in its fair value by business stagnation. 3. The manner in which the loan is to be repaid, which will have great influence in modifying the percentage of loan as related to its market value. If the time of payment is deferred for a long term of years, the percentage of the loan upon the market value must be much less than when the borrower commences to repay the loan the next month after it is made, and continues from month to month to make such payments until it is wholly repaid, or, what is the equivalent of such direct payment, he pays into the savings institution each month, in addition to monthly interest, a sum which the institution holds as a security for the payment of the loan in addition to the mortgage. Under these

conditions, a loan made upon real estate that is safe
at the time of the loan—a loan such as could be realized by an immediate foreclosure—is likely to remain
safe by reason of the increased security given from
month to month.

How shall the one who desires to pay for his home
become a safe borrower? Let us assume that seventy-
five per cent of the cash market value would be a safe
investment for the savings institution at the time of
making the loan, in cases where it was to be paid in
monthly payments, and interest payable monthly. If
the borrower has, to commence with, a margin of
twenty-five per cent on the value of the home he desires to purchase, he can buy at once, pay the margin,
and borrow the seventy-five per cent from the savings
institution, mortgage to them, and make his monthly
payment until all is paid for.

If he has not the margin of twenty-five per cent to
commence with, then he must commence to save his
earnings, and deposit them monthly or weekly until
the deposits so made, with the addition of the interest
or profits upon them, amount to the original margin;
then he can buy, make his mortgage to the association,
and proceed to pay for his home in monthly payments
—these monthly payments not much exceeding in
amount the sum he was paying for rent. In a few
years the home will be paid for, free of all incumbrance.

Another advantage is offered by the co-operative
savings and loan associations: It frequently happens
that a member may want to borrow a sum for which
he has no real estate to offer as security. He has
shares in the association upon which he has been

paying promptly for many months. He has friends who are willing to indorse for him, but their indorsements might not be thought good at the bank or with the money loaner. Moreover, he wants the loan on a basis that will enable him to repay in monthly installments. His friend or friends also hold shares in the association, and have no present use for the money accumulated in the association upon their shares. They are using it simply as a savings institution. They have confidence in their friend who' wants to borrow, and are willing to pledge their shares to the association as a collateral security for the repayment of the loan. They can do so, if the amount paid in upon all the shares thus pledged exceeds the amount of the loan. This makes the association absolutely secure, and places the borrower in the best condition possible for repaying his loan.

We have endeavored in this chapter to outline some of the benefits resulting from co-operative savings and loan associations. We have studiously avoided portraying them in vivid colors. Many benefits will accrue from them that we have not mentioned. Many other co-operations, through their instrumentality, will be made. The members will become trained in business habits and methods; accumulations will be made, which may be joined together in business co-operations. Not least among their manifold benefits is the stimulus they will give to endeavors of temperance, industry, and frugality.

CHAPTER III.

TYPICAL "CO-OPERATIVE SAVINGS AND LOAN ASSO-
CIATIONS."

THE purpose of the present chapter is to give a general outline of the scheme upon which co-operative savings and loan associations are conducted. There are so many modifications of the general scheme that an attempt to refer to them all would confuse the reader. A particular class has therefore been selected, a class that is typical, and involves the fundamental principles of all. In a subsequent chapter we shall point out the important divergencies from this typical form.

The Legislature of the State of New York, in 1887, · passed an act entitled "An act providing for the formation of co-operative savings and loan associations." It is known as Chapter 556 of the Session Laws of 1887. We shall select the scheme which this act embodies for our general outline. We do so because we believe it embodies the true principles upon which this form of co-operation should be conducted.

Co-operative savings and loan associations are corporations. Every member of an association is a stockholder, and holds a certificate of stock, stating the number of shares owned by him.

In an ordinary business corporation the stockholder

buys his stock and pays its full value at the beginning of his membership, making no further payment upon it while he owns it. He buys it as an investment, and his profits from the investment come in the form of dividends from time to time. If the business of the corporation is successful, and gives promise of large and steady dividends in the future, the value of the shares advance; and the reverse will occur if no dividends are paid, and the outlook for the success of the enterprise in the future is foreboding.

In the co-operative savings and loan association the stockholder pays only one dollar when he buys a share of stock, except under circumstances hereafter explained, and then continues to pay one dollar each month upon it to the association, until the small sums thus paid, increased by the dividends added to them by the association, amount to the sum of two hundred dollars. When this amount is reached the stockholder surrenders his share of stock and the association pays him two hundred dollars in one sum.

The one dollar which is paid in each month is called *dues*, and when the share has reached the value of two hundred dollars it is called a *matured share*. It represents two hundred dollars of accumulated savings. Thus it appears clearly that the capital of the association consists of the accumulated savings of its members, paid to the association upon shares of stock, and increased by interest which the association has received from loans made by it from the savings of its members thus paid to the association, and from other minor sources of income. It follows that the amount of the capital of the association will vary from month to month and year to year.

The stock of the association is issued in series. The first stock issued is series No. 1; the next, series No. 2, and so on during the life of the association. It is usual to issue a new series at the beginning of each fiscal year. All stock issued during the fiscal year will belong to that series. After a new series is issued no stock will be issued in a prior series.

All persons taking shares of stock at the first monthly meeting in the year will pay at the time of getting their shares one dollar dues on each share. Persons taking shares at the second monthly meeting will pay two months' dues. If obtained at the fourth monthly meeting, four dollars dues will have to be paid. Stocks taken out after the sixth monthly meeting, in addition to paying dues to the same amount they would have paid if they had taken the stock at the first monthly meeting, are charged a certain amount of interest, the amount of interest being usually the same as that which the association pays to a shareholder who withdraws from the association after he has made six months' payment of dues and before the end of the fiscal year.

The reason for charging dues upon all stock issued during the fiscal year, the same as the shareholder pays if he takes his stock at the first meeting in the year, is to make the amount of dues paid to the association upon each share issued in each series and outstanding at the close of the fiscal year, precisely the same, so that all shareholders in the series are entitled to the same amount of dividend in the distribution of profits.

A distribution of profits and losses should be made before the issuing of a new series. Some associations issue semi-yearly series, and even quarterly series. To do so simply requires the distribution of profits and losses to be made before the issuing of a new series.

We have now described the system as to a shareholder who continues to pay his dues until his share of stock has reached the value of two hundred dollars, when his accumulated savings are paid to him and he surrenders his stock. But suppose that at any time before such matured value is reached the shareholder finds himself unable to continue the payment of his dues, or he wishes to use the money he has already accumulated, or for any other cause desires to withdraw from the association! What then?

Every share of stock outstanding has upon the books of the association a *holding* value and a *withdrawal* value. The *holding* value is made up of all the dues that have been paid in, plus all the profits that have been added in the distribution of profits. The *withdrawal* value is the sum which the association will pay to the shareholders who withdraw before their stock has reached its matured value.

It is not customary to allow the withdrawing shareholder all the profits which have been added to his stock in determining its holding value. Some portion of them is usually retained by the association. When no part is retained, the *holding* and the *withdrawal* value will be the same. Each association determines for itself what portion, if any, of the profits it will retain from the withdrawing shareholder. The share of the profits retained, deducted from the holding value, will give the withdrawal value. In some associations the by-laws prescribe a certain definite percentage of the profits to be retained; in other associations the board of directors are empowered by the by-laws to determine from time to time what this percentage shall be.

In some associations the withdrawal value of each share of stock is determined at each distribution of profits, that is, at the same time the holding value is declared. The withdrawal value thus declared will continue until the next distribution of profits. Shares withdrawn at any time after such declaration of their withdrawal value and before the next distribution of profits will have added to such declared withdrawal value any dues paid and a certain rate of interest on such dues and on the withdrawal value as declared down to the time of their withdrawal. This rate of interest should be fixed by the by-laws.

All associations require at least thirty days' notice of a desire to withdraw, before the association becomes liable to pay. Only a certain portion of the receipts of the association are applicable to paying off withdrawing shareholders without the consent of the directors. In associations that have no matured shares calling for payment, one half of the receipts are applicable to the payment of withdrawals; and only one third, when they have matured shares awaiting payment.

When the demands of withdrawing shareholders exceed the funds applicable to their payment, they are paid in the order in which their notices of withdrawal were filed with the secretary of the association.

Only one third of the receipts are applicable to the payment of matured shares without the consent of the directors; and when the funds are not sufficient to pay all matured shares at once, the directors determine in what order they shall be paid; and, from the time they reach their matured value until paid, they draw a certain rate of interest, determined by the by-laws. The object of thus apportioning the receipts is always to have a certain part of them to satisfy the wants of shareholders desiring to borrow.

Shares of stock which have not been pledged to the association for a loan are called unpledged, or " free " shares. Shares that have been pledged to the association are called " pledged," or " borrowed " shares.

For the purpose of preventing a few heavy shareholders from obtaining and holding control of the association, the number of free shares which any one shareholder can hold is limited to ten in any one series, and the number of borrowed shares to twenty.

It is customary to charge what is known as an entrance fee, not exceeding twenty-five cents on each share of stock issued. Its object is to aid in defraying expenses.

All shareholders sign the by-laws upon taking shares of stock. They may sell their shares of stock, if unpledged, to any person, and upon such transfer being made upon the books of the association, and the transferee signing the by-laws, he will become a shareholder in the association. A transfer fee not exceeding twenty-five cents a share is usually charged by the association.

All *dues* upon stocks are paid to the association at a regular stated time in each month. A committee of the board of directors receive these dues, and receipt for them in a pass-book which is issued to each shareholder. When the hour has passed for receiving dues, they pass the receipts of the evening over to the treasurer of the association, and take his receipt therefor. All interest upon loans made by the association is paid in monthly installments, and paid at the same time with the dues; in short, all the receipts of the associations come in at the stated meetings each month. No officer has the right to receive funds for the association except at the stated meetings, except that the treasurer may receive payment of loans at any time; but, when not paid at such a meeting, interest has to be paid upon the loan until the next stated meeting.

For the purpose of securing prompt payment of dues and interest, the association imposes a fine, not exceeding ten per cent of the amount of dues or interest defaulted. The amount of the fine is fixed by the by-laws.

The funds of the association are loaned only to its shareholders. The loans are usually made in sums of two hundred dollars, the value of a matured share, or a multiple thereof. Some associations, however, make the minimum limit of a loan fifty dollars, or one fourth of the matured value of a share; and the next grade in amount one hundred dollars, or one half a share.

Every shareholder has the right to become a borrower, upon giving the required security, to an amount equal to the matured value of the shares owned by him. Thus, if he owns ten shares, he may become a borrower to the extent of two thousand dollars.

While all shareholders have the right to become borrowers, all will not want to borrow at the same time; but it will often occur that there will not be sufficient money to meet the wants of all who do wish to borrow. As all who have adequate security to offer stand on equal ground, it becomes an important question, relating to the harmonious workings of the association, to determine in what manner the first right to a loan from the funds of the association shall be decided. The common, and we believe the most equitable and satisfactory mode is to decide it by an open bidding of a premium—the one bidding the highest premium to have the money; in short, awarding the loan or loans to the highest bidder or bidders.

Upon the subject of the kind of premium bid and how paid, there is great divergence in the "building associations," "co-operative banks," "mutual loan associations," etc. We can not stay to explain them at this time—it would confuse rather than otherwise. We will describe the scheme at this time of the co-operative savings and loan associations of New York. It already appears that the value of a matured share, two hundred dollars, is the unit in all loans. If the loan is less than two hundred dollars, it is a definite fractional part, one fourth or one half of that sum. So that the language of the borrower, when stating how much money he wants to borrow, describes it by naming "one share," if he wants to borrow two hundred dollars; "five shares" if he wants to borrow one thousand dollars; "one quarter of a share" if he wants to borrow fifty dollars, etc. This is simple, when the premium bid is so much a share; it is readily understood and the amount is easily computed by all interested. Thus, if there are two thousand dollars to loan and two or more shareholders want it, the proper officer offers the money for sale: A bids "fifty cents," B "seventy-five cents"; A raises his bid to "one dollar"; if no one bids above him, the money is struck off to him. The premium he has agreed to pay for the loan is one dollar per share. If the number of shares he is borrowing is ten, the total premium is ten dollars, and the total amount of money he will receive will be two thousand dollars, less the premium. Although he receives but nineteen hundred and ninety dollars, he will give a security for two thousand, and pay interest on that sum. The "premium per share" retained passes to the profit-and-loss account of the association.

When there is no competition for the money the borrower will simply bid "par," and no one raising his bid, he will be awarded the money, and will receive the full sum of two hundred dollars per share. Under this system the only purpose of bidding a premium is to decide who shall have the money when several desire it. The securities received by the association, in fact, call for the payment of the principal sum named therein, and interest upon the same; and the whole subject of premium is closed when the loan is perfected. We shall explain the other systems of premiums in a subsequent chapter.

Immediately following the receipt of dues and interest at each stated monthly meeting, all the funds of the association that can be loaned at that meeting are offered to borrowers, and bids therefor invited. The person or persons to whom a loan or loans are awarded at once submits a statement of the securities proposed. At once following the sale of money to borrowers, the directors hold their regular monthly meeting for the transaction of the business of the association. The directors have power to pass upon the securities at their meeting, but the usual course is to refer them to the finance committee. This mode is always pursued in reference to real-estate security.

The form and kind of securities required by the associations are as follows :

1. In all cases a bond conditioned upon the payment of the loan and the interest thereon, according to the provisions of the scheme of the association.

2. In all cases also the assignment to the association of the shares of stock borrowed upon, as collateral security for the payment of the loan.

3. A first mortgage upon unincumbered real estate, containing the same conditions as the bond and collateral thereto.

4. Or in lieu of the mortgage, other shares of stock of the association may be pledged, provided their withdrawal value, added to the withdrawal value of the shares borrowed upon, shall exceed the amount of the loan, and interest thereon, for six months. This gives absolute security—the association having the money with which to make good the loan in case of default by the borrower.

A loan secured by a pledge of shares is known as a *stock loan ;* and when secured by a mortgage on real estate, as a *mortgage loan.*

In associations where the premium bid is per share, as before described, the rate of interest charged is six per cent per annum, payable in monthly installments. The interest on a share for one month is one dollar.

To illustrate the simplicity of this scheme, suppose A to be the owner of five shares, upon which he is paying his monthly dues, amounting to five dollars. He becomes a borrower to the extent of one thousand dollars, securing the same by pledging his five shares, and a mortgage upon real estate. The interest upon each share of his loan—two hundred dollars—is one dollar a month, or five dollars on the five shares; his dues are five dollars, making his monthly payment to the association ten dollars. If he continue paying five dollars dues on his stock, and five dollars interest on his loan until his stock has reached its matured value—the sum of one thousand dollars—the value of his stock becomes the equivalent of his loan, and they balance each other. He surrenders his stock, and the association cancels his securities.

The safety to the association of the security of a loan, constantly increases from the next meeting after the loan is made, by the increasing value of the shares borrowed upon, from the payment of dues thereon. But the borrower is not obliged to retain his loan until his shares of stock reach their matured value. He may repay his loan in full at any time, or one share thereof. If he so pays, except at a stated monthly meeting, he must pay interest up to the next meeting. When he has paid his loan in full, his shares will be released from the pledge for the loan, and he will hold them again as unpledged or free shares.

But instead of paying his loan in full, and still retaining his shares of stock, he may wish to have their value applied in part payment of the loan. In that event he will apply at a stated monthly meeting, and give proper notice of his desire to pay his loan and have the shares borrowed upon applied in part payment. Their withdrawal value will be allowed to him upon his paying the balance of the loan, and his shares of stock will be canceled, and the association will surrender his bond and give a discharge of the mortgage.

But suppose a borrower from any cause does not keep up the payment of his dues and interest. What then? When he becomes six months in arrears for interest and dues or either, the whole loan becomes due at once, at the option of the directors, and the association may commence an action to foreclose upon the securities. In this action the withdrawal value of the shares borrowed upon, at the time of commencing the action, will be applied upon the debt, and the stock canceled, and the decree taken for the balance. The usual and ordinary procedure of the courts in such cases controls the case thereafter.

The associations may become purchasers at a public or private sale of any real estate upon which they have a lien, or in which they have any interest, and thereafter to hold, lease, mortgage, or sell the same, as any individual might do. If for any cause at a sale of the mortgaged premises in the foreclosure action a sufficient sum is not bid for the premises to satisfy the costs and mortgage claim, a judgment for any deficiency may be taken against the borrower upon his bond.

We now come to the subject of the distribution of profits.

The gross profits of the association will consist of interest, premiums, share of profits left by withdrawing shareholders, fines, transfer and entrance fees. The principal item, of course, will be interest.

Under the system we are outlining premiums will not usually amount to a large sum. It is not desirable that they should, because large premiums mean that the borrower will, in effect, pay large interest; and, when he does so, it works injustice as between the borrower and the holder of free shares, by giving to the latter large profits at the expense of the former. Of this we shall speak more at length hereafter. Dues paid can not, of course, be reckoned as profits; they are capital.

For the purpose of illustration, we will first describe the distribution of profits, at the close of the first fiscal year, in an association which issues a yearly series only. The expenses of conducting the business should always be paid in full up to the time when the distribution is made. We will assume the association has issued during the year eleven hundred shares of stock; that some of these have been withdrawn, so that at the end of the fiscal year only one thousand shares are outstanding. Upon each of these shares there has been paid during the year twelve dollars in dues, making the total upon all the shares twelve thousand dollars. It may prove that the dues are in arrears on some shares; if so, the amount so in arrears, and fines thereon, should be treated as an asset, because it is a sum due the association, and will be paid. The assets of the association will consist of loans, for which it holds securities, cash on hand, dues, interest in arrears, and fines accrued thereon. The sum of these will constitute the assets on hand; but, to be absolutely accurate and just in the distribution, there is another item that should be included in the assets for the purpose of the distribution of profits, namely, the interest on the loans for the last month of the fiscal year, which will not be paid until the first meeting of the new fiscal year— that is, the fiscal year for convenience should commence with the first meeting in the year and will end at the beginning of the first meeting in the next fiscal year. The interest paid at the first meeting of the next fiscal year accrued during the last month of the old fiscal year, and should be counted among the assets of that year in ascertaining the exact profits of the year. Adding the interest upon the loans to be paid at the next meeting to the assets above named, we have the total assets for the purpose of distribution. Deduct the twelve thousand dollars liability for dues paid, which constitutes in fact the capital of the association, and the remainder will show the net profits of the year's business. Now, if we divide this net profit by the number of shares outstanding, viz., one thousand, the quotient will be the sum that should be added to each share as a dividend in the distribution of profits.

This is a simple method, but another method may be pursued, viz., dividing the net profits by the total amount of the capital—namely, the twelve thousand dollars—and the quotient will then be the percentage to be added to each dollar of the capital as a dividend. In case of an association having several series outstanding at the time of the distribution, this method must be followed. When the dividend has been added to the twelve dollars of dues paid during the year, their sum constitutes the " holding value " of each share of stock at the beginning of the next fiscal year, and the sum of such " holding value " of all the shares will constitute the capital of the association at the beginning of the next year. In this distribution we have assumed that there were no liabilities except the capital stock. If the association owes borrowed money, the amount would be treated as a liability in making the statement to find the net profits for distribution.

We will next illustrate the distribution of profits in an association issuing a yearly series at the end of its third fiscal year. The association will have outstanding three series of stock. The holding value of each share of the first and second series was determined at the last distribution of profits, and if we take the holding value of one share in the first series and multiply it by the total number of shares outstanding in that series at the end of the third fiscal year, we have the total holding value of the first series. Performing a like operation in reference to the outstanding shares in the second series, we ascertain the total holding value of that series at the beginning of the year. By adding together these two results, we have the total holding value of the first and second series, which constituted the total capital of the association at the beginning of the third fiscal year, and upon which monthly interest has been received during the year.

Upon each of these shares outstanding at the close of the third year there has been paid twelve dollars of dues. There have also been paid twelve dollars of dues on each share outstanding in the third series of stock. These dues are not only a liability, but they have been added to the capital, and are entitled to share in the profits, and we must treat them in this double aspect. The treatment of them as a liability in making up the statement of liabilities and assets is simple. By multiplying the total number of shares outstanding in all three series by twelve, we have their sum total as a liability. We also have it as capital. By adding their sum total to the total holding-value of the first and second series as above found, we have the total liability of the association on account of capital. If there are any other liabilities of any kind, they should still bo added to this total for the purposo of making tho statement of liabilities and assets. Having ascertained the total liabilities, the next stcp is to ascertain the total assets. These will usually consist of securities for loans, dues, interest, fines unpaid, and cash on hand. As explained in our illustration of distribution when there was but one series of stock to share in the dividend, we must include in the statement of assets, to bo wholly accurate, tho interest which becomes due and payable at the first meeting in the next year. This will be, of course, in the scheme we are outlining in this chapter, as many dollars as there aro shares borrowed upon. In addition to these items, we should include in our assets the fair cash value of any real estate or other property that the association may chance to own. Having ascertained the total assets, we deduct therefrom the total liabilities, and the remainder is the net sum of the profits for the year to be declared as a dividend upon the capital.

It is apparent that each dollar of the capital represented by the first and second series of stock is entitled to the same dividend. It has been invested the whole year. That part of the capital made up of the dues paid during tho year has not been invested during the whole year. It has been paid from month to month during the year, and invested from the time, as it was received. We must find what sum invested for a year would be their equivalent. That the illustration may be simple and clear, wo will first take the dues paid upon a single share, viz., twelve dollars. The first dollar paid at the beginning of the year has been invested twelve months; the next dollar eleven months;

the next, ten months; and so on to the twelfth dollar, which has been invested one month. Now $12 + 11 + 10 + 9 + 8 + 7 + 6 + 5 + 4 + 3 + 2 + 1 = 78$. Thus we find that the twelve dollars received and invested during the year in monthly installments, each installment being paid and invested at the beginning of each month, is equivalent to one dollar invested for seventy-eight months; and one dollar invested for seventy-eight months is equivalent to $6.50 invested for one year. Multiplying the total number of shares outstanding in all the series by $6.50, we have a sum which, if invested for the whole year, would produce the same income that the total dues will produce when received in monthly installments, and invested from month to month. By adding this equated sum, obtained as above described, to the total value of the first and second series, we have the total sum by which to divide the net profits, and the quotient will be the dividend percentage to be made upon each dollar of the capital invested during the whole year.

Taking now the " holding value " of a share in the first series at the beginning of the year, and multiply by the dividend percentage on one dollar, and we have the total dividend to be made on said share, except the dividend on account of dues paid during the year. To find this, we will multiply $6.50 (the reason of which was above explained) by the dividend percentage, and the result will give us the dividend to be made on account of the dues paid in during the year. Adding together the holding value at the beginning of the year, the dividend made thereon, the dividend on the dues paid during the year, and the dues themselves, and we shall have the holding value, which is also the capital value, of the share at the beginning of the fourth fiscal year. Multiplying this value of one share by the number of shares in the first series, and we have the total holding value of the first series after the dividend has been added.

Next taking a share of the second series, and performing in reference thereto the same operations above given in reference to the share in the first series, and we shall obtain the same result in reference to the second series.

In reference to the third series, we simply multiply $6.50 by the dividend percentage, and add the result to the $12 of dues, and their sum constitutes the holding value of a share in the third series of stock at the beginning of the fourth fiscal year. Multiplying by the total number of shares in the third series, we have the total value of this series. Now, adding together the totals of the three series, we shall have a sum equal to the sum of the total assets with which we started, if our computations have been correct. If they balance, it proves the correctness of the computations. If they do not balance, it demonstrates that we have committed errors, and must find them.

The procedure here outlined is applicable to a distribution of profits in an association having any number of series outstanding. The same operations are to be performed with reference to each series, except the last series, which have been described with reference to the first and second series of stock in the foregoing discussion; and the operations with reference to dues paid during the year upon all series will be the same as above described, and they will be the same with reference to the last series. The same operations will also be pursued in case of a half-yearly or quarterly series scheme in the distribution of profits before the issuing of a new series. The only variation will be in equating the monthly payments. The equation will have to be made for the shorter term instead of for one year.

In ascertaining the dividend percentage, if there is a small fraction it is often advisable not to use it, but carry over as an undivided profit the sum to which it would amount. In the foregoing illustrations we have assumed a distribution of all the net profits. Some associations, and we deem it a wise course to pursue, deduct from the net profits a small percentage before making the distribution and carry it over as undivided profits, gradually increasing the amount thus carried over as undivided profits from year to year, and thereby making what may be properly called a " guarantee fund "; and if any losses are sustained during the year, charge them up against this fund, thus distributing the effect of any loss that may occur in such a manner as not to impair seriously the steady distribution of a fair dividend at the close of each fiscal year, or before a new series is issued.

Upon this subject we refer the accountant to the ninth chapter, devoted to the subject of " How to keep Accounts."

We should allude to the liability of these associations to suffer loss. We know of no business undertaking, co-operative or otherwise, free from all liability of loss.

It is important to every one interested in the subject of co-operative savings and loan associations that he should understand the liability of loss that attaches to the scheme in its practical workings. The first liability to loss is one common to every corporation —the possibility that the officers who handle the money will prove dishonest and steal the funds. In this the liability in these associations is at the minimum. The funds received by the association are received at the stated meetings by the committee of the directors; one of their number has receipted in the pass-books of the members for all received; another member has checked the amount off in another book where it was charged against the shareholder at the beginning of the meeting; a third has counted the money as received. Immediately at the close of the receipts, they balance the cash received with the amount checked as paid, and pass the cash over to the treasurer, and take his receipt. The book upon which the amounts paid have been checked is kept by the secretary. The total receipts of the evening are at once reported to the directors at their meeting. Loans, as before stated, may be repaid to the treasurer at any time. At no time will a large sum of money be on hand in the treasurer's custody, as compared with the total assets of the association. A bond is required of him, much larger than any sum that will be in his hands at any one time, with two sureties approved by the directors. We assert there is no business concern handling the same amount of money in which the liability for loss is less than in these associations. No moneys can be paid out by the treasurer except upon the order of the directors, which order must be signed by the president and secretary.

The next liability is the possibility of the securities taken for loans not being good, and the full amount of the loan not being realized in the event the borrower defaults in paying the loan. This liability is incident to the savings-bank, and to every institution that loans money; but here again we assert these associations are safer than any other scheme for savings yet devised. We have before alluded to the fact that all loans made upon a pledge of shares of stock, the withdrawal value of which exceeds the amount of the loan and six months' interest thereon, were perfectly safe. As an association advances in age, the percentage of its loans thus secured will increase. Now as to liability to loss on mortgage loans. The same care as to titles is required as in any corporation loaning money on real-estate security. Whether the value of real estate offered is sufficient is determined usually by a duly appointed committee of the directors. Every one of them is personally interested in the safety of the security; his reputation is also at stake with his fellow shareholders; he receives no benefits by deciding that the real estate offered is a sufficient security which he would lose by deciding otherwise. He stands in a position to be absolutely unbiased, except that his every interest is in the direction of securing only a good security. His judgment may be at fault, but the committee consists of three men; they are passing upon the value of real estate in their own town; they know its market value, its advantages and disadvantages. More important than these facts is the one that the payment of the loan, except as to a part, is not long deferred. At the next monthly meeting the borrower begins, in effect, paying his loan; the shares of stock borrowed upon are increasing in value. If the loan was safe at the time it was passed, the chances are very small that it will ever become unsafe. If it was an unsafe loan at the time when passed by the committee, it will constantly grow safer so long as the borrower continues the payment of his dues and interest. It should have been stated before that these associations make loans only in their immediate vicinity, so that many shareholders know constantly of all loans made, and all may know who desire. Another fact should not be forgotten in this connection, that the moral risk of a class of men who have planned for themselves a steady course of saving, or the paying for a home by monthly savings, is far above the average moral risk of a mortgage in the usual mode. In the event of the association having to bid in a parcel of real estate to secure its debt, it has a great advantage in selling it again, by getting a small down payment and the purchaser becoming a shareholder and paying for it in the monthly sums upon dues.

For the foregoing reasons we believe the scheme of these associations, in their practical workings, is more free from liability of losses than any other scheme in operation.

The question naturally arises, in case there are no borrowers, what then? Such a contingency will seldom arise, and, if it does occur now and then, it will be temporary in its duration. The worst result from such a contingency is a failure, for the time being, to make profits; the principal sum of dues paid is not impaired. The scheme of the association, however, provides for such a contingency if it arises and continues, and that is by compelling withdrawals in series that have attained a certain age. What share shall be withdrawn is determined by lot, the shareholders thus compelled to withdraw being paid the " *holding* value " of their shares. It is very seldom in the experience of these associations that this remedy has to be used. In the natural course of business, if the association is not making fair profits, shareholders will begin to withdraw at the withdrawal value of their shares, thereby leaving such portion of the profits which have been added to the dues paid as the by-laws of the association provide. The profits thus retained help to increase the profits to be divided at the next distribution among the shares that remain outstanding.

There can not be anything like a "run upon a bank" upon one of these associations; it matters not how many want money on withdrawals, each shareholder must wait his turn; he must give the thirty days' notice of his desire to withdraw, and if there is not sufficient money applicable to the payment of withdrawals to pay all who have given notice, they are paid in the order of the time when their notices of withdrawal were filed with the secretary. The association will pay them as rapidly as possible, because the one withdrawing is surrendering some portion of his profits, which accrues to the benefit of the shareholders remaining; hence, the payment of withdrawals is always a profitable use of the funds received into the treasury. The nature of the scheme does not admit of that combination of facts which must occur to produce the feeling of uncertainty, doubt, and suspicion, which breed the panic and sudden rush of depositors in a bank to obtain their money.

The management of the association is in the immediate control of the board of directors, consisting usually of nine members, with the president, secretary and *treasurer and vice - president as additional *ex officio* members thereof, making seven members a quorum for the transaction of business. These officers are elected annually. In their election each shareholder has one vote for every share of stock owned by him not in arrears for dues. The president appoints from the nine directors a finance committee of three members, which serves for four months, thus using upon this committe during the year all the nine members of the board. The president is also, *ex officio*, a member of every finance committee, and the secretary of the association acts as its secretary.

This committee receives and receipts for the moneys at the monthly meetings, and passes them over to the treasurer. They pass upon the sufficiency as to the value of all real-estate security offered, and, in conjunction with the attorney of the association, upon the titles of the real estate proposed to be mortgaged to the association; their report is made in writing, and signed by them. As a rule, no compensation is paid to any officer except the treasurer and secretary, and their salaries are not large ; their amount will be governed by the volume of business the association is doing.

One of the strong elements of success in associations organized and conducted on this scheme is the interest which is aroused in all its members to aid in its success; and first-class men will always be found to fill its offices, men who will take pride in faithfully performing the trust reposed in them.

We have now spoken of the general features of the scheme upon which the co-operative savings and loan associations are organized and conducted, necessarily in this general outline omitting many details which will fully appear in subsequent chapters.

We submit to the reader with confidence in our assumption that no scheme has been devised for financial co-operation among men of small means that excels the one we have thus outlined in simplicity, in safety, in accomplishing an equitable division of benefits, and in the certainty of success.

We have not outlined an organization to be formed upon some finely wrought theory, but one that has been most thoroughly tried and very uniformly met the expectation of those united in the enterprise. It is not an organization for a few to make large profits at the expense of the many; or one wherein the borrower pays a large interest for the benefit of the shareholder who does not borrow. All stand upon equal footing. It does not encourage speculation, but steady savings; and to attain them, there must be industry and frugal habits. It encourages home-building and all the blessings that naturally flow from it.

CHAPTER IV.

At the present time the data requisite for writing a full history of the growth and spread of the co-operative savings and building-loan associations in the United States can not be obtained. We can only give a brief outline. Their operations and development have been so quiet and unobtrusive they have not attracted general attention until within the last three years. Among the great mass of American citizens their existence even has been unknown. As a rule, they have not been under State supervision, and no public record has been kept of their number, or of the business transacted by them. Even in the localities where they have been most numerous and best managed, the beneficial results flowing from them have not, until recently, been to any great extent spread before the public. As a factor in co-operation they have not received the attention they deserve.

In 1887, the American Economic Association gave them due prominence in their monographs upon co-operation. During that year they began to attract the attention, quite generally, of the daily

4

press, and at the present time no form of direct co-operation is attracting the attention of the public so generally as these associations. The scheme under which they were first conducted has undergone many changes and modifications. Of this feature in their history, we shall speak in the next chapter. With these changes, have arisen changes in their names. The first name given to them was "Building Associations." This was succeeded by "Building and Loan Associations." This has been the most universal name by which they have been designated; but a great variety of other names have come into use, such as "Mutual Loan Associations," "Savings-Fund and Loan Associations," "Homestead Aid Associations," "Co-operative Savings and Loan Associations," "Co-operative Banks," etc. The best generic term now in use seems to us, is the name adopted by the New York State League, viz., "Co-operative Savings and Building-Loan Associations." This name gives the four conspicuous objects in their business, namely, co-operation, for the purpose of stimulating savings, for building homes and making loans therefor.

From data * that seem reliable, we learn that the first building association in this country was organized in a suburb of the city of Philadelphia, called Frankford, January 3, 1831, and named the "Oxford Provident Building Association." The scheme was simple. There was a single series of stock, entrance fee of five dollars, monthly dues on each share of stock three dollars, and matured value of shares $500. The shares reached their maturity in ten years and six

* A book entitled "How to Manage Building Associations," by Edmund Wrigley, of Philadelphia, published in 1873.

months, and the association was dissolved. A new association of the same name was formed at once.

Another similar association was formed in the same place in 1845, called the " Franklin Building Association," in which the matured value of the shares was placed at $200 and monthly dues at one dollar. In 1847, an association similar to the Franklin was organized in the Kensington District of Philadelphia. The number of shares was limited to five hundred; the matured value of shares $200, and monthly dues of one dollar.

During the last years of that decade, the organization of these associations in Philadelphia was very rapid. Until 1849 or 1850 none were incorporated. They were simply voluntary associations, holding their property through the medium of trustees. Yet so rapid had been their growth in that city that fifty or more were organized between 1831 and 1849. The laws of the State of Pennylvania passed in 1850, providing for their incorporation, limited the number of shares which an association could issue to five hundred. In 1859 the law was amended by increasing the limit to 2,500 shares, of $200 each matured value. In 1874 the law was further amended by removing the limit as to the number of shares, but limiting the aggregate value of the stock an association might have outstanding to $1,000,000.

We have no data at hand of the number of associations chartered from 1850 to 1859 inclusive; but during the decade of 1860 to 1869 inclusive one hundred and forty-eight associations were chartered ; and from 1870 to 1875 inclusive three hundred and seventeen were chartered. In 1876, the centennial year, there were in active operation in Philadelphia alone at least four hundred and fifty associations. We believe it a safe estimate to make, that such number exceeded the total number of associations in all places in the United States. M. J. Brown, editor and proprietor of the " Building Association and Home Journal," now places the total number of associations in the State of Pensylvania at nine hundred, of which four hundred and fifty are located in the city of Philadelphia, and four hundred and fifty in other parts of the State. Hence it can be said with great fitness that Philadelphia has been the "breeding-place" of these associations in America.*

Prof. F. B. Sanborn, Secretary of the American Social Science Association, in 1888 asked Mr. Brown the question as to the amount of capital invested in these associations in Philadelphia and in all Pennsylvania, and we quote the following from Prof. Sanborn's report: " M. J. Brown has undertaken to answer this question, and his figures, although partly estimates, are of great value. He examined the sworn accounts of one hundred and twenty building associations with the following results : Aggregate capital, $8,749,337; average capital, $72,911; aggregate shares, 151,680; average shares, 1,264. Applying this ratio to the three hundred and thirty Philadelphia associations, their aggregate capital becomes $32,810,017, and the total number of their shares 568,800."

The total estimate for the State reaches $60,000,000 of capital, and nearly 1,000,000 shares.

* Prof. F. B. Sanborn's report on "Co-operative Building," read at the September meeting of the American Social Science Association at Saratoga in 1888.

Dr. R. T. Ely, in his "Labor Movement in America," published in 1886, says : "Six years ago it was officially stated that 60,000 comfortable homes had been constructed in Philadelphia alone through the aid derived from the building associations, and it is certain Mr. Barnard did not exaggerate when he entitled the chapter describing them, in his work on 'Co-operation as a Business,' 'One Hundred Thousand Homes.' "

The influence of these associations has been most potent in encouraging home-owning and home-building among the wage-workers of Pennsylvania; and it is asserted that there is no city in the Union of its size, or approximating to it, where so many of the wage-earners own their homes as in Philadelphia. We believe it a fact to be noted, that in no city of its age or approximate population does the anarchist or extreme socialist find so few followers as in this city.

From Pennsylvania these associations have spread into almost every State in the Union.

New Jersey.

The Bureau of Statistics of Labor and Industries of New Jersey is to be commended for the interest and enterprise it has manifested in collecting statistics relating to this form of co-operation in that State. No bureau of labor or statistics in any other State, except Massachusetts, has, until the present time, deemed them of sufficient importance to demand attention. In 1880, 1882, 1884, and 1886, the New Jersey Bureau collected data regarding these associations. We quote as follows from their report for 1886:

In 1880, when the bureau first endeavored to collect information from the building and loan associations in this State, there were reported to be in existence one hundred and six of these societies, but less than one half (fifty-one) favored us with returns. These aggregated, in net assets, $4,002,647, and about forty-seven thousand shares, or an average of $78,483 assets and nine hundred and twenty-one shares to the association. Previous to the year mentioned, no such statistics had been available, and, except in the immediate localities where they flourished, no one had any idea of the extent or condition of the New Jersey co-operative building enterprises—something which had much to do with intercepting their development.

Our publication, incomplete as it was, met with much favor and attracted considerable attention throughout the State to this form of co-operation. And when, two years later, in 1882, we again investigated the subject, one hundred and eighteen secretaries, without exception, cheerfully sent in replies. According to our estimate, there were during that year one hundred and twenty-eight New Jersey building and loan associations, of which twelve "terminating" ones were reported to be closing up, that is, their shares had matured. The aggregate returns from the one hundred and eighteen organizations, of which the majority were serial or perpetual, gave 102,075 shares, owned by 20,000 members, of whom fully 6,000 were borrowers. The assets amounted to $6,748,775. The averages were, therefore, eight hundred and sixty-four shares, one hundred and seventy shareholders, and $57,192 assets—an apparent decrease, easily accounted for by the fact that very many small societies, not reporting in 1880, made returns.

In 1884 there were said to be in existence one hundred and twenty-nine building and loan associations, a number of which had been organized since the statements for 1882 appeared, while several of the terminating societies running at that time had been "wound up." . . . It was estimated that the net assets of all the New Jersey associations in 1884 amounted to $7,000,000, and that of our wage-workers who had secured homes, at least 4,000 were then engaged in paying off mortgages with assistance obtained as shareholders.

The fourth census of our building and loan enterprises was made by the bureau at the close of the present year. On October 1st a circular was sent to the various associations, the names of the newly-organized ones having been obtained from the county clerks, asking for the information tabulated in the tables below, which give the statistical details of one hundred and fifty-six organizations in active operation at that date. . . . The number stated, one hundred and fifty-six, therefore includes all the active associations at the beginning of the fall. Since then and up to the close of the year, several more have been incorporated, so that the total at present can not be far from one hundred and seventy—a very rapid increase within the past two years. From the reports which have been forwarded to the bureau, these New Jersey associations are generally in a very prosperous condition, and a great benefit, not only to the individual members, but to the community at large ; for they are increasing the number of tax-paying, property-owning citizens, and making it comparatively easy for an industrious workingman to own a home. The improvement has been noticeable in the northern part of the State, especially in Essex and Hudson Counties, where the number of the associations has doubled since 1884, and both Jersey City and Newark now each support a building and loan journal—the "News" and "Advocate"—the only newspapers of the kind published in the State. . . . A summary of the statistics of the one hundred and fifty-six New Jersey associations shows the following results : 37,730 shareholders holding 204,653 shares, or an average of two hundred and forty-two members and over thirteen hundred shares—five and a half to each shareholder. The net assets foot up $9,349,517.46, or nearly $60,000 to an association. Of the members, nearly two thirds are wage-earners, and 8,562, or over one fifth, are borrowers. Of the latter, 5,354, or over sixty per cent, are workingmen. Over one fifth of the shares, or 42,373, have been borrowed on. The profits of one hundred and forty-two associations (net assets, $8,915,120) were $1,706,649, or an average of $12,018 for $50,764 paid in dues; that is, 23.7 per cent for the average time (two years and a half) the shares have run—about nine and a half per cent a year. The incidental expenses have averaged, for one hundred and ten associations, $353 annually.

From the tabulated statements of facts in said report, relating to the one hundred and fifty-six associations that reported in detail to the bureau in 1886, we learn that about fifty-six were organized on the single series, or terminating plan, and about one hundred on the serial, or permanent plan; that the county of Camden had twenty-four associations, all upon the permanent plan; the county of Essex twenty-four, of which eight were on the terminating plan; the county of Hudson twenty-one, of which all were on the terminating plan except six; the county of Middlesex fifteen, all of which were of the terminating kind except two; the county of Burlington had thirteen, of which all were of the permanent plan except two.

One of the largest associations in the State, at the date of the report, was the "People's Building and Loan Association," at Harrison. This association was organized in 1873 on the serial plan. At the date of its annual report, in 1886, it had outstanding 5,017¼ shares, held by 1,046 shareholders, distributed into eleven series, and of the aggregate value of $192,947.31. The matured value of shares is $200, and monthly dues are one dollar. The whole number of shareholders were reported to be wage-earners. The constitution of this association is printed in the bureau's report, in full, with the remark, that "the constitution of this association is reproduced below, and, as it is generally considered to be a very good one, may serve as a model for new enterprises." *

The first association in New Jersey was organized prior to 1847, but that was the year in which the Legislature first passed an act authorizing their incorporation; another act was passed in 1849, which was revised in 1875. The law for incorporation is very general in its terms, and permits an endless variety in the schemes upon which the business may be conducted. Their growth and prosperity in this State continues, and at the present time there are not less than one hundred and eighty associations.

Massachusetts.

We are able to obtain full statistics with reference to loan associations in the State of Massachusetts from the reports of the Commissioners of Savings-Banks of that State.

The Hon. Josiah Quincy, now deceased, became deeply interested in these associations as a means of stimulating the wage-workers in the matter of savings, home-building, and home-owning. As the result of his endeavors, a general act providing for their incorporation was passed in 1877. By that act, they were named " Co-operative Saving-Fund and Loan Associations." In 1883 the act was amended, so that they were named " Co-operative Banks," and this is the name by which they are now designated in this State.

This general act for their incorporation was carefully prepared by experts in Philadelphia, as we are

* See Appendix.

informed, and outlines a definite scheme for the organization and conduct of their business. Under this scheme, the associations are permanent—issuing quarterly, semi-yearly, or yearly series, as the association shall determine. The matured value of shares is $200, monthly dues are one dollar, and the accumulated capital is not to exceed $1,000,000.

From the report of the Savings-Bank Commissioners of Massachusetts, dated December 31, 1887, we learn that on October 31, 1887, the total number of co-operative banks was fifty-one—a gain of eleven during the last year; that their total assets were $4,211,-948.86—a gain in one year of $982,982.24. The total number of shares outstanding, 134,864; the total number of shareholders, 20,735, of whom 3,797 were borrowers.

From the date of that report up to September 1, 1888, it is authoritatively reported that thirteen new co-operative banks were organized, making a total of sixty-four.

The first of these banks, organized under the act of 1877, was the Pioneer Co-operative Bank of Boston. The largest of these banks is at Waltham; its assets, October 31, 1887, were $337,647.29; number of shares outstanding, 8,893; number of shareholders, 1,488, of whom 288 were borrowers.

Of the sixty-four banks, about eleven are in Boston, and the rest are well distributed throughout the cities and large towns of Massachusetts—there being three in Worcester, three in Taunton, two in Fall River, and one each in Lowell, Lynn, New Bedford, Cambridge, Chelsea, Somerville, Springfield, Holyoke, Westfield, Fitchburg, Waltham, Woburn, etc. But three of the twenty-five cities of the State are without one, while many of the larger towns where skilled workmen are employed have each one of these banks. The number of these savings institutions is now increasing more rapidly than ever. They are all conducted upon the same scheme, except that the law admits of the bank deciding for itself whether it will adopt the installment premium plan or the interest premium plan. They are under State supervision. Massachusetts now justly ranks at the head in its legislation relative to these associations. Under its laws, the danger of wild speculative schemes coming in vogue is wholly averted.

Maine.

Loan associations have not developed yet to any considerable extent in Maine, there being but ten or twelve in the State at the present time. These have been principally organized during the last five years.

New Hampshire.

In New Hampshire there are but four associations, all organized since 1887.

Rhode Island.

There are said to be but three associations in this State, the leading one being at Providence.

Vermont.

There is at present no law for the incorporation and organization of loan associations in Vermont, and, so far as we have been able to ascertain, none have been organized.

Connecticut.

Prof. Sanborn, in the report before cited, says: " In Connecticut there are six or seven associations in different parts of the State; one at New Haven having a special charter, and the rest are voluntary associations, having no incorporation." There is one located at Meriden, called " The Meriden Permanent Building and Loan Association."

Much interest in these associations is now developing in this State, and without doubt a law authorizing their incorporation will soon be passed. Connecticut passed through an unfortunate experience with building associations in former years; but the schemes upon which they were organized and conducted were widely apart from the scheme of the true building and loan association. C. F. Southard is our authority for saying that the methods of these old associations resulted in so much of popular feeling against them that the Legislature instituted a searching investigation concerning them, and, as a result, in 1860 savings and building associations were forbidden to receive deposits after January 1, 1862, and in 1865 they were required to return all deposits on or before July 1, 1866, which practically wound them up. The law under which they were organized was repealed.

The associations now forming in this State are organized upon safer methods. So much of interest is aroused in them that a newspaper called " The Building News and Household Journal " is now published at Meriden, devoted to the Meriden building and loan associations and co-operative and fraternal societies.

New York.

Of the early history of loan and building associations in New York very little reliable data are to be obtained. An act was passed for their incorporation in 1851. There were some associations in the State at that time. Between 1849 and 1859 a large number of associations were formed, but the act of 1851 outlined no definite scheme. It was so general in its provisions that it permitted the incorporation of any scheme, whether good or bad. The bad schemes, and especially those of a speculative character, came into great prominence. Promises were made by the organizers of the associations which could not be fulfilled. Heavy losses were sustained in many places by the confiding shareholders, and generally the expectations of those investing in them were not realized. They consequently fell into popular disfavor. C. F. Southard is authority for saying that such disfavor culminated in the Legislature appointing a committee of three to investigate them, and that such committee reported in favor of revoking the charters of all; but the report was not adopted. The number in the State at the time of the investigation was one hundred and twenty-four.*

It is certain that in 1870 there were very few associations in the State of New York. The city of Rochester and vicinity is now the banner locality in the number and success of these associations, in proportion to the population. They number at the present time eighty-three, and are forming so rapidly that before this statement is printed their number may reach a hundred.

The first association in this city was organized in

* C. F. Southard in an article in the " New York Star," September 9, 1888. See also "Assembly Documents," 1856, vol. iii, No. 46.

1852, but did not continue long; not meeting the expectation of its stockholders, its affairs were closed up. The next association was not organized until 1871. There was quite a " boom " for a few years in their growth. During 1871 and 1872 some " building lots " associations were formed in that city; that is, associations which bought a tract of land, and then sold lots to be paid for in monthly or weekly sums, much after the manner of the true building and loan associations. Many of the shareholders built houses. The associations ran in debt for the land, giving a mortgage upon it. Several proved financial failures, and in due time the mortgage was foreclosed, and the savings of those who had invested were lost. These were confounded in the public mind with the true building and loan associations, and injured them much. It was not until 1882 that they began to increase again. " The Homestead Loan Association of Rochester," organized upon the terminating plan, was then reorganized upon a permanent plan, and has taken the lead of all associations in the State. According to its annual report, October 7, 1887, it had 1,506 shareholders, of whom 261 were borrowers; it had outstanding 17,512 unmatured shares and 502 matured shares, and its assets amounted to $270,266.51.

The first association in Buffalo was organized Aug. 6, 1851, the second in 1860. They have been very successful in that city. While there are no accurate statistics as to the number, and estimates differ widely, the lowest estimate is one hundred.* One of the old-

* From a search recently made in the clerk's office of Erie County, we learn that the total number which have been incorporated in that county amounts to 327. Until recent years they

est, if not the oldest, association in the State now doing
business was organized in Elmira in 1875, and called
" The Chemung Valley Mutual Loan Association." It
was organized upon the scheme of issuing a yearly series
of stock; matured value of shares, $200; monthly dues
of one dollar, and monthly interest at six per cent. It
is now in its fourteenth financial year, and eminently
successful. From it as a model others have been organized in the Southern Tier counties. The president
of this association drafted the New York Act of 1887
for the incorporation of co-operative savings and loan
associations before mentioned; and many of the recently
organized associations have organized under its provisions. The passage of this act through the Legislature
drew attention to the associations throughout the State.
About the same time persons in New York became interested in them, and began to write them up in the
daily press. About two years ago the publication of a
monthly paper was commenced in the city of New
York, known as the " Building and Loan News." It
has served as a channel for the exchange of views between those interested in the subject, and its publisher
and his friends have done much during the last two
years to arouse public interest therein. About the
same time several of the New York dailies began writing the plan up, and associations were formed by employés of several of the papers. The " Star " became
a notable champion through the graceful pen of C. F.
Southard, who has done much for co-operative association in New York and its vicinity.

were organized upon the single-series plan, and nearly all associations organized more than ten years ago have matured their stock
and ceased to exist.

As a result of all this movement there has come to pass a regular "boom" in building and loan associations in the cities of New York, Brooklyn, and neighborhood, and it is now extending throughout the whole State. At the present time there are thirty associations in New York, eighteen in Brooklyn, four in Westchester, and in the whole State of New York about two hundred and seventy-five. They are now organizing with great rapidity, and I have no doubt that on January 1, 1890, there will be four hundred associations in the State of New York.

A State League was organized in June, 1888, which promises to have great influence in legislation affecting these associations. Mr. George W. Elliott, of Rochester, is president of the League, and Charles O. C. Hennessy, of New York, is its secretary.

Ohio.

Ohio ranks next to Pennsylvania in the number of its associations. No accurate statistics, however, have been gathered with reference to them, and only a proximate estimate can be made as to their number. Prof. F. B. Sanborn, in his report before mentioned,* says it is supposed that their number in Ohio exceeds six hundred. Of this number, about four hundred are in Hamilton County. The first association in the State was organized in 1857 in the city of Cincinnati. Dr. P. A. Peck was the promoter of its organization, and became the champion of these organizations in their early history in that city.

It seems they have outrun his expectations, and

* Report to American Social Science Association in September, 1888.

have increased in numbers beyond the requirements of
the community. In writing of his work for these associations three years ago, he said: " There are too
many building associations. At the time I started the
system I thought that five or six societies would be
enough for the needs of the people of this city; but
now there are so many I think a great many people
suffer by it. . . . Some of the members, instead of
paying their debts, put their weekly earnings into these
associations. . . . It is my opinion that societies nowa-
days pay too much in the way of salaries and current
expenses."

It is estimated that the shareholders in Cincinnati
exceed seventy-five thousand. In this city these associations far outstrip the savings-banks in the amount
of their investments and the number of their depositors. There is located at Dayton one of the largest, if
not the largest, association in the United States. It is
called the " Mutual Home and Savings Association."
The scheme upon which its business is conducted is
widely divergent from the true scheme of the building
and loan association. It issues shares of $100 and $500
matured value. It also permits shares to be paid up
in full at one payment, and then pays cash dividends
upon such shares. It has an office open during business hours for the receipt of dues, interest, etc. It
amounts, in fact, to a bank, involving in the conduct
of its business many of the beneficial principles belonging to the true building and loan association; but
instead of being purely a co-operative savings and loan
association, it becomes an institution in which the
capitalist can invest a considerable sum of money in
one lump in the purchase of paid-up stock, and hold

5

the same as an investment. The true co-operative savings and loan association allows only weekly or monthly payments to be made for the purpose of accumulating savings. The law in Ohio, under which these associations are conducted, was amended in 1886 after much discussion. They have not, however, as yet, been brought under State supervision.

Illinois.

The first building and loan association organized in Illinois, and in fact in the West, was in 1849, in Chicago, under the name of "The Chicago Building Association." It conducted business without a charter until 1851, when it was chartered by special act of the Legislature. The next association in this State was organized at Jerseyville, in 1852, and the third at Chicago in 1857. It was not until 1869 that a general act was passed authorizing their incorporation; but prior to that many had been incorporated by special act of the Legislature. The statute of 1869 authorized the incorporation of associations for purposes widely divergent from the true building and loan association, as the following quotation shows. It authorized a number of persons to "form themselves into an incorporated company for the purpose of accumulating a fund for the purchase of real estate in large tracts, paying off incumbrances thereon, the improvement thereof into lots and parcels suitable for homesteads, and the distribution of such lots or parcels among the shareholders."

Then follows provisions covering the legitimate building and loan association. In 1872 a law was passed, patterned after the laws of Pennsylvania at that time, which superseded the law of 1869. In 1874 this law was repealed, it is claimed, through the influence of those interested in savings-banks. In 1879 the law, substantially of 1872, was re-enacted. In 1880 a member of an association at Monticello, incorporated under the act of 1872 while in force, refused to pay his loan, alleging that the following section of the act of 1872 was in conflict with the Constitution of the State. " Corporations organized under this act being of the nature of co-operative associations, therefore, no premiums, fines, nor interest on such premiums that may accrue to the said corporations according to the provisions of this act shall be deemed usurious, and the same may be collected as any other debt of like amount may be collected by law in this State."

In the lower court the claim of the refractory borrower was sustained ; and this decision was affirmed in the Supreme Court of the State. At that time there were twenty associations in the State. By union of action on the part of some fourteen of this number, a reargument was obtained in the Supreme Court, and upon such rehearing the court reversed its first ruling, and held that the statute was constitutional. This decision marks the beginning of a new era in building and loan associations in Illinois. It called into existence the Illinois Building Association League, which has done much to advance the interests of associations. Through its influence two amendments to the law were passed in 1888, one authorizing the installment plan of paying premiums, and the other exempting the stock and mortgages of the associations from taxation. The provisions of the law do not provide for State supervision. That subject is now being agitated.

Since the decision before mentioned, building associations have increased in number with great rapidity, until there is claimed to be over two hundred and fifty in Chicago and nearly three hundred in other parts of the State. From my own investigations, I am led to believe that the number is as large in Illinois as in Ohio. A local league of the associations in Chicago and vicinity has recently been formed. One of the best newspapers in the country devoted to these associations is published at Chicago, under the name of " The American Building Associations News." *

Wisconsin.

The Secretary of State has kindly furnished us a list of all the associations in this State that have filed certificates of incorporation in his office up to the month of November, 1888. The total number at that date was forty-two. They were located in twenty cities and villages. Milwaukee had twenty of this number; Chippewa Falls, Superior, Lacrosse, and Oshkosh two each, while each of the remaining localities had but one.

It is somewhat remarkable that over one half, or twenty-three, of the total number were incorporated in 1887. Five were incorporated in 1886; four in 1885; three in 1884; and two in 1883. Five were incorporated in 1888 up to the month of November.

This list shows the oldest association was incorporated October 17, 1883, located at Appleton, and called " The People's Saving-Fund and Building As-

---

* For many of the facts in the foregoing relating to Illinois we are indebted to a report prepared by Prof. Jenks, of Galesburg, for the American Social Science meeting in 1888.

sociation." We are led to believe that there must
have been some associations in this State before that
date, but they were not required to file their certificates
of incorporation in the office of the Secretary of State.
We are led to this conclusion from the course of
legislation. The Revised Statutes of the State, adopted
in 1878, authorized the incorporation of these associations. The statute provided that the capital stock
should not exceed $500,000, and should be divided
into shares of $200 each. In 1882 the law was amended,
providing that the capital might be divided into shares
of not less than twenty-five dollars, nor more than two
hundred dollars. Other amendments were made at
this time. This legislation occurred before the organization of the associations at Appleton, and was undoubtedly had to meet the wishes of some association
or associations then in existence. The law was again
amended in 1885, providing that the capital stock
might be five millions.

The law was further amended in 1887, and, among
other provisions, exempted the capital and investments
of the associations from taxation, except in the case of
real estate bid in by the association under some lien
held thereon by the association. This exemption from
taxation may account for the great " boom " in their
organization in 1887. It seems that the reverse of the
experience of most States is occurring in Wisconsin.
Secretaries report to me that earlier associations were
established on the serial plan of issuing stock, and that
many of the latter associations are upon the terminating plan.

Michigan and Indiana.

Concerning loan associations in Michigan we have no data beyond the fact that some were established there many years ago; that the result of their business, as a whole, has not been satisfactory, and they declined in popularity; but at present their number is increasing again, and at the time of this writing a movement is on foot to form a State league.

In Indiana their number has been increasing recently with great rapidity, especially in the city of Indianapolis. Their number has become numerous enough in that city to bring into existence a paper called the "Building Association Register." Some time ago this paper stated that they were organizing at the rate of one a day in Indiana. By far the larger number were organizing upon the terminating plan. The law of the State provides no uniformity in plan, and the result is the same here as elsewhere—there is a great diversity in the schemes upon which their business is conducted.

Our data is insufficient to warrant us in giving any facts further than we have already stated.

Minnesota.

In Minnesota, loan associations have attained their greatest development in the twin cities of Minneapolis and St. Paul. No statistics have so far been collated by an official bureau of the State.

The fullest information we have been able to obtain is from a monograph by Albert Shaw, published in September, 1886, by the American Economic Association, entitled "Co-operation in a Western City." He says: "The form of co-operative enterprise that has attained far greater results in the United States than all others combined is that of the well-known and almost invariably successful building and loan association. Several of the most flourishing building and loan associations to be found anywhere in the country are established in the cities of Minneapolis and St. Paul In the former city, the first was organized in 1874."

Mr. Shaw tells us that, in Minneapolis, "about one thousand homes have thus far been secured for workingmen by the building and loan associations, and their operations have only fairly begun. It may be reasonably estimated that two hundred and fifty more families will be domiciled through the agency of the associations in 1887, and that the number will increase a hundred a year thereafter for some years to come, producing results not only of great consequence economically, but of inestimable moral and social value."

The first association was organized in St. Paul in 1869. The idea' was taken there by one Theodore Sanders from Philadelphia. There are now over forty of these associations, and their total membership "must exceed six thousand, representing fully one fourth of the families in the city. Mr. Shaw further says: "The estimate that from eight to ten thousand homes in St. Paul have been, in whole or in part, secured to their owners with money advanced by the building societies might seem extravagant; but I must conclude that the facts bear it out." The associations in these two cities continue, without any material change, the present Philadelphia systems of building associations. Associations have been established at Duluth and other places in the State.

Iowa, Kansas, and Missouri.

The number of loan associations in Iowa is not large. The first was organized at Burlington in 1870, and the second at Keokuk and Oskaloosa in 1872. There are some at Des Moines and in other parts of the State. There has recently been organized at Des Moines what is called the " Suburban-Home Building Association," the plan of which is to buy a tract of land and build houses thereon, and sell the same to stockholders, who make payments weekly or monthly upon the general plan of the true building and loan association. Schemes such as this, have, as a rule, brought more evil than good to the stockholders. In the State of New York, at Rochester, "building-lot associations," through failure, for years, placed the true building and loan associations in disfavor. The associations of this class are very largely speculative, and hence wholly outside of the class of associations which uniformly prove a blessing to those engaged, and friends of true co-operation should regard them with suspicion.

In regard to Kansas we have no data that is reliable.

In Missouri, loan associations have been growing with great rapidity for a few years. Of the precise number we are not informed, but they exceed fifty and may reach one hundred. A question of great interest to them is now in litigation in the courts of the State. On March 31, 1887, the laws authorizing their incorporation were amended in many particulars. The amendatory act contained a provision exempting these associations from taxation, on the ground that they were benevolent associations, and consequently might

be so exempted under Article X, section 21 of the
Constitution of the State. The Secretary of State
disagreed with such interpretation, and refused to issue
certificates of incorporation until the tax upon the
capital was deposited with the State Treasurer, to be
held by him until the courts passed upon the validity
of the act. This arrangement was entered into by
some thirty-four associations. The result of this litigation will have great influence upon the future of
these associations in the State of Missouri.

Maryland.

The first act for the incorporation of loan associations was passed in Maryland, April 17, 1843; but
according to data received by us from that State no
association was formed until March, 1846. An association was then formed—the organizers meeting in a
church on St. Charles Street—and named " The Baltimore Building and Loan Association." As elsewhere,
so here, the first associations were upon the terminating plan, but of late the serial plan is taking the lead,
until three fourths of the associations issue their stock
upon that plan. The matured value of a share is
usually fixed at $100, and dues twenty-five cents.
weekly, payable to the society prior to the stated
weekly meeting, or at the meeting. Weekly interest
on a borrowed share is placed at twelve cents.

Those associations have been quite uniformly successful in this State. In the city of Baltimore their
membership is largely artisans, clerks, and railroad
men—men working for wages. In the rural parts of
the State there are some associations embracing in
their membership many of the prominent men in the

community. The total number of associations in the State at the present time, as we are informed upon trustworthy authority, is one hundred and ninety-one, of which one hundred and fifty-eight are located in Baltimore.*

Southern States.

We have no data relating to the extent of loan associations in the Southern States beyond that contained in Prof. F. B. Sanborn's report, before mentioned, to the " American Social Science Association." We quote from it as follows :

For various reasons, some of which are stated by R. T. Hill, of Texas, in his report concerning provident institutions in the extreme Southwest, there have been few accumulations of savings in the form of money in the greater part of the South. The number of savings-banks there is small, and building associations are recent and, as yet, comparatively few. Mr. Hill estimates that there are fifty in Texas, which is probably more than in any of the former slave-holding States, unless Maryland be an exception. They are numerous in Missouri, and a few are found in Arkansas, Mississippi, Kentucky, Tennesee, Lousiana, Alabama, Georgia, the Carolinas, and the Virginias. From these States, however, the committee have only scanty reports. There are twenty or more associations in the city of New Orleans, several in Atlanta, one at Georgetown, S. C., one at Key West, Fla., one at Pensacola, one at Selma, Ala., one at Fort Smith, Ark., one at Lafayette, La., one at Parkersburg, W. Va., one each at Yazoo City and Columbus, Miss., and no doubt many

* These figures are widely divergent from estimates of their numbers which I have seen. Rosenthal's " Manual for Building and Loan Associations," published in August, 1888, at Cincinnati, places the number at five hundred in Baltimore. We believe the figures above given to be correct.

others in the above-named States. In Louisana it seems that as long ago as 1873 a building association was formed, which ran its course in ten years, and divided its profits among its members. But the first of the existing New Orleans associations was organized in September, 1882, and has since been very prosperous, having now about six hundred members, who have built or purchased more than one hundred homes during the six years of its existence. Several others of the twenty or thirty New Orleans associations have from three hundred to six hundred members. In Tennesee the associations organized in 1880–81 and in 1885, in order to secure favorable legislation, formed a State union, which, at its organization, included six associations at Memphis, four at Nashville, and four or five others in different parts of Tennesee. There are now five or six in Chattanooga, which during seven years past have provided homes for two hundred and fifty families, and in all Tennesee there must now be upward of thirty associations.

Pacific Coast.

Our data is meager with reference to the Pacific coast. Loan associations have been established at various points, although in many cases the scheme upon which they are conducted is unlike that of the true building and loan association. The element of real-estate speculation enters into their scheme to some extent. In 1887 there were in California eleven associations, with assets of $2,595,488, represented by 30,000 shares.

General Remarks.

Certain facts have become well established in our investigations. 1. That, as a rule, the current newspaper statements and some of the book literature relating to loan associations exaggerate their number in localities and States where they are most numerous. 2. That, in their early development in almost every State, they have in some degree become speculative in relation to real estate, which in the end has generally proved unsatisfactory, and in many cases losses were sustained by the shareholders, and building and loan associations ceased to be popular. Pennsylvania has been an exception to some extent, and explanation is found in the fact that in that State there has been a closer following of the true principles. The law of the State so limited the number of shares and the matured value of the share that large speculative associations could not be formed under the law. It has been most fortunate for their success in that State. 3. The State of Massachusetts has the most uniform scheme throughout of any State, although now only about ten years old. The early history of co-operative associations in the State, before the present law, was not satisfactory. New York has one law for their formation as good as Massachusetts; but its trouble lies in the fact that the old law of 1851 remains unrepealed, and admits of all sorts of schemes. 4. There is at the present time a " boom " in these associations throughout a large part of the United States. They are attracting attention everywhere, and, as a factor in co-operation among wage-earners and the encouragement of savings, they are fast becoming the most prominent and influential. The amount of savings already paid into them in the form of dues in many States exceeds the deposits in savings-banks.

The total number in the United States, January 1, 1889, will not be far from four thousand. To speak of the total number of shares outstanding, or the total number of shareholders, or the total accumulations in these associations throughout the whole country, would be mere guess-work, and we will not enter upon it. We earnestly hope that the next census will include statistics of these associations, when we may hope for reliable data concerning them as a whole throughout the country.

CHAPTER V.

A REVIEW OF THE DEVELOPMENT OF THE SCHEMES
UPON WHICH CO-OPERATIVE SAVINGS AND LOAN
ASSOCIATIONS HAVE BEEN AND ARE NOW CON-
DUCTED.

IT is our aim in this chapter to present a review of
the advancement made in the manner of conducting
the class of associations under discussion. This calls
for an examination of various schemes which have
been and are now in operation, and the reasons that
have led to their development from the simple building association. We can not refer to all the modifications that have arisen in the various schemes. It is
the principal schemes, and the more important modifications, that we shall discuss. We will first refer to
the manner of issuing

Stock.

In the primitive building associations of Philadelphia, there was but a single series of stock issued;
every person taking shares of stock, subsequent to the
date of the first issue of shares, was obliged to pay back
dues in order to be in the same position he would have
been had he taken his stock at the date of the first

issuc; so that each shareholder paid the same amount
per share into the association regardless of the time
when he took his shares. The money was loaned only
to shareholders. Inasmuch as only one series of stock
was issued the lifetime of the association was limited
to the time that it took for the shares to reach their
matured value. This scheme necessarily involved the
condition that every shareholder remaining in the
association at the time the stock matured must be a
borrower to the amount of the matured value of shares
held by him. Let us make this clear. Suppose the
charter of the association limited the number of shares
it could issue to five hundred, and that during its lifetime it had issued that number. After the payment
of its running expenses, the funds received could be
used for only two purposes, namely, the making of
loans to its own members and paying shareholders who
withdrew. Suppose that, of the five hundred shares
issued, three hundred had been withdrawn, leaving two
hundred outstanding when attaining their matured
value. Assume the shares were $200 each at their ma-
tured value. Now two hundred shares at $200 each, is
$40,000. Before the shares can be matured, the asso-
ciation must have $40,000 of assets. The assets con-
sist of the money due from the shareholders to the
association upon loans. As no shareholder can borrow
a larger sum than the matured value of the shares held
by him, it follows that no shareholder can owe the
association for borrowed money a larger sum than the
association will owe him when his shares of stock have
matured; therefore, each shareholder must owe the
association a sum equal to that which the association
will owe him upon his matured shares. The only limi-

tation or exception to this statement of the case will arise in reference to the dues paid at the last meeting. The amount of those dues will not have been borrowed and will be due to some shareholder or shareholders in excess of the amount owing by him or them to the association.

But as the association progresses from year to year towards the maturity of its stock, it might not happen that there are shareholders who desired to borrow. What then? It would not do to have the dues paid in from month to month remain uninvested; no profits would accrue, and the result would be unsatisfactory. Under the scheme of a single series, the association has the power to compel shareholders to borrow the funds. They are called forced loans; and their articles of association and by-laws determine who should become the borrower when there are no shareholders wishing to borrow.

This scheme is known as the *terminating plan*. It involves three serious defects which it was very desirable to obviate, namely, the dissolution of the association when the stock matured; the large amount of back dues which the new stockholder would have to pay who took stock after the association had been running for some time, and, lastly, the making of forced loans—that is, compelling the shareholder to become a borrower, whether he wanted to do so or not.

To overcome these defects, the serial scheme was developed. Under this scheme, a new series of stock was issued at the beginning of each fiscal year, or half-yearly. In some instances series have been issued quarterly, and even oftener.

This is known as the *serial plan*. This change in

the scheme obviated two of the defects in the single-series scheme. It permitted the association to become perpetual, and it furnished a new series of stock so often that one taking stock at any time in the current series did not have a large amount of back dues to pay to place him in the same situation that he would have been had he taken his shares at the first. As a matter of practical experience, the serial plan also obviates, except in rare cases, the third defect. It permits of the accession of new stockholders, who become such for the express purpose of becoming borrowers. In the single-series scheme, when an association had become two or more years old, the amount of back dues that they would have to pay on their stock in order to become shareholders, so that they might become borrowers, was a serious obstacle; while under the serial plan, the amount was not large at any time. In a well-managed association, having the confidence of the community, there is usually no difficulty in finding those who wish to borrow the funds. But the scheme provides a mode to obviate an accumulation of funds that can not be loaned by providing a mode for compelling withdrawals. In the serial scheme it is deemed advisable, when a series matures, to have but comparatively few outstanding free shares.

Hence, it is deemed a wise policy to encourage withdrawals in series approaching maturity. This is accomplished by increasing the percentage of profits which the withdrawing shareholder is allowed as the series approaches its maturity.

In addition to this policy, many associations have provided that the withdrawal of stock may be compelled after a series has attained a certain number of

6

years. In the case of a compulsory withdrawal, the shareholder is allowed all the profits. The scheme of the Massachusetts co-operative banks has this provision, the number of years being placed at four or more. The scheme of the New York co-operative savings and loan associations has the same provision, and places the age of the series at four years or more.

While it is wise to thus provide a mode for compelling withdrawals, if necessity requires it, to prevent the accumulation of uninvested funds, there will seldom be occasion for an association to avail itself of the provision.

The single-series, or terminating plan, has been almost wholly abandoned in localities where these associations have been in operation long. Most of those that remain in such localities were formed years ago, and have not had time to run their course to a natural dissolution by the maturing of their stock.

In some cases where an association is formed upon the serial plan, each series has been conducted separately, as though it was the only series of stock the association had outstanding, thereby making, in effect, as many terminating associations running under one management as there are series issued. This cumbersome mode of conducting the business has arisen from the fact that those who organized and conducted the association did not fully comprehend the proper mode of conducting the business in cases where all the series are run together, forming, in effect, a partnership.

There is still another scheme, which has assumed the name of the *permanent plan.* Under this scheme, stock is issued at any time when there is a demand for it. The largest association in the State of New

York, the Homestead Fund Association of Rochester, and the largest in the State of Ohio, the Mutual Home and Savings Association of Dayton, issue their stock upon this scheme. The latter association is one of the oldest, most successful, and largest associations in the United States. This scheme no more deserves the name "permanent plan," than the serial plan, as both make the existence of the association perpetual. The associations above named provide in their scheme for paying cash dividends upon matured stock. The Dayton company also allows the face of a share to be paid at one payment, and issues thereupon "paid-up stock" upon which it pays dividends

These are features which do not belong to the true co-operative savings and building-loan associations. Especially is this true of the feature of issuing paid-up stock. This plan allows the capitalist to make investments in its stock in the same manner that he would invest in the stock of any corporation for the purpose of deriving profits from the dividends declared. This is not allowed in States where a well-drawn statute has been enacted to regulate the business of loan associations.

Matured Value of Stock.

In both the terminating and permanent plans there have been various modifications as to the matured value of the shares. In the first building association—the Oxford Provident Building Association, in Philadelphia—the matured value of the shares, we have seen, was $500. The third one formed—the Franklin Building Association—placed the matured value of shares at $200. This has been a very common "matured value" throughout the United States; but associations have been formed in which the matured value has been placed at $10, $50, $100, $105, $250, $300, $500, and even $1,000. There has been and is now great diversity as to the matured value of shares.

Amount and Payment of Dues

Both the terminating and permanent plans admit of many modifications in the amount and payment of dues, and many have been developed. We have already noted, in Chapter IV, that the dues in the Oxford Provident Building Association were three dollars a month on each share, and that the new association that succeeded it upon its dissolution placed the monthly dues at the same, and that the Franklin, organized in 1845, placed its dues at one dollar a month on each share. A very common rate of dues has been and is now, in all forms of these associations, one dollar a month on each share.

In order to provide for smaller savings than one dollar, many associations have been formed providing for weekly dues of twenty-five cents on each share; and when the matured value of a share has been fixed at ten dollars, monthly dues have been placed at five cents a share.

Early in the history of these associations in Pennsylvania, the laws of the State fixed the matured value of shares at $200, and monthly dues at one dollar a month on each share. In the first building association, according to our information, the monthly dues were all paid on a certain evening in each month, between seven and nine o'clock. At these monthly meetings all the business of the association was transacted, except the perfecting of its loans. This has been the most common mode as to time and manner of paying dues; but other modes have come into use in many places. One has been for the association to have a regular office at which the secretary or treasurer could be found at certain hours, or all the time, to receive and receipt for dues, and they were treated as if paid at the regular monthly or weekly meeting. This involves greater expense in conducting the business, and from this mode have developed associations much unlike the true building and loan associations, although classed with them.

We most earnestly indorse the mode of making the dues payable once a month, and that all dues be paid between certain hours, usually in the evening, to be fixed by the by-laws; and that they be received and receipted for by a committee of the directors, the secretary and treasurer assisting them if the committee desire their aid.

Premiums.

There have been various modifications in the development of the scheme of building associations relating to the premium paid by the borrower. These modifications have related both to the amount and the time when paid. Let us inquire as to what is a premium? In the common language of the business mart it is a bonus which the borrower pays to the association in addition to interest for his loan. Is there any necessary reason, existing in the scheme, which calls for the payment of any premium or bonus by the borrower at all? None whatever, beyond the question of the most satisfactory and practical method of deciding who shall borrow a certain sum of money, where several, having equal right to borrow, are competing for it. What is the effect of a premium by a borrower? It increases the profits of the association and the amount of the dividends to be added to the shares. Who pays the sum that thus helps to swell the dividends beyond legal interest? The borrower, of course, who pays the premium. Does the borrower get any of it back? Yes, a small part of it. How? In the dividends added to his shares. How great a part of it does he get back? The part that he gets back will bear the same proportion to the amount paid by him that the value of the shares he borrowed upon bears to the value of all the shares of the association outstanding at the time the next dividend is made after he pays the premium. Suppose all shareholders became borrowers for the same amount, and paid the same amount of premium. What then? Each one would receive back in dividends upon his shares the full amount of premium, and no injustice would be done; all would share equally in the benefits of the bonus, and each bear equally its burden.

But will all shareholders become borrowers to the amount of their shares? No; except in the single-series plan, where they are compelled to borrow. In the serial plan only a small part of the shareholders can become borrowers. What becomes of the greater part of the premium paid to the association in this plan? It inures to the benefit of the non-borrowing shareholder. Do premiums work equity between the non-borrower and the borrower? Certainly not. The dividends of the former are increased without bearing any of the burden that increases the amount.

It is in this matter of premiums that many modifications in the scheme of building associations have worked a most conspicuous inequality and injustice in the benefits accruing to shareholders. They have justly rendered the building and loan association in some places odious. Premiums should not, we insist, be charged or allowed except for one purpose. If there is $2,000, or any other sum, to loan, and only one shareholder that wants to borrow the sum at the time it is offered for loan, he should have it without one cent premium or bonus. If two or more shareholders wish to borrow it, the right to loan it should be sold by an open bidding per share; and this is justifiable only upon the ground that in the long run it will prove the most satisfactory and practicable method of deciding between shareholders desiring to borrow the money offered for loaning. The association should discourage the bidding of large premiums.

Inequality of benefits to the shareholders is not the only evil effect to be charged to the system of premiums; but some of the modifications, in fact nearly all, have complicated the whole scheme, and made it hard to be comprehended by the uneducated, and has prevented their rapid growth and the extended beneficent results that would flow from a just scheme.

The several schemes relating to the subject of premiums may be grouped under five heads, namely, "The Gross Plan," "The Net Plan," "The Installment Plan," "The Interest Premium Plan," and "The New York Plan."

The four names used first in this classification are familiar names in describing the schemes they designate. The fifth we have assigned to the plan embodied in the New York Co-operative Savings and Loan Association scheme. No better name occurs to me to use than the name of the State where it has been definitely adopted by a general law. Let us first examine

The Gross Plan.

We shall assume the matured value to be $200. In this plan the borrower, at the time of bidding off his loan, bids a certain per cent on the matured value of the share, or a certain sum per share, according as the scheme of the association provides. The amount thus bid is deducted from the matured value, and the borrower receives only the remainder, but gives security to the association for $200 a share, and pays interest on that sum. To illustrate: Suppose the successful bidder at the sale of the money bids twenty-five per cent, or $50 a share. He receives $150, and gives security for $200 a share, and pays monthly interest at the rate of six per cent per annum on $200. If he continues to pay his dues and interest until his shares of stock mature, the value of the shares borrowed upon equal the loan, and one cancels the other. Now, the real cost of the loan to the borrower will be determined by the length of time it takes the shares in the series borrowed upon to mature. The length of that time will be determined by the profits of the association, the amount of which will be largely determined by the premiums bid on money loaned. If all the money loaned by the association obtained as high a premium as above mentioned, the share would mature in eight or nine years, and the dues paid would amount to from $96 to $108 upon each share, the balance of the matured values of the shares being made up by the profits added to the shares in dividends. But suppose the borrower, in the case above assumed, paid a much higher premium than was generally obtained at the sales of money; then it would take a correspondingly longer time for his shares to mature, and he would have to continue his payment of dues and interest a longer time accordingly, and the expenses of the loan would be increased in the same proportion.

This was the plan adopted in the first building associations, and in those associations there was but a single series of stock. The association terminated with the maturity of the shares.

As we have seen before, all shareholders remaining in the association until their shares matured must necessarily become borrowers to the amount of their stock, less only the dues and interest paid at the meeting when the stock matured. If all paid the same premium, no serious injustice would be done; but if competition was spirited at one meeting, and a high rate of premiums was given—such as the $50 a share assumed in the foregoing illustration—and at another meeting a borrower had no competition and obtained his money at par, there would arise great inequality in the expense of a loan, and also a consequent uncertainty as to the length of time it would take the shares of stock to mature. To limit this uncertainty and prevent the borrower, at a time when there was no competition, from obtaining his loan without the payment of a premium, the custom sprang up of fixing in the constitution or by-laws a minimum premium at which the bidding for loans must start. When the serial or permanent association came into existence, it adopted this custom, and fixed a minimum premium bid.

The first association with which the writer had an

acquaintance was organized and conducted for some years on the scheme of requiring a minimum premium of $40 on each share. The highest sum the borrower could obtain was $160 a share.

In the early days of building and loan associations, as compared with these times, money commanded a high interest, and the rate of six per cent per annum, which the borrower paid in the association, was below the legal rate; hence, if he obtained his loan without any premium, the association would not obtain legal interest. It seemed eminently proper, therefore, that the borrower should pay a premium of some amount.

At that time the values of real estate, as a rule, were advancing in the localities where buildings were being erected with money borrowed from loan associations, and it was felt that the non-borrower was entitled to large interest upon the money which he paid into the association, and which enabled the borrower to obtain his loan, and thereby be able to own his home, and, while paying for it, also obtain the benefit of the rise in value of his real estate. For these reasons a high rate of premiums obtained in the early history of the building and loan associations.

The question may well arise in the mind of the inquirer, in the event the borrower desired to repay his loan before his shares attained their matured value, did he have to pay the full two hundred dollars on each share of his loan? To require this of the borrower would manifestly make the burden of the borrower so heavy as to have a disastrous effect upon the success of the whole scheme. To obviate this, a system of rebates was adopted. By the law of Pennsylvania, passed in 1859, under which thereafter building and loan associations were organized and incorporated in that State, it was provided that a borrower repaying a loan within eight years after the organization of the corporation should have returned to him one eighth of the premium for each of the eight years unexpired at the time of such repayment.

This law evidently contemplated a single-series system; but the principle is equally applicable to the serial system. Instead of " organization of the corporation," we have only to insert within eight years after the series, to which the shares borrowed upon belonged, was issued, and the plan of rebates applies.

This rule contemplates the maturing of shares in eight years; and the system of rebates which it provides for is simply this: If the borrower has paid a premium of $50 a share, as we have before assumed, that premium is divided into eight parts—being $6.25 each. If the borrower repays during the same year he borrowed, he repays the $150, and $6.25 in addition, namely, $156.25. If he repays during the second year, he must pay $162.50, and so on, increasing $6.25 each year. The same principle applies to any premium bid.

But still another question arises. Suppose the shares were issued for some years before the owner borrowed upon them. In the serial plan, when money is offered for sale, there may be several shareholders competing for the money, and the shares of stock held by each have been issued in different series; one, for instance, may have just come in and taken stock in the current series for the purpose of becoming a borrower; another one may have had and paid dues upon his stock for four years. Suppose both are successful bidders at $50 premium. From what we have stated above, it is clear how the rebates apply to the borrower in the current series; but as to the one holding shares four years old, the above rule would not apply. As to him, the rule is applied in this manner: The borrower is allowed at the time of borrowing a rebate of one eighth of the premium for each full year the series has run at the time he borrows. Thus, on the $50 bid, if the series in which the shares were issued, upon which the borrower is obtaining a loan, is over four years old and less than five years, he receives $150 a share and four eighths of the premium bid by him— so that he would receive in all $175. If the shares were one year and less than two years old, the borrower would receive $156.25.

The same rules we have stated apply to a system based upon a scheme in which it is assumed that the shares will mature in ten, or any other number of years. The premium bid is divided into as many parts as the scheme assumes it will take for the shares to mature, and whenever a loan is repaid, a rebate is made of as many of these parts of the premium as there are years remaining of the time it is assumed it will take the shares to mature; and a rebate is likewise made from the premium bid at the time of borrowing, of as many of these parts of the premium as the shares borrowed upon are years old. It is apparent that the gross plan, with its system of rebates, complicates the book-keeping of the association.

To illustrate: Take an association upon the serial plan, in which it is assumed that eight years is the requisite time for a share to mature, and which issues a new series of stock each year. Suppose a loan is made upon ten shares belonging to the current series, at a premium of $50 per share. A security is given to the association for $2,000. This is the face value of the asset. If it run until the shares borrowed upon mature, $2,000 will be paid upon it; but, if repaid the same year it was given, $1,562.50 will cancel it. If not paid until the next year, it will take $1,625 and so on, increasing $62.50 each year until the eighth, when it will take $2,000. Suppose at the close of the fiscal year the association holds $20,000 of mortgages, at their face value, what is their actual value? We certainly can not say their actual value exceeds a sum that will cancel them if paid to the association. To determine what sum will cancel them, we must ascertain how much rebate each share borrowed upon in making up the $20,000 of loans is entitled to be allowed on repayment. The total of such rebates deducted from the $20,000 will give us their actual value; but, to ascertain the sum total of rebates, we must know the amount of premium bid on each of the one hundred shares borrowed upon, and the age of each of the shares. From these intricacies of the system there came into use the terms "apparent profits" and "actual profits," "unearned premiums" and "earned premiums." Assume each of the one hundred shares above to have sold at a premium of $50; it is clear it only took $15,000 of money to secure the $20,000 of mortgages. Here is an apparent profit of $5,000, but, as we have before seen, if all the shares borrowed upon belonged to the current series, $15,625 would cancel the $20,000; and the actual profits from the premiums is only $625 instead of $5,000. Of the $5,000 of premiums only $625 is "earned," and the remainder, $4,375, is as yet "unearned."

In our illustrations we have assumed the simplest conditions that could arise under the rebate system. Increase the mortgages to $100,000, and made in five different series, and each loan paying a different premium, and the expert accountant will be appalled with the complexity, unless he has become an expert in these particular accounts, and has clearly understood the difference between " earned " and " unearned " premiums, and opened his books and kept the month at basis.

One of the rocks upon which many building and loan associations have run and nearly foundered has been this "unearned premium." Until very recently many associations opened and kept their accounts as though the whole premium had been paid, and reckoned their assets in declaring their dividends at the face value of their securities, instead of the " actual value "; and as the years ran by and rates of interest declined, and the rate of the minimum premium had to be lowered in order to obtain borrowers at all, and the earlier borrowers from any cause repaid their loans, the rebates which had to be allowed to them necessarily came out of current profits, and the result was to make dividends very small and greatly to damage the prosperity of the association, without the shareholders, as a mass, being able to clearly understand what was the difficulty. This consequence was obviated by keeping the books so that the securities were only reckoned at their actual value; but this was more difficult than many secretaries and organizers knew well how to do. The gross plan, with its system of rebates, is too complex for the ordinary wage-worker to readily understand, or for any one, without careful study; and

by reason of its intricacies, and sometimes rank in-
equalities of benefits between borrower and non-borrower, it has greatly retarded the growth of loan associations upon simpler and more equitable schemes.

The Net Plan.

The net plan was the next to develop. Building
and loan associations came into existence in such great
numbers in Philadelphia that they necessarily had to
compete with each other for shareholders; and hence
there was a constant tendency to modify the original
scheme so that the new association, with a scheme
changed from the older scheme, would appear to be
better for the borrower. The borrower could readily
perceive that when he was paying six per cent on $200
a share and had received only $150 or $160, he was in
fact paying seven or eight per cent for the use of his
money. To obviate this apparent high rate of interest, a new scheme was devised of only charging six per
cent interest upon the sum actually received. The
security would be given to the association for the principal sum of $200 a share and for the payment of in-
terest upon the sum which he actually received after
the amount of his premium bid was deducted. This
came to be known as the "net plan," from the fact
that interest was paid only upon the net sum the borrower received. The system of premiums, with the
minimum bid and rebates of the gross plan, remained
unchanged. If the borrower was making his loan upon
shares in a series four years old, he was allowed four
eighths of the premium bid, if the association was organized on the basis of eight years to mature its shares.
If organized on the basis of nine years to reach ma-

turity of shares, he was allowed four ninths of the premium; if organized on the basis of ten years, then four tenths were allowed; that is, the net sum he would receive would be $200 a share, less the premium bid, plus four eighths or four ninths or four tenths of such premium, according to the scheme of the associations.

If borrowing in the current series—that is, the last series issued—the net sum received would be $200 a share, less the total premium bid. The same rebates from the face value of the security were allowed on repayment of the loan as under the gross plan. In brief, the net plan varied from the gross plan only in charging the borrower interest on the net sum received, instead of charging him interest on the face value of the security, that being for the matured value of each share borrowed upon. This scheme was better for the borrower, provided he was not induced by reason of the apparent advantage to him in the matter of interest to run up the premium bid to a higher rate than he would have done under the gross plan. This interest advantage was a tempting delusion in the matter of bidding high premiums.

It will be seen that the net plan involved all the intricacies and complexities of the gross plan. It was an improvement to the borrower who understood the plan fully, and was not induced thereby to bid a higher premium than he would otherwise have bid; but to the unthinking it often proved a delusion and a snare.

The Installment Plan.

The third plan evolved in the history of building and loan associations relating to premiums is known as the "installment plan." Associations organized and conducting their business under the installment plan are subject to two classifications. In the first the borrower bids a premium in the same manner as under the gross and net plan; but instead of the whole amount of the premium bid being deducted from the matured value of the share, and he receiving upon his loan only the balance, the premium bid is divided into as many parts or installments as the scheme of the association assumes that it will take months for the shares to mature; and the borrower at each payment of his dues and interest pays one of these installments of the premium bid by him. Under this arrangement, the borrower receives $200 a share upon his loan, or whatever sum constitutes the matured value of the shares, and pays interest upon that sum and gives a security to the association for the payment of the principal sum, and, in addition thereto, for the payment of the installments of premium, with his dues and interest. Thus, if a borrower in the current series should bid a premium of $50 a share, $200 being their matured value, and the scheme of the association assumes that nine years are required for the shares to mature, the $50 premium would be divided into one hundred and eight installments, of which one part would be paid with each payment of dues and interest. If the association assumes that it would take ten years for its shares to mature, then the $50 would be divided into one hundred and twenty parts or installments, and one installment would be paid with each payment of dues and interest.

This plan was a great advance upon the gross plan and the net plan; under it, the borrower received his

7

full $200 a share, and he could readily determine how much the installment of premium for every month increased his rate of interest paid for the use of the money.

The second class of associations organized under this plan modified the first scheme by dropping out the assumption that the shares would mature in a certain number of months, the premium bid not being a gross sum divided into installments for the purpose of determining the amount of the installment to be paid each month. The bid is made solely on the amount that the borrower will pay each month for the use of the money, in addition to the legal interest. The borrower receives $200 a share and pays interest thereon, and, in addition thereto, such sum every month as the bid made by him requires. The latter form of the installment plan has justly become the most popular of the two, and we think is now generally adopted in associations throughout the country where the installment plan is in operation. Under this plan the borrower who wishes to repay his loan at any time before his shares of stock have matured simply pays the installment of premium up to the time of the payment of his loan. It will be observed that this plan or scheme eliminates the complex system of the gross and net plan with reference to rebates, and very much simplifies the account-keeping of the association, and also simplifies the whole scheme of the association to such a degree that it can be readily understood by men of ordinary intelligence.

The second form of the installment plan was the one adopted by the law of Massachusetts, providing for the incorporation of what is now known as the "co-operative banks" of the State of Massachusetts; and, so far as we are advised, is the plan generally pursued by associations in St. Paul, Minneapolis, and Philadelphia.

Premium Interest Plan.

The fourth plan or scheme relating to premiums, which has developed in recent years to some extent and is gaining ground in some localities, is the "premium interest plan." This plan was incorporated into the Massachusetts scheme of co-operative banks in 1882. That law provides that any corporation organized under the act providing for the incorporation of co-operative banks may provide by its by-laws that the bid for loans "at its stated monthly meetings shall, instead of a premium, be a rate of annual interest upon the sum desired, payable in monthly installments. Such bids shall include the whole interest to be paid at any rate not less than five per centum per annum."

The original act which this amends provided for that form of the installment plan in which the bid was a certain per cent upon the amount loaned, payable each month. Under the amendments referred to, the co-operative banks are given the option of the installment plan or to confine the bidding to the rate of interest to be paid by the borrower, the money to be struck off to the borrower who bids the highest rate of interest and furnishes satisfactory security. It will be noted that under the premium interest plan of Massachusetts the minimum rate of interest shall not be fixed by the by-laws at less than five per cent per annum.

Associations under the old law of the State of New York may be organized upon any of the plans or schemes to which we have already referred; and of late some associations have been organized upon the premium interest plan, the minimum rate of interest being fixed at five per cent and the bidding for the loans commencing at that sum. This plan of premium is a great advance upon the gross plan and net plan with their system of rebates; and it is claimed by its friends to be also an advance upon the installment plan, as it simplifies the scheme by confining the bidding of the premium solely to the rate of interest. The borrower receives $200 per share, and pays such rate of interest per month as his bids call for.

There are many things connected with this plan to commend it, and its friends speak very strongly in its favor. As to which of these schemes is the best we shall discuss in the next chapter.

The New York Premium Plan.

As we have before stated, we name the fifth plan relating to premiums " the New York premium plan," for the reason that it is the plan incorporated into the general law of this State providing for the incorporation of co-operative savings and loan associations. The general scheme incorporated into the statute contemplates that the only object or purpose of a premium being paid by the borrower is to determine who shall become entitled to borrow the money where there are several bidding for it who are equally entitled to become borrowers. That the selling of the money at auction to the highest bidder is the most practicable manner of determining who shall borrow the money, assuming,

of course, that each borrower has ample security to
offer for his loan according to the requirements of the
scheme of the association. The borrower, at the time
of his bidding, clearly understands that whatever
premium he bids is in the nature of a bonus, and that
the amount that he bids is deducted from his loan
at the time, and he gives security to the association
for $200 a share, and pays interest thereon, and
the whole premium transaction is closed. Under this
system, high rates of premium will not be bid, and
a very large share of the loans made will pay no
premium at all. The general law provides that the
rate of interest to be paid shall be determined by the
by-laws of each association. The object of this provision is to allow associations to reduce their rates of
interest as the general legal rate of interest shall decline. At present the legal rate of interest in New
York is six per cent; and associations now organizing
under this statute fix their rate of interest at that
sum; but in case the rate of interest should be placed
at five per cent by legislative enactments, the associations formed under this act could, by their by-laws,
change their rate of interest accordingly. Under this
plan the face value of the securities represents their
actual value, and every security held by the association
bears the same rate of interest. No delusions nor snares
are held out to the borrower to lead him to bid a high
premium on the ground that it will be returned to
him. The whole scheme of an association is simplified
to such a degree that it may be readily understood by
all. We shall further discuss the merits of this plan
hereafter.

We have now described the five plans relating to

the subject of premiums. There are various modifications of these several types; but it is not our purpose to enter into the discussion of them in detail.

Many associations exist which seek to be known or classified as associations of the class we are discussing which should not be so classified.

It is an essential feature of building and loan associations, co-operative banks, and the co-operative savings and loan associations that each share of stock of the same age, whether borrowed upon or not, shares equally in the distribution of profits; but there is a class of associations where the borrower is excluded from any share in the profits. As an illustration of such a scheme we quote from a communication to the "American Building Association News," dated at Mt. Vernon, Ind., February, 1888:

We have two associations here working on the following plan : Par value of shares $100, dues payable weekly, twenty-five cents per share. A fixed amount of $65 is loaned on each share borrowed on and the loans run five years from date of series in which loan is made ; $65 you will notice is the amount returned to the association in dues during a period of five years. The borrowing members pay 6 per cent weekly with their dues on the net amount of loan ; for example, a loan of ten shares, $650, the interest for the first year at 6 per cent is $39 ; the second year interest on $520, $31.20 ; third year interest on $390, $23.40 ; fourth year interest $15.60 ; fifth year interest $7.80 ; no premium is paid by the borrower, and each series of stock is liquidated at the end of five years from the time of issue. The borrowers have their mortgages cancelled, and the non-borrowers receive the net amount of profits or losses, as the case may be, up to that time on each share held, including dues paid on the same.

An association of this nature could not be conducted under the laws of Pennsylvania, Massachusetts, or New York.

Another scheme for associations usually classed as building and loan associations, but improperly so, allows the shareholders to pay a gross sum at the beginning of a series, in lieu of monthly or weekly dues, which invested at a certain rate of interest will amount to the matured value of a share in the association in a certain number of years, the time which the association assumes that it will take the stock in the series in which the shares are issued to mature.

An association of this kind is speculative and in conflict with the true object and spirit of building and loan associations. All features of speculation should be eliminated from these associations, so far as possible, in order to make them continuously popular and successful. The capital of all associations should consist of the monthly or weekly savings of its members, with profits derived therefrom in loaning to its own members or shareholders. Much injury has come to the fame of the true co-operative associations for savings and home-building by schemes that assume their name and many of the forms of doing business, but which are in reality only schemes by which the money-lender obtains large interest from the borrower. They should be discouraged by every friend of true co-operation among wage-earners.

CHAPTER VI.

WE have now before us a general outline of the several schemes upon which the class of associations under discussion have been and are now conducted. We have seen something of their history and development. The literature on the subject is very meager, and hence the field of our investigation has been limited. We have passed over without describing many modifications of several schemes which do not appear to have assumed sufficient importance to merit a separate classification and name. We have sufficient data before us, however, from which some safe conclusions may be derived.

Before proceeding to describe in detail how to organize these associations, the details of management, and the proper methods for keeping the books of account, let us examine which of the several schemes or their modifications presented seems to be the best.

That scheme is undoubtedly the best which secures an *equality of benefits* between the borrower and non-borrower, *simplicity* in its practical workings, and *safety* in the highest degree. These three essential requisites must exist in any scheme to become deservedly popular.

Safety of the Scheme.

All the schemes we have described have the essential requisite of safety in nearly the same degree. They all require, as a rule, the same kind of security for their loans, namely, first bond and mortgage, or a pledge of their own stock upon which there has been paid into the association a sum equal to the amount loaned and six months' interest on the loan. The latter gives to the association absolute security, as we have seen; all risk upon the loan is, in fact, eliminated.

The safety of loans made upon bond and mortgage depends in all the schemes on the same conditions. These conditions may be briefly stated as follows: 1. The good judgment, experience, and integrity of those who examine and appraise the value of the real estate offered to the associations as a security for loans. 2. The knowledge and accuracy of those charged with examining titles and making abstracts of the same. 3. The percentage of margin which is required between the value of the mortgaged premises and the amount loaned. 4. The condition of the real-estate market, when the loan is made, as to whether it is normal, inflated, or depressed. 5. In those loans where the fire insurance upon the buildings is a part of the security relied upon, the watchfulness of the officer, whose duty it is to see that the insurance does not expire and leave the building without insurance; and carefulness in selecting companies to carry risks that are able and willing to pay in case of loss.

All the foregoing conditions of *safety* may be fulfilled under any scheme, either carefully or negligently, intelligently or ignorantly, honestly or dishonestly. The intelligence and character of the officers whom the shareholders select to conduct the affairs of the association are of first importance always; and no scheme can relieve the shareholders from the greatest care in this selection. The most that any scheme can do is to provide all the elements of safety possible.

Receiving Dues, Interest, and Fines.

We have seen that two modes are pursued in receiving dues, interest, and fines.

The first is for the board of directors, or a committee thereof, to hold regular stated meetings, weekly or monthly, according to the scheme of the association, for the receipt of dues, interest, and fines, and of installments of premium when the scheme is upon that plan. No officer has the right, on behalf of the association, to receive payments from the shareholders at any other time.

The second mode is to require the payments to be made to the secretary or treasurer, or permit them to be made at any time during the week or month at the office of the association, the officer, in order to accommodate the shareholder, having regular office-hours for the purpose.

Of these two modes, it is proper here to inquire which is best. It is manifest that if the receiving of dues, interest, fines, etc., is devolved upon a single officer, such as the secretary, and he has an office, and is to be found there during business hours, and also at stated times in the evening, it gives to each stockholder the advantage of selecting his own time during the week or month, according to his convenience, for making his payments; and again, it is clear that if an association is prosperous and increases the number of its shareholders without any limitation, they may become so numerous that there will not be sufficient time at an evening meeting for any committee to receive and receipt for all the payments then due. In such cases a regular officer, located in an office for the receiving of dues, interest, fines, etc., becomes a necessity.

The answer to the question raised will be made differently by different persons, according to their conception of the true mission of loan associations. For myself, I do not believe that the shareholders of any association should be permitted to become so numerous that payments can not be handled in a single evening by the proper committee. For a single officer to receive the dues at any time must inevitably tend to centralize the running of the association in the hands of that officer. It is with him that all the stockholders become acquainted, and not with the other officers to the same extent; nor do they become acquainted with one another. They go and pay their dues when convenient, and then go about their business. It becomes to them much like depositing in a bank. It necessarily involves additional expenses in conducting the business, while it leaves a door wide open for defalcations and ring methods in the management of the association.

On the other hand, the stated meeting for the payment of dues and the receipt thereof by a proper committee tends to bring all the stockholders together at regular intervals. They meet one another and all the board of directors. When it is not convenient to attend a meeting the money and pass-book can be sent by some friend. By this means all become better acquainted with the scheme of the association, and more interested in the manner in which its business is conducted. When the sales of money immediately follow the receipt of dues many persons will remain to attend the sales. If there is a slack demand by borrowers the interest of shareholders will be aroused in looking about among their friends for those who wish to borrow, and soliciting them to join the association, explaining to them its workings and the benefits to be derived from joining it. Under such conditions the association becomes an educator.

These are some of the reasons which lead us to prefer the stated meeting for the receipt of dues ; and we believe its wisdom is completely established by the. fact that in those localities where that method has been most commonly followed loan associations have attained their greatest success. There is an element of safety in it which can not be obtained under the other mode.

Weekly or Monthly Dues.

An examination of loan associations through the country will show the fact that weekly dues are most often associated with the scheme of a single officer receiving the dues. There are classes in some localities with whom weekly dues are advantageous, but in most instances the monthly scheme answers every end.

Simplicity of the Scheme.

Of two or more schemes, each having the essential requisites of securing an equality of benefits between the borrower and non-borrower, and safety in sub-

stantially the same degree, that scheme is best which
is least complex in its practical workings. These associations are intended for the wage-earning classes; for
men of moderate means, men whose business experience is not large or varied, and hence the scheme
adopted should be one that can be readily understood
by them. The issuing of stock and the payment of
one dollar dues on each share until it arrives at the
value of $200 is a simple arrangement. In case of a
withdrawal, the giving of a thirty days' notice and receiving back the dues paid and a certain percentage of
the profits which have accrued, is a simple proceeding
that all can understand. The loaning of money at
each meeting to the highest bidder is easily understood, when the premium bid is treated as, and understood to be, a bonus, and the borrower receives $200 a
share less the premium per share he has bid, and gives
a security for the $200 and pays interest monthly at 6
per cent or any other rate fixed by the association,
and continues to pay his dues until the shares are matured and one cancels the other—or if he repay his
loan before the shares mature and the amount to pay
is the sum he has given security for, the whole proceeding is simple and straightforward. The book-
keeping in cases like this is simple, and a stockholder
or auditing committee can easily at any time arrive at
the condition of the association.

But change this form of premium to a system
whereby it is assumed that it will take ten years for
the shares to mature, and then divide the premium
into ten parts, and deduct them all from the amount
of money the borrower receives, if he is borrowing
upon shares in the current series, and require him to

give a security for the full $200 a share and pay interest on that sum, and tell him that if he wishes to repay his loan before the shares borrowed upon mature the association will allow a rebate on the premium bid of as many tenth parts of the same as there are full years remaining out of said ten years at the time he repays the loan, the whole proceeding becomes complex, and can not be comprehended in its full effect without a study more difficult and patient than the average artisan will give it. Such is the gross plan, with its system of rebates. It is complex beyond ordinary comprehension, and complicates the accounts of the association to such a degree that an ordinary business man, when placed upon an auditing committee can not verify the accuracy of the annual statement without greater labor than he can or will bestow upon it.

It does not relieve the complexity by adopting the net plan—the only change in this being that the borrower pays interest on the actual sum which he receives. This, in fact, still further complicates an examination of the accounts. Before an auditing committee can determine whether John Doe, a borrower, is paying or has paid the amount of interest he ought to pay, they must ascertain the amount of premium he bid on his loan, and deduct that from $200 to ascertain the amount upon which he should pay interest; and not only that, but they must ascertain how old the series was when he borrowed, so that they may determine the amount of rebate he had on the premium bid. This must be done with reference to every loan outstanding.

This complication is somewhat relieved under the installment plan, in which the borrower receives the full sum of $200, and pays the premium in monthly installments, with his dues and interest; but it still remains complicated. It involves the examination as to the amount of premium bid upon each loan, in order to determine whether the installment actually paid is the right one.

The fourth plan, which is regarded with much favor in many localities, and especially in the co-operative bank scheme of Massachusetts, where the premium bid may be, if the association so elects, upon rate of interest to be paid for the loan, is subject to the same objection as the installment plan. To determine the amount of interest which ought to be paid, the amount of interest bid on each loan must be ascertained.

Many associations in New York, under the old law, adopted the policy of fixing a low rate of interest as the minimum, and then borrowers bid up the rate in the competition for money. There are many things to commend premium - interest bidding, but this scheme is at the expense of simplicity in the practical workings of the business of the association. As regards the essential requisite of simplicity in the practical workings of the associations, it seems clear that the scheme of the co-operative savings and loan associations of New York is superior to any other.

Equality of Benefits.

Equality of benefits between the borrower and the non-borrower must be secured in these associations to justly entitle them to the name of co-operative associations.

If the scheme upon which they are conducted involves the fleecing of the borrower by the free share-holder—the one who does not borrow—they cease to be what is claimed for them. The effect in the stimulation of savings and in furnishing facilities therefor, in encouraging home-building, and making the attainment of a home possible to the wage-worker, has been so great that these associations have been almost uniformly successful, accomplishing much good, notwithstanding considerable injustice involved in the practical workings of the system between borrower and non-borrower—the former paying a very large interest and the latter receiving it. The borrower too often undertakes obligations which he does not fully comprehend until it is too late for him to recede, and if he attempts to free himself from the burden he only still further swells the profits of those who do not borrow.

We shall assume that the scheme which has the essential elements of simplicity in its practical workings and safety, and, at the same time, secures the greatest equality between the borrower and the free shareholder, is the best. We assume this, because it seems to us to admit of no dispute.

The total sources of profits of an association arise from premiums, interest, fines, entrance - fees, and transfer-fees. If, perchance, in the course of its business in the enforcement of securities upon defaulted loans, it becomes the owner of real estate, rents received, as well as any advance realized upon its resale above actual costs to the association, belong to profits. But these are chance profits; they are not the sources from which, under the ordinary workings of the scheme, profits are expected to be realized, so we shall not refer to them again, but shall leave the enumeration above to stand, with one addition thereto—while the sources above enumerated constitute all the sources from which the business of the association derives gain, as between the stockholders, there is yet another source of profit, and an important one.

We have, in Chapter III, fully explained the difference between the *holding* value and the *withdrawing* value of shares. Now, whenever a shareholder withdraws he leaves in the treasury of the association the difference between these two values, which inures to the benefit of the shareholders who do not withdraw, and constitutes a portion of the profits to be divided at the next distribution.

The necessary expenses of conducting the business of an association will, as a rule, exceed the sum received from entrance-fees, transfer-fees, and fines, so that the amount of profits to be divided at each distribution will not exceed the sum received since the last distribution from premiums and interest and profits left by withdrawing shareholders.

Now let us cast out of these items the premium paid, and assume that the interest paid is simply the legal rate. It is manifest that the borrower and non-borrower are receiving equal benefits. The borrower pays his monthly interest, and has value received, in return therefor, in the loan that has been made to him. The non-borrower, who is availing himself of the association as a place to accumulate his savings, is obtaining better advantages than he can obtain elsewhere, when he is able to secure the legal rate of interest upon his savings paid in from month to month.

The borrower obtains the advantages of being able

8

to pay interest in small sums from month to month, and likewise monthly payments in addition as dues upon his stock, which in time shall wipe out his loan. This secures equality between the borrower and non-borrower, and both reap a benefit without loss to the other. The distribution of interest and the profits left by the withdrawing shareholder, in the form of dividends to the holding value of the respective shares held by the borrower and non-borrower, is just, and works equity between all parties concerned; but it is otherwise with the item of premiums.

If all borrowers bid the same premium and the premium received by the association was distributed among the shares borrowed upon, then there would be an equality of benefits; but such is not the scheme. Premiums, as well as other items of profits, are bunched and divided among all the shares outstanding according to their holding value.

It needs no array of figures to show that when the free shareholder receives 10 per cent interest on his savings in a community where the legal rate is but 6, that the borrower has paid either in premium or interest far above the current rate. We have in Chapter IV written to some extent on this question. It is inevitable that if the association is one in which free shareholders obtain large interest it is one in which the borrower will pay large interest, either under the name of interest or premiums.

It may be of service in the consideration of this subject to obtain some correct notion of the relative number of borrowers and non-borrowers in these associations.

At the date of the annual report for 1886 of the

Savings-Bank Commissioners of Massachusetts, there were forty co-operative banks in that State, having 14,805 shareholders; of this number only 2,960 were borrowers. There were outstanding 98,783 shares of stock; but, unfortunately, the fact is not compiled as to the number of shares borrowed upon. From an examination of the report of the " Bureau of Statistics of Labor and Industries " of New Jersey for 1886, wherein they have tabulated certain facts with reference to 156 building and loan associations in that State, we find the total number of shareholders 37,730, of which only 8,562 are borrowers. The total number of shares outstanding is 204,653, of which only 42,373 have been borrowed upon.

There is located at Elmira, New York, an association organized upon the serial plan : Matured value of shares, $200 ; monthly dues, one dollar ; issuing a new series of stock each year, and has matured three series of stock. It now issues and matures a series each year. Its thirteenth annual report shows outstanding 3,510 shares in all series, of which 812 have been borrowed upon.

From our investigation and from the necessity of the scheme of these associations, we conclude that the ratio of non-borrowers to borrowers will, on the average, exceed four to one.

From this it follows that excessive interest and premiums paid by the borrowers may be divided into four parts at least, and only one of these parts will be returned to the borrowers in dividends to their stock while the remaining three parts will be divided to the free shares. While this conclusion is not accurate, it is approximately so.

We feel it needs no argument to prove that the old gross plan, requiring a premium bid of $25 a share, or even more, and payment of interest on $200—while the most the borrower could receive on his loan was $175 a share—worked rank injustice.

The first association in which the writer was a shareholder required a minimum premium bid of $40 a share. The promise was held out to the borrower that he would get his premium back in dividends upon his shares. We have seen that he would not get back more than one fourth of it. The free shareholders received the other three fourths. Under this system the free shareholder who remained until his shares matured would receive from 12 to 18 per cent interest.

The system could not prosper except in localities in which real estate was rapidly advancing, and the borrower obtained an advantage from the advanced value of the real estate he was paying for.

As we have before stated in the last chapter, the net plan relieved somewhat the rank inequality of this system. While excessive interest was not required, the large premiums still remained. This in turn yielded to the installment plan. In this the borrower obtained and paid interest on $200, but with each monthly payment was an installment of premium. Under either plan, whatever premium he did pay, not over one fourth came back to him. The free shareholders obtained the lion's share.

We have before spoken of a modification of these schemes that placed the interest paid from month to month at less than legal interest. This system proves but a delusion and a snare to the borrower. In addition to the fact, which was always fallacious, that he would get his premium back in dividends upon his shares, he was shown that he was obtaining a low rate of interest, and that he could afford to bid a high premium. Under these conditions, and the stimulus of an open competitive bidding, the premium would be run up until the borrower paid an excessive sum in premium and interest for his loan. Such are the dangers attendant upon this scheme.

The fourth plan, the premium interest plan, is free from this evil where the minimum rate of interest is placed at the legal rate. The only objection we urge to this scheme is the want of *simplicity* that we have before discussed, and the further fact that it is liable to breed dissatisfaction to have borrowers year after year paying different rates of interest on the same sum of money.

But whenever in this scheme the minimum rate of interest is placed below the legal rate, there still remain the conditions before stated which prove a delusion and often a snare to the borrower, and it is also open to the objection of being wanting in simplicity. It has some advantages that are urged in its favor that should be noticed. The advocates claim for it the advantage of adapting itself to the fluctuation in the money market. When money is plenty, the borrower may obtain his loan below legal interest. When money is scarce, he will have to pay more, and that it is equitable that he should do so. There is some force in this claim; but in some of its bearings it is fallacious. If the borrower only continued to pay the higher interest while the increased demand for money continued, or the low rate while the demand was small, then the claim would have greater force; but he continues to pay the high or low rate of interest so long as he continues his loan. If he has obtained a low rate, he will not change it. If he has been compelled to pay a high rate to obtain the loan, he will be watching for an opportunity to pay off the loan and obtain a new one at a lower rate. But when the scheme requires a uniform rate of interest and the premium bid is understood to be a *bonus* to be paid at the time, the amount of that bonus will be controlled by the condition of the money market. If money is plenty, he will not pay a high bonus; he will usually get it without the payment of any; but if the demand for money is greater than the supply, he will have to pay a bonus accordingly. The increased or decreased premium, upon this scheme, therefore more accurately and equitably adjusts itself to the money market than the high or low rate of interest in the interest premium plan.

Loans in small sums, to be repaid in driblets, as loans are made in these associations, can not as a rule be made elsewhere. The rate of interest upon loans of this character are not subject to much fluctuation from the legal rate. The borrower will always be willing to pay legal interest when coupled with the other advantages offered him.

We, therefore, prefer the plan of the co-operative savings and loan associations of New York. Premium should not enter into any scheme for the sake of profits, but simply as a mode of deciding who shall have the money. It should be understood to be a bonus, and when bid, that not more than one fourth is coming back to the borrower. When money is plenty, no bonus will be bid.

Before me lies the reports of the association at Elmira, New York, before mentioned, for the years of
1886 and 1887. It loaned for the fiscal year ending
in February, 1886, $40,750; rate of interest 6 per
cent, and the total premiums paid, $62.

For the fiscal year ending in February, 1887, it
loaned $53,400, and the total premium was $232.45;
and the report of both years states that the demand
for loans during the year exceeded the amount of
money the association had to loan.

It may be urged that this system admits of high
bidding by the borrower, and excessive interest resulting therefrom. That is true; so does any system yet
devised; but it holds out no false or delusive incen-
tives to rash bidding. The borrower understands he
is bidding a bonus; and understanding this, he will
not bid high—and in the practical workings it will
be very seldom that any premium will be bid at all.

We have not discussed in this chapter the merits
of the terminating plan, as compared with the permanent plans for issuing stock, for the reason that we
assume it will be conceded by all that either of the
permanent plans are superior to the terminating plan.

We prefer the serial plan to the plan of issuing
stock at any time. The only object of issuing at any
time is to allow persons to become shareholders without paying back dues. This is sufficiently obviated in
the issuing of a series once in six months. Under
this plan, any stockholder ascertaining the number of
shares outstanding in each of the series can determine
very closely at any time the amount of the accumulated capital of the association. We prefer it for its
simplicity; and it is the plan generally adopted wher-

ever these associations have been carefully regulated by the laws of the State.

Voting by the Stockholders.

There are two modes of voting. The first is to allow the stockholder to cast one vote and only one, whether he holds one or twenty shares of stock. The second is to allow him to cast one vote for each share of stock held by him. The advocates of the one-vote system claim that it prevents a few stockholders holding large blocks of stock from combining to control the association. This is true; but, on the other hand, it allows ten men holding one share apiece to have the same voting power of ten men holding ten shares apiece. The limitation of ten free shares in any one series is a sufficient check upon the attempt of a few to control its policy. We believe each stockholder should be allowed to cast a vote equal to his interest in the association, to the extent of casting one vote for each share of stock held by him. If no limitation were placed upon the number of shares a stockholder might hold, we would agree with the one-vote plan; but we prefer to place the limitation in the holding of shares, and then each share have a vote.

In conclusion, then, we express our preference for the scheme which issues its stock in series, matured value $200, monthly dues of one dollar, money loaned without a premium when there is no competition and when competition occurs, the premium bid being treated as a bonus and deducted from the loan; interest at 6 per cent, payable monthly. Hence we approve, in the main, the scheme of the co-operative savings and loan associations of New York.

CHAPTER VII.

IT is our purpose to explain, first, in detail, how to organize a co-operative savings and loan association under the general act for their incorporation, passed by the Legislature of the State of New York in 1887. The act itself will be found in the Appendix.

The first section of this act provides: " That any fifteen or more persons, being of full age, may form an association as provided within this act. All associations formed under the provisions hereof shall be known as co-operative savings and loan associations, and the name of every association so formed shall contain, as a part thereof, the words, ' co-operative savings and loan association.' "

The first step therefore is to find fifteen or more persons of full age who will unite to form an association. The only condition which the statute provides for membership is one of age.

Any person desirous of forming a loan association in his own locality should prepare a paper in language substantially as follows:

" The undersigned, being of full age, hereby express a desire to unite in the formation of a co-operative savings and loan association under the provisions of the act for their incorporation known as Chapter 556 of the laws of 1887 of the State of New York, and upon the due incorporation of said association and the adoption of by-laws, we hereby severally agree to take the number of shares of stock in said association set opposite our respective names."

Below the written matter the paper should be ruled and headed as follows:

NAME.	RESIDENCE.	NO. OF SHARES.

The paper being thus prepared, it is ready for signing by those who will join in the formation of the association.

While only fifteen are necessary for the formation of an association, it is well to obtain as many more as possible. The greater the number who will join in the organization the greater will be the interest in the enterprise in the community, and a larger issue of stock will be secured at the first meeting for issuing the same.

The question will arise as to how large a community should be to undertake to conduct an association successfully. Any business center having a population of five hundred can maintain one of these associations; and it will be especially adapted to the wants of the community if a large element of the population belongs to the wage-earning classes.

The requisite number having been obtained to join in the formation of an association, the next step is incorporation.

Section 3 of the statute provides that "said association shall become incorporated by the said fifteen or more persons making, signing, and acknowledging, in the manner and form prescribed for the acknowledgement of deeds in this State, a certificate wherein shall be stated the name of said association; that the association is formed under and for the purposes prescribed in this act; the town, village, or city where the association is located within this State; and the limit of the number of shares of stock it shall have outstanding at any one time.

" When made as aforesaid, said certificate shall be filed and recorded in the office of the Secretary of State, and upon said certificate being so filed and recorded the Secretary of State shall issue a certificate in proper and suitable form, declaring the facts contained in said original certificate, and the filing and recording thereof in his office, and which latter certificate shall thereupon be recorded in the county clerk's office of the county where said association is located; and, upon the same being so recorded, the persons named in the certificate first above mentioned, their associates and successors, shall become a corporate body."

The procedure for incorporation is thus clearly pointed out in this section of the statute.

The drafting of the certificate is the first thing to be done. The law enumerates the facts which it must contain. 1. The name of the association. If no common understanding has come to pass as to what the name shall be, this can be left blank, except the part which the law prescribes must appear in the name of every association, viz.: " co-operative savings and loan association." The completion of the name need not be determined until a meeting is called for that purpose, and to execute the certificate. In deciding upon a name it is well to identify the locality of the association by the name adopted, as " The Albany Co-operative Savings and Loan Association "; or, if the association is organized by a special class, as " The Albany Railway Co-operative Savings and Loan Association," or " The Albany Clerks' Co-operative Savings and Loan Association," etc.

2. The statement that the association is formed under and for the purposes prescribed in Chapter 556 of the laws of New York for 1887, entitled an act " providing for the formation of co-operative savings and loan associations "; and in the event such act has been amended at the time of the making of the certificate, there should be added, " and the acts amendatory thereof."

3. The name of the town, village, or city where the association is located.

4. The limit of the number of shares of stock the association shall have outstanding at any time.

Section 5 of the act provides, " that the total number of shares outstanding at any time shall not exceed ten thousand." This fixes the maximum limit.

We perceive no advantage to be gained by fixing the limit at a less number, except it arise out of the laws relating to taxation. As the laws stand at this writing in the State of New York, no advantage is gained in that direction. These associations are " institutions for savings," and therefore not liable under the general corporation tax act, and are especially exempted from the provisions of Chapter 143 of the laws of 1886, which is an act taxing the privilege of organizing a corporation.

However, outside of cities, it will rarely occur that an association will wish to have more than five thousand shares outstanding at one time, and in small villages they will seldom exceed three thousand shares. We suggest the following as a form for the certificate of incorporation :

This memorandum certificate of incorporation, made this .... day of ......, 18.., certifies that we, [here insert names], being of full age, have agreed to unite, and do hereby unite, to form a co-operative savings and loan association, as follows, to wit:

1. Said association is formed under the provisions and for the purposes prescribed in Chapter 556 of the laws of 1887 of the State of New York, and any acts amendatory thereof.

2. The name of the association is The [insert name] Co-operative Savings and Loan Association.

3. The said association is formed to conduct the business thereof in the [town, village, or city] of [name], in the State of New York.

4. The number of shares of stock which said association shall have outstanding at any one time shall not exceed the number of ....

We ask that the Secretary of State of the State of New York shall file and record this certificate in pursuance of the provisions of section 3 of said Chapter 556 of the laws of 1887.

In witness whereof, we have hereunto set our hands and seals the day and year first above written.

.... (seal)   .... (seal)
.... (seal)   .... (seal)
.... (seal)   .... (seal)
.... (seal)   .... (seal)
.... (seal)   .... (seal)
.... (seal)   .... (seal)
.... (seal)   .... (seal)
.... (seal)   .... (seal)

etc.   etc.

State of New York, } *ss.*
County of ......

On this .... day of ......, 18.., personally appeared before me the undersigned, a notary public in and for said county [insert names of all who signed above], to me personally known to be the same persons who signed the foregoing certificate of incorporation and severally duly acknowledged that they executed the same.

....
Notary Public.

Execution of the Certificate.

A meeting of those who have agreed to unite in the organization should be called at some convenient hour and place, at which time the name of the association should be decided upon, if it has not been before, and, upon the same being inserted in the certificate, all should sign their full names, and a seal should be affixed opposite each name. A notary public should be in attendance and take the acknowledgments of the signers as to a deed.

While together, the members should designate some three of their number as a committee to call the next meeting of the incorporators, which will occur after the incorporation has been completed, and such committee should also be directed to prepare by-laws for the consideration of the incorporators.

The certificate should be next taken to the county clerk for his certificate, to be annexed as to the official acts of the notary who has taken the acknowledgment. The paper is then ready to be forwarded to the Secretary of State, to be filed and recorded.

With it should be sent the amount the Secretary of State is entitled to for filing and recording it and issuing the certificate, which said third section provides he shall issue, to be recorded in the county clerk's office.

Unless the Secretary of State shall prescribe a different form for use by him, we suggest the following as a form for such certificate, and that it be sent with the original certificate to the Secretary of State, so that all he will have to do is to execute and return the same. We hope these associations will become so general that the Secretary of State will prepare and have printed a certificate that shall to some extent be artistic, as it will constitute the charter of the association when the memoranda of the county clerk showing that it has been recorded in his office has been indorsed upon it.

FORM OF CERTIFICATE ISSUED BY SECRETARY OF STATE.

To all whom it may concern :

This instrument duly certifies that [insert names of those who executed certificate filed and recorded in his office], have duly filed in this office, and the same has been duly recorded, a certificate for the purpose of incorporation, under the provisions and for the purposes prescribed in Chapter 556 of the laws of 1887, and any acts amendatory thereof, providing for the formation of co-operative savings and loan associations.

That the certificate so filed and recorded duly sets forth that the name of such association is "The ...... Co-operative Savings and Loan Association."

That such association is formed under the provisions and for the purposes prescribed in Chapter 556 of the laws of 1887, and any acts amendatory thereof.

That such association is located in the ...... of ......, in the County of ......, in the State of New York.

That the capital stock of said association outstanding at any time shall not exceed ...... thousand shares, and upon the recording hereof in the county clerk's office of the county of ...... in this State, the incorporation of said association will be complete.

In witness whereof, I have hereunto set my hand and affixed my official seal at the city of Albany, in the State of New York, on this ...... day of ......, in the year of our Lord one thousand eight hundred and eighty- ....

....

Secretary of State.

Upon the receipt of this certificate from the Secretary of State, it should be forthwith recorded in the county clerk's office of the county mentioned in the certificate; and upon being so recorded, the incorporation of the association will be complete.

By-Laws.

The next step in completing the organization is the framing and adoption of by-laws.

Section 17 of the statute provides that: " The association as soon as duly incorporated shall possess power to adopt by-laws, not inconsistent with the provisions of this act, regulating the due conduct of the business of the association, defining the duties of the officers and committees, times of meetings, mode of determining and declaring the withdrawing value of shares, and in relation to all other matters having reference to the conduct of the business, although not specifically mentioned in this act."

In the case of building and loan associations in this State, formed under the provisions of Chapter 122 of the laws of 1851, it is necessary to have what was termed, " articles of association." In familiar speech these are called the " constitution " of the association, and are filed in the office of the county clerk, as a part of the steps to become incorporated.

Under the act of 1887 this is not required. The act itself constitutes the constitution.

The reason of this is clear when we consider that the provisions of the act of 1851 admitted of great variety in the schemes upon which associations could be conducted, and the particular plan or scheme of the association was outlined in the articles of association; while under the act of 1887, but one general scheme is allowed, and that is definitely outlined in the act itself.

But the act of 1887 allows of minor variations in the details of the scheme, and these are to be described

9

in the by-laws. There will be found in the Appendix a complete set of by-laws as a form.

We shall here discuss only such portions of them as seem necessary to give those seeking to organize an association a clear understanding of what the by-laws should contain, the reasons therefor, and the duties of officers thereunder.

Officers.

Section 4 of the act provides that: "The officers of the association shall consist of a president, vice-president, treasurer, and secretary, who shall be *ex-officio* members of the board of directors, which shall consist of nine members, exclusive of said *ex-officio* members. Other officers may be authorized by the by-laws.

"The duties and compensation of the officers, their terms of office, the time of their election, and the time of periodical meetings of the officers and shareholders, shall be determined by the by-laws, except that the board of directors shall determine each year the compensation of the secretary and treasurer."

Term of Office.

Under the terms of this section, the by-laws will determine the length of time for which officers may be chosen. We think no question will arise as to the term of office of the president, vice-president, treasurer, and secretary. The term of one year is so universal that no one would suggest otherwise. The term should be for one year. It is easy to re-elect a good officer, and it is the easiest mode to get rid of an inefficient one by electing some one else.

As to the nine members of the board of directors,

there may arise a difference of opinion. It may be claimed that it would be unwise to elect a full board each year; that it would admit of bringing in an entirely new body of men, who would not have the experience that those who had served upon the board would have, and that it would be better to elect for three years, thereby making it possible to bring in only three new men each year. On the other hand, that mode allows of the possibility of a ring being formed in the board; or, if an inefficient member has been elected, he can not well be got rid of under three years. We believe the best method is to elect all annually; you can re-elect the good members and drop those who have not been satisfactory, either in their conduct of business or in inattention to their duties. There can not be a change unless the owners of a majority of the shares outstanding desire it, and that is not likely to occur unless there is good ground for the change. The usual course is to continue from year to year the board of directors with few changes. This has been the practice in building and loan associations generally. We therefore recommend that the by-laws prescribe for the annual election of all officers, and that all officers shall hold office until removed or their successors qualify.

Should it be determined to adopt a three years' term of office for directors, then the by-laws should provide for a casting of lots among the nine directors elected at the organization, in order to determine who should hold office for the term of one year, who for two years, and who for three years; and provide that at each annual election thereafter there shall be three directors elected for the term of three years.

The by-laws should also prescribe in what manner a vacancy occurring in the board of directors or other officers shall be filled, until the next annual election. This may be done by a special meeting of the shareholders held for such purpose, or by the board of directors. We recommend the latter course as being the simplest, and not involving the expense attending the calling of a meeting. It is unnecessary to discuss here the ordinary duties of the several officers. These will be expressed in general terms in the by-laws. The form which we give contains such provisions as we deem proper. (See Appendix.)

Treasurer.

The treasurer must give bonds in such sum as the board of directors prescribe. These bonds should be twice the amount of any sum of money which it is anticipated will be in his hands at any one time during the year. We recommend at least two sureties, and one at least should not be connected with the bank where the treasurer deposits his money. The reason of this last provision is, that in case the bank fails both sureties will not be involved.

The president and secretary should sign the certificates of stock and all orders for money drawn upon the treasurer. They should have no authority to issue an order upon the treasurer, except in pursuance of an order of the board of directors, except in the case of loans; and as to these orders, the by-laws should provide that an order should not be issued until the securities have been approved by the committee and attorney who have to pass upon their sufficiency; and, in case of real-estate security, the mortgage has been left with the county clerk for record.

The by-laws should provide that every order drawn should be dated when drawn, and specify the purpose for which made and the name of the payee.

The Secretary.

It is unnecessary to discuss here the duties of the secretary in keeping the books of account or what books he should keep. We refer the reader to the ninth chapter, where the matter is fully treated.

At each stated monthly meeting of the board it is desirable to have a report from the secretary showing the number of shares outstanding, the number borrowed upon, the receipts of the last meeting, and the balance of cash on hand. A form for this report may be made which can be used through the fiscal year. Any member of the board desiring to keep fully informed on the details from month to month, can do so by having one of the forms for this report, and making himself, or have the secretary make for him, the entries from month to month. Many other items of information may be embodied in this monthly report. It need not be entered in the minutes. Its object is to give the members of the board full information from month to month, and in such form that, with experience, they will be enabled to so keep track of the details of the association that they can detect at once any departure by the secretary, or treasurer, or president from strict adherence to the by-laws. For a form for such monthly report see Appendix.

The annual report of the secretary should be a full and complete report of the transactions of the year, showing the total receipts in detail, so that the amount received from each source of income will clearly appear, as well as the total disbursements, and the purposes for which they were made. This report should be printed, and distributed to stockholders before or at the beginning of the annual meeting. For a form for such report see Appendix.

Accompanying the report, the president may make any review of the business of the year, and any suggestions or recommendations which seem to him wise. In this connection it is proper to refer to the manifest importance of having a good secretary. He should be a fair accountant at least, and thoroughly post himself at the outset of his work. It is simple work to keep the accounts if a proper system is adopted; but if an inadequate system is adopted in the beginning it will complicate and lead to tangles in after years that will prove very annoying, involving much labor and vexation. He should comprehend fully the scheme upon which the association is based, and be able to explain it to others; he should at all times be affable, and cheerfully explain, to all who ask him, questions about the workings of the association. The details of the work done are largely under his care. There must be absolute accuracy in all his entries, and promptness in doing his work. Under the law, only he and the treasurer can receive compensation for their services, and usually the pay of the treasurer is nominal. The secretary should receive a sum that pays him fairly for the work done.

In many places where the old building and loan associations have flourished, and are now flourishing, one man will be secretary of two or more associations;

and under such arrangement he is able to devote his entire time to their work. The same thing occurs under the co-operative bank scheme of Massachusetts; and there is no objection, in cities that can maintain several associations, to the same thing being done under the recent law of New York, or wherever that scheme may be adopted.

Finance Committee.

The nine members of the board of directors should be divided into three finance committees, each committee serving for the term of four months. This committee will have charge of the receipts of dues, interest, and fines, and must pass upon the sufficiency of securities offered for loans. Its duties are important. In the matter of receiving dues, etc., the by-laws should give it the right to call upon the secretary and treasurer to aid them. In passing upon securities, it will receive the assistance of the attorney; the duties of the latter, however, being confined to the examination of abstracts of title furnished by the borrowers from the county clerk, the drawing of the bonds and mortgages, and, when the loan is finally passed, seeing that the mortgages are at once recorded in the proper clerk's office.

The detail of passing upon securities is as follows: At the time the borrower bids off his loan, he should describe upon suitable blanks, furnished by the association, the real estate offered as a security, or, in case of a "stock loan," the shares of stock of the association. The loans proposed to be secured by stock can be disposed of by the whole board at once if desired. The secretary would be able to inform the board whether the borrower owned the stock which he proposed as a security, and the withdrawal value of the same; but if no one asked for an immediate consideration of a stock loan, the descriptions of proposed securities would be handed to the finance committee. The by-laws should prescribe the time when the committee shall meet, following each stated meeting, to pass upon securities. Before the time of such meeting arrives, each member of the committee should examine with care the real estate proposed, and appraise its fair market value. In making this appraisal there should be exercised great caution and intelligent judgment. The following conditions should be carefully ascertained and noted : Is the tendency of value of real estate where the property is situated upward or downward ? Is its present value speculative or substantial ? Is it the result of a " boom," or of an undue depression ? Is its particular location one where property is liable to advance or decline in value ? Is it vacant, or built upon ? If built upon, what is the character of the buildings ? Are they well or cheaply constructed ? And what is their rental value, and the class of tenants which occupy them ? If not, are they to be occupied by the borrower as a home ? And, lastly, what are the antecedents and habits of the borrower, his ability, and prospects of securing a steady income to meet his dues and interest ? All these questions enter into the examination of real estate offered as a security, and should have weight in accepting or rejecting the proposed security for a loan. Each member of the committee having thus examined the property and made his appraisal is prepared to vote intelligently when assembled to pass on the loan.

In determining whether the security offered for the loan is sufficient, the question arises, What percentage of value shall be loaned? Here two courses are open under the law of New York. A maximum limit may be fixed by the by-laws, as seventy-five per cent; or it may be left wholly to the discretion of the committee. My own conviction, arrived at after much experience, is that the safest way is to leave the responsibility wholly with the committee, the guiding rule being that a sufficient margin should be required between the value and the amount loaned to make the loan safe under all reasonable probabilities. There is no way of escaping the fact that the association must rely upon the good judgment and integrity of its committee. If the committee is corrupt or visionary as to the value, no by-law can restrain or guide it. To evade the by-laws, when the percentage to be loaned is fixed, it is only necessary to appraise the value sufficient to bring the case within the letter of the by-law. It is better to place the responsibility of making a good loan squarely upon the committee, without any fetters save those dictated by a sound judgment and a cautious prudence. If the committee on consultation approve the security offered, then the attorney takes charge of seeing that the title is good, and of the preparation of the necessary papers to perfect the loan. The by-laws may allow the attorney to make the abstract of title or require the borrower to produce to the attorney an abstract from the county clerk which the attorney shall examine and pass upon.

We prefer the latter course, under the laws of the State of New York. If the attorney finds the title satisfactory, he will prepare the bond and mortgage and have them executed, together with an assignment of the shares of stock borrowed upon, and leave the mortgage at the clerk's office for record. If any insurance is required by the terms of the mortgage, this should be procured, whereupon the order for the loan will be drawn and delivered to the borrower. All securities, except the mortgage, should be passed by the attorney at once to the secretary, who will obtain the mortgage from the clerk's office as soon as recorded, make the proper entries in the security book, and then turn over the same to the treasurer in whose custody they will remain. The charges of the attorney for his services must be paid by the borrower. The amount may be left to his discretion, or the by-laws may empower the board of directors to fix a schedule of rates.

Meetings.

The by-laws should fix the times for all the regular meetings of the shareholders and of the board of directors. The first annual meeting of the shareholders will naturally occur soon after the last stated monthly meeting in the fiscal year, for the receipt of dues, sufficient time being allowed after the monthly meeting to permit the officers to get their books properly balanced up and the annual reports prepared.

In fixing the time of the monthly meeting for the receipt of dues, etc., the question presented is, at what time in the month will the wage earners as a general rule be best able to pay their dues and interest? When do they usually receive their pay? In railroad centers the time should be fixed after the monthly pay-day. Attention at the beginning to this question

will often enable men to become shareholders who
would not if the monthly meeting was before "pay-
day," and will prevent the trouble of amendments of
the by-laws to meet these conditions after the association has been formed and begun operations. The
manner of calling special meetings of the shareholders
and of the board of directors will be provided in the
by-laws.

Withdrawals.

Section 7 of the general act of incorporation,
among other things, provides that, " The withdrawing
shareholder shall be paid the amount of the withdrawing value of his accumulations as determined under
the by-laws at the last distribution of profits before
the notice of withdrawal, together with all dues paid
since such distribution, and such interest on the value
of the shares at the time of the last distribution and
on the dues thereafter paid, as the by-laws shall determine."

From a reading of the section it will appear that it
makes full provisions as to the manner of giving notice of withdrawal, and when the amount of the withdrawal shall be paid. It is left to the by-laws to determine the manner in which the withdrawal value shall
be determined. The questions that arise for consideration in forming the by-laws upon this subject may
be stated as follows :

1. Shall the withdrawing shareholder be allowed
all the profits that have accumulated upon and been
added to his shares in the form of dividends, or, only
a part of such profits?

2. If he is not to be allowed all the profits, what
part shall be retained?

3. If a part is retained, shall it be a uniform percentage, applying to all withdrawals regardless of the age of the shares when withdrawn?

4. Shall the part retained by the association be arranged upon a plan whereby, as the share advances toward maturity, a smaller percentage shall be retained?

5. If the latter course is adopted, shall the by-laws fix the amount for each year that a series has run?

Or, Lastly: Shall the whole matter be devolved upon the board of directors, for them to determine the withdrawal value in each series, to remain in full force until the next distribution and another declaration of withdrawing values?

If the withdrawing shareholder is allowed all the profits which have been added to the dues paid into the association, the by-laws would simply so declare, and fix the rate of interest to be allowed upon the value of the shares, as determined at the last distribution and upon the dues paid in since that time.

If the association should deem it wise to have the association retain a uniform percentage of the profits from the withdrawing shareholder, regardless of the age when withdrawn, the by-laws would name the percentage to be retained, and determine the rate of interest to be allowed as above since the last distribution of profits.

If, however, it is deemed best to adjust the rate of percentage retained according to the age of the series when the share is withdrawn, allowing a larger share of the profits as the share advances toward maturity, and at the same time it is thought best to fix the rate by the by-laws, the amount to be retained during each year of the progress of a share to its maturity must be named, together with the rate of interest to be allowed on the value of the share at the time of the last distribution, and upon dues thereafter paid until the withdrawal.

If, however, the whole matter of determining what shall be paid upon withdrawals falls upon the board of directors, then the times of declaring such withdrawal value by the board should be appointed, together with any limitations as to rates of interest that may seem desirable.

In the history of building and loan associations it has been the usual custom to retain from the withdrawing shareholder a part of the profits. We deem it proper and prudent to do so. There is possibility of loss upon loans that have been made while the withdrawing shareholder was a member, after he has withdrawn. If he takes out all the profits that have accrued up to the last distribution before his withdrawal, the remaining shareholders take the burden of all the risks thereafter upon loans from which the withdrawing shareholder has received his full share of profits. For this reason it seems just to retain from the withdrawing shareholder, a share of the accrued profits.

But we observe under the Massachusetts co-operative bank scheme that some of the associations, or co-operative banks, as they are now called, allow to the withdrawing shareholder all the accrued profits; but the greater number retain one fourth; some retain one tenth, while others grade the amount retained according to the age of the share when withdrawn. We believe it the wisest course to leave the whole subject to the board of directors. It is advisable beyond question, it seems to me, to encourage withdrawals in series nearing maturity by allowing a larger percentage of profits to be withdrawn.

When a large number of free shares remain in a series at the time it matures, they call for a large amount of money; and it will take so long to pay them off that discontent is often produced among the holders of the shares. It has always been the policy of building and loan associations to encourage withdrawals in series approaching maturity. When discretionary power is lodged in the board, they can stimulate withdrawals from series wherein a large number of free shares remain, by increasing the share of profits allowed to be withdrawn. On the other hand, it may be urged with force that when the percentage of profits allowed to be withdrawn is fixed in the by-laws, all know from the outset just what share they will be allowed on withdrawing. It is possible that our bias in favor of leaving the subject of withdrawal values with the board, to be fixed at each distribution, arises from the fact that such is the plan under which the writer has had his practical experience. We should not quarrel with any one who disagrees with us.

Fines and Entrance Fees.

In section 6 of the general act is the following: " The association shall have power to impose and collect a fine, not exceeding 10 per cent for each month in arrears, for every dollar of dues or interest which a shareholder shall refuse or neglect to pay at the time it is due. They shall also have power to charge an entrance fee of not exceeding twenty-five cents on every share of stock issued by the association."

It is most desirable that all dues and interest should be paid promptly at the designated time each month. Promptness is a good business habit to cultivate. To insure this promptness it is very beneficial to provide for a money penalty in case of failure. In most cases where there is a failure to pay at the appointed time it is the result of forgetfulness. Now, there is nothing that is so efficacious in overcoming forgetfulness as to make it cost money. Hence it has been almost a universal feature in associations of this kind to attach a fine to each failure to pay dues and interest at the time fixed for such payment.

The association formed under the act in question, by its laws determines the amount of the fine to the maximum sum of 10 per cent. It can not fix a larger sum, but it may a smaller. We believe 10 per cent is none too large. Yet many associations place it at a less per cent. An entrance fee may be placed at a less sum than twenty-five cents a share, but in our judgment twenty-five cents is the best sum. It helps out in the necessary expenses of the association, and is not felt by the shareholder. The same is true of the transfer fee.

Annual and Semi-annual Series.

The general act allows a new series to be issued annually or semi-annually. We prefer the annual series. The only advantage of the semi-annual series is that the new stockholder can come in at any time without paying so much of back dues. But where there is an annual series there will be no serious obstacle in that direction. The new series will be issued at the first meeting after the annual distribution of profits. It is simpler than the semi-annual series, and that is most desirable.

We have now discussed quite at length matters in which the general act allows of variations in the scheme of associations formed under it, and which are to be defined and regulated by the by-laws. It has been our aim to aid in framing the by-laws. In the form of by-laws found in the Appendix we have followed the scheme which we deem wisest; but they can be readily modified for any scheme allowed by the general act. The three cardinal principles to be kept always in view are safety, equality, and simplicity.

Adoption of By-laws and Election of Officers.

The committee appointed to frame the by-laws being in readiness to report, a meeting of the incorporators should be called to adopt by-laws and elect officers. It is wise to give a general notice of this meeting, inviting all who may wish to learn about the workings of the scheme to be present. The explanations given by the committee in making their report, and the discussions that are likely to arise, will aid much in giving a clear idea to those in attendance of the beneficent objects of the association, and may induce many to become shareholders at the first meeting for issuing stock. The by-laws will fix the first meeting for issuing stock and paying dues. Sufficient time should elapse between the meeting when officers are elected and the meeting for issuing stock and paying dues, to permit of the by-laws being printed. There should be adopted at the meeting for the election of officers a form of seal for the association.

Passbooks and Certificates of Stock.

The certificates of stock should be nicely printed on good paper, in two colors of ink, with such adornments as may be practicable where the printing is done. As a suggestion for a form, see form in Appendix. They must be signed by the president and secretary, and also bear the imprint of the seal of the association. There will be issued to every shareholder at the time he receives his stock a passbook. For suggestion as to the form and manner of preparing passbook, see Appendix.

10

CHAPTER VIII.

HOW TO ORGANIZE ASSOCIATIONS UNDER THE NEW YORK ACT OF 1851, AND IN ANY STATE WHERE THE LAW DOES NOT PROVIDE A DEFINITE SCHEME.

THE act of 1851 is very general in its terms. It is so broad that it will permit of the incorporation of an association upon any scheme that has been or may be devised for conducting the business of a building and loan association, or an accumulating fund association.

Unless one is somewhat familiar with the character of these associations he will not be able to form a correct impression respecting them by reading this law for their incorporation. This is a defect common to the laws of most of the States of the Union authorizing the incorporation of such associations.

Section 1 of the act of 1851 provides as follows:

Any number of persons, not less than nine, may associate and form an incorporated company for the purpose of accumulating a fund for the purchase of real estate, the erection of buildings, or the making of other improvements on lands, or to pay off incumbrances thereon and removing incumbrances therefrom ; and for the further purpose of accumulating a fund to be returned to its members who do not obtain advances as above mentioned, when the funds of such association shall amount to a certain sum per share, to be specified in the articles of association.

The second section provides what shall be contained in the articles of association, and is as follows:

Such persons shall severally subscribe articles of association, in which shall be set forth the name of the corporation, the time of its regular meetings, and how special meetings may be called, and what shall constitute a quorum to transact business at meetings ; the qualification of members, and how constituted ; what officers, trustees, and attorney there shall be, and how and when chosen, and their duties, and how removed or suspended from office ; the entrance fee of new members and new shares, the monthly or weekly dues per share, the redemption fee on shares on which advances shall be made, and fees to be paid on the transfer of shares ; the fines or penalties for non-payment of dues or fees, or other violation of the articles of association ; the manner of redemption of shares by advances made thereon, the mortgaged security to be taken on such advances, and how the same may be redeemed or changed ; the manner of the transfer or withdrawal of shares ; the manner of investing funds not required for advances on shares ; the qualifications of voters at meetings, and the mode of voting ; the ultimate amount to be paid to the owners of unredeemed shares ; the manner of altering or amending the articles of association, and such other provisions as shall be necessary for the convenient and effective transaction of the business thereof ; provided that the same shall not in any respect contravene the Constitution or laws of this State.

The third section provides for the authentication of the articles of the association when they are executed, and where they should be filed, and reads as follows:

A true copy of such articles, signed by the officers of the association, together with a statement showing when the association was organized, and the place of the transaction of its business, and the names of the officers and trustees at the time of making of such statement, which shall be verified by oath or affirmation before any officer authorized to take affidavits, to be used in courts of justice, shall be filed in the office of the clerk of the county in which such association shall transact its business ; and thereupon the persons who have subscribed the articles of association as aforesaid, and such other persons as shall become members of the association, and their successors, shall be a body corporate by the name specified in such articles of association, and shall possess the powers and privileges, and be subject to the provisions of title third of chapter eighteen of the first part of the Revised Statutes, so far as those provisions are consistent with the provisions of this act, and they shall by their corporate name be capable in law of purchasing, holding, and conveying any real and personal estate whatever which may be necessary to enable said company to carry on their operation named in such certificate.

The whole act, with the acts amendatory thereof, will be found in the Appendix.

The first step in the work of organization is to secure nine or more persons who will unite in the undertaking. Whoever becomes interested in forming such an association, and it will usually be one person in the beginning, in casting about among his friends to find others to join with him, should keep clearly in mind the importance of securing good men to become incorporators, men who stand well in the community, and who will make good officers for the association. It is not well to stop when nine are secured. There ought to be a much larger number, and the larger the number the better. Having secured as large a number as is practicable, the next step is the meeting for the adoption of the articles of association, and for the election of officers. The drafting of these articles and their adoption is a most important matter. The articles not only constitute the charter of the association, but must outline the scheme upon which the business of the association is to be conducted. It usually occurs that the person who has been active in having the association formed is more or less familiar with the operation of these associations, and has a printed copy of the articles of association of one of them. If the incorporators wish to organize upon the same scheme, these articles may be easily changed in the matter of names, dates for meetings, etc., and then adopted. If no such copy is at hand, it may be obtained by writing to the secretary of some other association, and requesting a copy.

But by this method the faults in the scheme of one association are often perpetuated in another. It has been a common occurrence to adopt articles of association which the incorporators did not understand, and from want of proper information upon the subject they were not competent to judge whether the provisions contained in them were good or bad, or whether they accurately outlined the scheme upon which they wished the business of their association to be conducted.

There are probably in the State of New York at the present time not far from 270 associations incorporated under the act of 1851. An examination of their articles of association will show an endless variety in their language and their provisions. To select the articles of association of any one of them as a precedent and stop at that would not be sufficient for my purpose. It is my aim to give such information upon the subject as will enable those forming an association to frame articles that will be suitable to the scheme upon which they desire to conduct their business. To accomplish this there is no better way than to give a precedent for the articles of association or constitution, as they are sometimes termed, section by section, and under each section explain the variations and the phraseology in the section necessary to adapt it to the principal schemes upon which these associations are conducted. In this way we shall hope to accomplish better results than by placing precedents in the Appendix, and discussing them here in a general way. The beginning of the articles of association is properly a preamble, and we so name it.

PREAMBLE.

We, whose names are hereto subscribed, under the provisions of the laws of the State of New York, and especially an act entitled "An act for the incorporation of building, mutual loan, and accumulating fund association," passed April 10, 1851, and the acts amendatory thereof, do hereby associate ourselves and form an incorporate association for the purposes named in section 1 of said act, viz., for the purpose of accumulating a fund for the purchase of real estate, the erection of buildings, or the making of other improvements on lands, or to pay off incumbrances thereon, or to aid its members in acquiring real estate, making improvements thereon, removing incumbrances therefrom, and for the further purpose of accumulating a fund to be returned to its members who do not obtain advances as above mentioned, when the funds of such association shall amount to a certain sum per share to be specified in the articles of association ; and we do hereby adopt the following articles of association for the government of such association and the management of its business.

An association organizing in any other State can adopt this preamble by simply changing the name of the State, and inserting, in lieu of the act therein quoted, the title of the act under which the association is to be formed, and the purposes for which the law authorizes an association to be created.

ARTICLE ONE.

NAME AND PLACE OF BUSINESS.

SECTION 1. The corporate name of this association shall be " The ...... Association," and its place of business at ......, in the State of New York.

Any name may be selected for the association which suits the fancy of those engaged in organization. Care should be taken not to adopt the name of any other association already existing in the same State. It is advisable to adopt as part of the name the name of the place where the association is located.

ARTICLE TWO.

CAPITAL AND STOCK.

SECTION 1. The capital of this association shall consist of the accumulated savings of its stockholders, paid in upon stock, with the profits arising from the investment thereof to be made as hereinafter provided.

SECTION 2. The matured value of shares of stock shall be ..... dollars. The stock shall be issued in ...... yearly series, and after a new series has begun to be issued, no stock shall issue in a prior series. The total number of shares of stock outstanding at any one time shall not exceed ...... thousand shares.

The amount of the matured share may be any sum, but for convenience it should be fixed at $50, $100, $200, or $500. The series may be issued quarter-yearly or semi-yearly. The limit of the number of shares should be controlled by the matured value of shares and the extent of business which the association expects. With the matured value of shares at $200, 10,000 shares is a proper limit.

Who may become Stockholders.

SECTION 3. Any person, except as hereinafter limited, who is acceptable to the board of directors, may become a stockholder, and thereby a member of the association by subscribing these articles of association, and taking one or more shares of stock, and paying the entrance fees and dues thereon, as hereinafter provided. Parents and guardians may take and hold shares in the association as trustees in behalf of their minor children or wards, provided the cost of such shares be paid from the personal earnings of such minor children or wards, or by gifts from persons other than their male parents. Married women may take and hold shares in the association, provided the cost of such shares be paid from their personal earnings, the personal earnings of their children voluntarily bestowed for such purpose, or from property bequeathed or given to them by persons other than their husbands. Such parents or guardians, as trustees for their children or wards, shall be members of the association, and entitled to all the rights thereof as though they owned the stock personally, except as hereinafter limited. Upon a minor child becoming of age, the stock so held for him shall be transferred to him, and he shall become a member, and the membership of his trustee, on account of such stock, shall cease.

The above provisions in reference to parents, guardians, and married women, and the sources from which payments made upon stock held by such classes of persons must be derived, is substantially quoted from section 6 of the act of 1851. Except for such requirement of the law, we should not insert it. In case of married women, the stock will be issued in their name. In the case of a minor child or children, it should be issued to ......, trustee for ......, the name of the parent or guardian being put in the first blank and the name of the child or children in the second blank.

SECTION 4. A certificate of stock shall be issued to every stockholder, signed by the president and secretary, and under the seal of the association. Such certificate shall state the number of shares it represents, and the number of the series of stock in which it is issued. An entrance fee of ...... cents per share shall be paid to the association upon the issuing of the certificate. Such certificate of stock may be assigned by the owner thereof, or his duly authorized attorney in the presence of the secretary or president of the association ; but such assignment shall be subject to all the rights of the association in the stock assigned. The assignee, having obtained the approval of the board of directors, may sign the articles of association, and upon complying with the requirements thereof shall become a member of the association. The association, at their option, may take up the assigned certificate and issue a new certificate to the assignee. For every share assigned, there shall be paid to the association a transfer fee of ...... cents.

A proper sum for the entrance fee is twenty-five cents per share, and for the transfer fee fifteen cents a share.

Payments on Stock.

SECTION 5. All payments upon stock other than entrance and transfer fees shall be known as "dues." Each stockholder shall pay upon each share of stock held by him, at or before every ...... meeting for the payment of dues, the sum of ......, until the share of stock has reached its matured value, when the association shall pay the same to him, as hereinafter provided in these articles of association.

Whether the payments shall be *weekly* or *monthly* depends upon the scheme adopted by the association, and the amount to be paid at each meeting will be largely influenced by the same consideration. It is usual, where weekly payments are required, to make the dues twenty-five cents, and when monthly, one dollar. The matured value of the shares will also influence the amount required for dues at each meeting. For convenience the dues should be twenty-five cents, fifty cents, one dollar, etc.

Free Shares, Borrowed Shares, and Limit of Holding.

SECTION 6. Shares of stock upon which no loan has been made shall be known as "free shares," while shares of stock upon which loans have been made shall be known as "borrowed shares." No stockholder shall hold more than ...... shares in any one series, except that he may, in addition thereto, hold ...... shares as trustee for a minor child or children ; but he shall not be allowed to vote upon such additional shares held as trustee, and except further that the board of directors may allow a borrower to hold ...... additional shares for the purpose of borrowing upon them. But no stockholder shall hold more than ...... borrowed shares altogether.

Limiting the number of shares is to prevent a few obtaining control. A safe limit is ten shares in each series. The limit to be placed upon borrowed shares should be controlled by the class of property upon which the association expects to make loans.

ARTICLE THREE.

OFFICERS : THEIR ELECTION AND DUTIES.

SECTION 1. The officers of this association shall be chosen from among the stockholders, and shall be a president, vice-president, secretary, treasurer, and nine directors, all of whom shall constitute the board of directors of the association. In addition thereto, the board of directors shall appoint a suitable attorney, who shall be subject to removal by them without notice at any time. Said officers shall be chosen annually at the annual meeting of the association in each year ; their election shall be by ballot, and each share of stock not in arrears, except as limited by these articles of association, shall be entitled to one vote. In case there shall be a failure for any cause to elect officers at the regular time appointed for the annual meeting, a special meeting of the stockholders may thereafter be called for the purpose of electing said officers. All officers shall continue in office until their successors shall have been duly elected and qualified.

Whether all the directors shall be elected annually or whether they shall be divided into classes and one part of them elected annually is a matter upon which the practice of associations differs. We have given our views upon that question fully in Chapter VII, and need not repeat them here. We think the majority of associations allow one vote only for each stockholder, regardless of the amount of stock held by him. If the incorporators wish to follow this rule, the above proposed section should be modified accordingly. If the incorporators deem it advisable to have the directors hold office longer than one year, the above section should be modified to conform to the scheme which they adopt.

Suspension and Removal of Officers.

SECTION 2. The board of directors, by a two thirds vote at a regular meeting, or a special meeting called therefor, shall have power to suspend any officer of the association for cause ; whereupon a special meeting of the stockholders of the association shall be called, in the manner prescribed by these articles, to consider such suspension. At the time of calling such special meeting, notice thereof, with the charges and specifications in writing against the offending officer, shall be served upon him personally, or left at his last place of residence. At such special meeting, or a meeting adjourned therefrom, the offending officer shall be reinstated or removed by a majority vote of the stock represented at such meeting.

In the event the association should adopt the mode of allowing each shareholder to cast one vote instead of voting upon his stock, the above should be changed to read " by a majority vote of the stockholders present at such meeting."

Vacancies.

SECTION 3. In case of a vacancy occurring in any office by the death, resignation, or removal of any officer, the board of directors shall have power to fill such vacancy until the next annual election, or until the stockholders shall hold an election to fill such vacancy.

Duties of President.

SECTION 4. The president shall preside at all meetings of the stockholders and of the board of directors, sign all certificates of stock and all orders properly drawn upon the treasurer for the payment of appropriations of moneys, see that each officer performs his duties and that the laws of the association are enforced, and, when directed by the board of directors, to duly execute discharges and acquittances of bonds and mortgages, and faithfully and impartially discharge all the duties of his office.

In some associations the articles of association provide that the president shall discharge any bond or mortgage, when entitled to be discharged, without direction from the board of directors. We prefer the course indicated above, which requires the board of directors to direct the discharge before the president has power in the matter. If the other course is preferred by those organizing the association in the place of the clause above relating thereto, the following may be used : " And it shall be his duty to discharge any bond or mortgage held by the association when the same is entitled to be discharged."

Duties of Vice-President.

Section 5. In case of the absence or disability of the president, the vice-president shall perform his duties. He shall also perform the duties of president in all cases where any proceedings are pending against the president for his suspension or removal.

Duties of Treasurer.

Section 6. The treasurer shall be the custodian of all funds, securities, contracts, and deeds belonging to the association, subject, however, to the direction of the board of directors. He shall receipt for all moneys paid to him, and pay all orders or drafts upon him ordered by the board of directors and signed by the president and attested by the secretary. He shall keep suitable and accurate books of account of all his transactions, subject to the direction of the board of directors as to the form and the manner of keeping the same, and shall make a report of the finances of the association to each regular meeting of the board of directors, which report shall be filed by the secretary. His books of account shall be subject to the call and inspection of the board of directors or any member thereof at any time, and shall be subject to the inspection of any stockholder at all reasonable hours. He shall give a bond with at least two sureties, one or more of whom shall not be connected with the bank where he deposits the funds of the association, in an amount directed by the board of directors, and in form and sufficiency of sureties subject to their approval. At the expiration of his term of office he shall deliver to his successor in office, within five days after the qualification of such successor, all moneys, books, and papers of the association in his possession ; and in case of his suspension and removal from office, he shall deliver the same to the board of directors upon his removal forthwith.

The above provision, requiring that one or more of the sureties should not be connected with the bank where the treasurer deposits the funds of the association, may be omitted if the incorporators do not deem it wise to require such a provision. It usually occurs that in case of a failure of a bank that all persons connected therewith become insolvent; and if all the treasurer's sureties upon the bond were connected with the bank, by a failure of the bank the bond would become worthless.

Duties of Secretary.

SECTION 7. The secretary shall be present at all meetings of the stockholders and board of directors in person, or have a proxy from the board of directors, and keep correct minutes of the proceedings, which shall be transcribed into a suitable minute-book and read at the next meeting for the approval of the board. He shall sign all certificates of stock and all orders directed to be drawn by the board of directors upon the treasurer, and receive the dues, fines, and interest and any other moneys coming to the association when so directed by the board of directors, and receipt for the same, or assist the board of directors or its committee in receiving and receipting for the same when so directed. He shall publish and serve all notices and advertisements when directed or required to be published or served ; he shall keep an accurate account of all moneys paid to the association ; he shall keep a true account between the association and the shareholders, and give to the shareholders at all times any desired information in relation to the financial affairs of the association ; he shall keep such books of account and in such manner and form as the board of directors shall require. His books of account shall be subject to the call and inspection of the board of directors or any member thereof at any time, and shall be subject to the inspection of any stockholder at all reasonable hours. When so directed by the board of directors, he shall have an office, known as the office of the association, and be in attendance thereat at such hours of the day as they shall direct. All moneys received by him shall be turned over by him to the treasurer within ...... hours after the receipt of the same. He shall make such reports to the board of directors as they shall require from time to time ; he shall make a detailed report of the business of the association at each annual meeting and all other meetings of the stockholders when requested so to do by any officer of the association. He shall have charge of the correspondence of the association, and shall deliver to his successor in office, within five days after the qualification of such successor, all books and papers in his possession belonging to the association, and, in case of his removal from office, he shall deliver the same to the board of directors forthwith.

In drafting the foregoing section we have endeavored to make it applicable alike to an association which has a regular office for the receipt of dues, interest, and fines, and allows the stockholders to pay the same to the secretary at any time prior to the regular meeting, as well as to associations which only permit dues, interest, and fines to be paid at the time of the regular meetings. In the latter case the secretary usually assists the finance committee of the board of directors in receiving and receipting for dues, etc. We believe it right in all cases to leave the general control of the whole matter to the board of directors.

Duties of Attorney.

SECTION 8. It shall be the duty of the attorney to make abstracts of title, or examine the same when procured by the borrower from the county clerk, of all real-estate which has been offered to the association as security for loans and approved by the board of directors or its finance committee, and, if satisfactory, to indorse his approval thereon. He shall prepare all securities given to the association, and see that all policies of fire insurance which are given to secure loans are in proper form and with proper indorsements for the security of the association. His charges for such services shall be reasonable at all times, and subject to the direction of the board of directors, and shall be paid by the borrower, unless the board otherwise directs. He shall see that all mortgages are properly entered for record before any advances are made thereon. He shall meet with the board of directors as required, but shall have no vote. He shall receive no compensation for meeting with the board from the association, except as they may direct.

The above clause, saying that the attorney shall have no compensation for meeting with the board of directors, except as they shall direct the same, is to obviate any implied agreement to pay him what his services are reasonably worth when he attends at their request. Under the section as it stands the board will havo to voto to givo him the compensation therefor before he would be entitled to any, although he should attend at their request.

Finance Committee.

SECTION 9. The president shall appoint from the nine directors, during the year, three finance committees of three members each, and each committee shall serve for the term of four months. The appointments shall be so made that each director shall serve upon one of said committees. Such committee, except when the board of directors shall otherwise direct, shall pass upon all securities offered to the association for loans, subject to the approval of the attorney as to the title of real estate. They shall examine personally all real estate upon which they shall pass, as to its sufficiency as a security. They shall hold a meeting on the ...... after each regular meeting of the board of directors, for loaning money, at ...... m. o'clock. They shall audit all bills against the association ; [they shall attend all regular meetings for the receipt of dues, interest, fines, etc., and receive and receipt for the same, and at the close of the meeting turn the same over to the treasurer, and take his receipt therefor;] they shall perform such duties proper for a finance committee, as the board of directors shall direct.

The clause above, inclosed in brackets, in reference to the receipt of dues, etc., by the finance committee, should be omitted when the association wishes to adopt the scheme of having dues, interest, and fines, received wholly by the secretary, when he has an office for that purpose, or under any other arrangements whereby the secretary is authorized to receive and receipt for dues, etc., and in its stead there should be a clause, in substance, as follows: "The finance committee shall audit the accounts of the secretary quar-

11

terly, and at such other times as the board of directors may order."

Auditors of the Annual Report.

SECTION 10. The president, at the time of the last meeting for the receipt of dues, etc., before the annual meeting, shall appoint three stockholders who are not officers in the association, who shall examine the books of account of the treasurer and of the secretary, and the annual report prepared by the secretary, and verify the same by an examination of the books of the secretary, and of the securities and funds held by the treasurer, and if found to be correct, indorse their approval thereon.

The object of this provision is to have a committee appointed from the stockholders who have had nothing to do with the management of the business during the year, for the purpose of verifying the results shown by the detailed annual report of the secretary.

ARTICLE FOUR.

MEETINGS OF THE ASSOCIATION.

SECTION 1. The annual meeting of the stockholders shall be held on the ...... day of ...... in each year, at ...... o'clock in the evening.

In fixing the time for the annual meeting, sufficient time should be allowed between the last meeting for the receipt of dues, etc., and the loaning of money in the fiscal year, to enable the secretary and treasurer to write up their books, and for the secretary to prepare his annual report and have it printed. It will be found advisable in the long run to allow at least two weeks for these purposes.

Board Meetings.

SECTION 2. The board of directors or the finance committee shall hold a meeting on the ...... day of ......, between ...... and ...... o'clock in the evening, for the receipt of dues, interest, and fines, and immediately following such meeting the board of directors shall hold a meeting for offering the money of the association to borrowers, and for the transaction of any other business of the association which comes before the board of directors.

This section relating to the board or the committee for the receipt of dues, etc., offering money for sale, and transacting other business of the association, will vary greatly according to the scheme adopted by the incorporators for conducting the business of the association. If the scheme is adopted whereby dues, etc., are paid to the secretary, then the meeting of the board should not be held until the time is up within which dues, interest, and fines, may be paid, and the meeting of the board will be for the purpose of offering the money for sale, and transacting the regular business of the association; or, instead of the meeting for this purpose at this time, the finance committee may be authorized to offer the moneys to borrowers, and the meeting of the board of directors be held at some other time for the transaction of such business as may come before them. Again, the section will be modified as the scheme adopted calls for weekly or monthly meetings. The section as given in blank may be filled up either for weekly or for monthly meetings.

Special Meetings of the Board.

SECTION 3. Special meetings of the board of directors may be called by the president at any time upon twenty-four hours' notice. Such notice may be given orally by the president or secretary, or by serving a written notice, stating the object and time of the meeting, upon each director, or by leaving the same at his residence, in the custody of some person residing therein, of suitable age and discretion. The president shall call a special meeting of the board of directors, when requested so to do by three members, in writing, specifying the purpose for which they desire the meeting to be called.

It may seem to some persons that the above provision for calling the special meeting of the board of directors allows but a very short time; but in the practical management of an association it will frequently be found necessary for the board of directors to come together to consider some matter upon short notice, and if a longer time than twenty-four hours is required, inconvenience at times will be caused.

Special Meetings of Stockholders.

SECTION 4. Special meetings of the stockholders may be called by the president, and shall be called by him whenever requested by ten stockholders, in writing, specifying the purpose for which they desire the meeting called. Five days' notice of any special meeting for any purpose shall be given by mailing, postage prepaid, to the post-office address of every stockholder, as it appears upon the books of the association, a written or printed notice, stating the time and place, and the business to be brought before the association.

Quorums.

SECTION 5. ...... stockholders shall constitute a quorum at all meetings of the stockholders, and ...... directors shall shall constitute a quorum at all meetings of the board of directors.

The number to constitute a quorum should be influenced by the expectations as to the number of stockholders.

Post-office Address of Stockholders.

SECTION 6. At the time of signing the articles of association, each stockholder and trustee shall write opposite his name his post-office address, and shall notify in writing any change made thereafter in his post-office address.

The object of this section is to make suitable provision for mailing any notices required to be given by these articles of association.

ARTICLE FIVE.

LOANS : TO WHOM MADE.

SECTION 1. The funds of the association available for loans shall be loaned only to its stockholders. Every stockholder who can give the required security shall have an equal right with every other stockholder to such funds to an amount not exceeding the matured value of the shares held and owned by him. Loans shall be regarded as advances upon the matured value of the shares borrowed upon, and shall be made only for the matured value of the shares, except, when necessary to make out the sum the borrower desires, the fractional parts of one fourth or one half of a share may be so advanced.

Under the foregoing, if the matured value of shares is $200, loans must be in the sum of $200 or a multiple thereof; except a borrower wanted $250, when one share and a quarter could be loaned. The borrower would have to own two shares of stock. If the matured value was $100, he would have to own three shares, and borrow upon two shares and one half of the third share. The section as proposed limits all loans to stockholders. In the event of an accumulation and no demand for loans, there should be forced withdrawals, which will be provided for under the head of withdrawals.

The Funds: How and when offered to Borrowers.

SECTION 2. All funds available for loans shall be offered to borrowers by the board of directors or their financial committee at an open meeting held immediately following the regular ...... meeting for the receipt of dues, etc., or at such other regular and stated times as the board of directors may direct ; but in the event all of said funds shall not be loaned at said stated meetings, the board of directors or their finance committee may hold special meetings for the purpose of offering such funds to borrowers.

The offering of the funds to borrowers may be devolved wholly upon the board of directors, in which case the words " or their finance committee " should be stricken out wherever it occurs ; or it may be confided wholly to the finance committee, in which case, in place of " the board of directors or their finance committee," the words " the finance committee of the board of directors " should be substituted ; or the conducting of the sales may be given to the secretary, in which case " the secretary " will be inserted instead of the " board " or its " finance committee."

Interest.

SECTION 3. Interest on all loans shall be at the rate of .... per cent per annum, payable in ...... installments at the same time that dues are paid upon the stock borrowed upon.

While legal interest remains at six per cent, we believe it best to make it the interest on loans. Fixing it at a lower rate will only tend to increase the amount of premium bid.

Premiums.

SECTION 4. The right to borrow the funds, when two or more stockholders desire the same at the times they are offered to the borrowers, shall be decided by the bidding of a premium per share; and the loan shall be awarded to the highest bidder, and the premium bid shall be deducted from the amount loaned at the time the loan is paid over to the borrower.

The plan proposed in this section is the gross plan, without the system of rebates. The borrower gives his security for the amount borrowed. The premium is deducted from the sum loaned, and the borrower thereafter has simply the interest on his loan and dues on stock to pay. If the incorporators prefer the installment premium plan, which is the most common at present, the following should be adopted in place of the above :

SECTION 4. The right to borrow the funds, when two or more stockholders desire the same at the times they are offered to borrowers, shall be determined by the bidding of a certain sum per share, to be paid monthly in addition to the monthly installment of interest during the continuance of the loan ; and the loan shall be awarded to the highest bidder, and the security given shall include the payment of such monthly installment of premium.

In the event the incorporators should prefer the interest premium plan, then the following should be used in the place of the foregoing sections 2 and 3.

Premium Interest Plan.

The right to borrow the funds when offered to borrowers shall be decided by a bidding upon the rate of interest to be paid per annum, payable in monthly installments, at the same time the dues are paid upon the stock borrowed upon. The

loan shall be awarded to the highest bidder, provided, however, that no bid shall be accepted for a less rate than ....
per cent per annum.

We have in preceding chapters fully discussed these several premium plans, and expressed our convictions as to the respective merits of each, hence we will not discuss them now. We give no form for the gross plan, with the system of rebates, for the reason that we do not wish to be responsible in any degree for continuing a system so complex and so misleading.

Naming Security.

SECTION 5. The person or persons to whom a loan or loans are awarded shall forthwith furnish to the board or their committee a full description of the security or securities proposed for the loan or loans.

The description of the securities proposed should be passed at once to the committee charged with the duty of passing upon their sufficiency. In place of " the board or their committee " above named should be inserted the precise officer or officers conducting the sale as fixed in the prior section.

Rejected Security.

SECTION 6. The borrower shall pay interest on his loan from the time the same is awarded to him at the sale of the funds. In the event he fails to give satisfactory security, he shall pay interest on the sum bid off until the first stated meeting for the loaning of money after the rejection of his securities, and his right to a loan under his bid shall be lost.

The borrower should pay interest as above provided, for the reason that the funds must be set aside for him at once upon awarding him a loan. In case the monthly installment premium plan is adopted, the first line in the section should be amended so as to read, "The borrower shall pay interest and the monthly (or weekly, as the case may be) installment of premium on his loan," etc. ; and also amended below so as to read, "He shall pay interest and the ...... installment of premium on the sum bid off," etc. A provision may also be incorporated in the above section providing that in case the loan is passed for a less sum than bid off, and the borrower accepts such reduced loan, he shall pay the interest and installments of premium, if any, upon the full amount bid off up to the first stated meeting for the sales of money after the acceptance of the loan. This latter provision has a wholesome effect in restraining borrowers from overestimating the value of the real estate they offer as a security.

ARTICLE SIX.

Security for Loans.

SECTION 1. The security for all loans shall be a bond in the penal sum of twice the amount loaned, secured by a first mortgage upon unincumbered real estate, accompanied by a transfer and pledge to the association of the shares borrowed upon and all accumulations that have or shall accrue thereon; or, in lieu of the mortgage, the borrower, or another, may transfer and pledge to the association free shares, the withdrawing value of which at the time of borrowing, added to the withdrawing value of the shares borrowed upon, shall exceed the amount loaned and the interest thereon for six months. All bonds and mortgages given to the association shall contain or refer to the conditions for the repayment of loans and the interest thereon prescribed by these articles of association.

In case the installment premium plan is adopted there should be added to the phrase " and the interest thereon," wherever it occurs, the words, " and installments of premium bid." If desired, a limit may be placed upon the amount of the mortgage as related to the appraised value of the mortgaged premises. To do this, there would be inserted after the words " real estate " in the second line, the words, " for not exceeding ...... per cent of its appraised value as appraised by the finance committee."

Payment of Loans.

SECTION 2. The borrower shall continue to pay to the association the ...... installment of interest (and ...... installment of premium) until the shares borrowed upon shall reach their matured value, unless the loan is otherwise paid before that time, when the association shall discharge the securities and the borrower shall surrender the stock borrowed upon. A borrower may repay a loan and all arrearages of interest (and installments of premium) and fines thereon, or one share thereof, at any stated meeting for the receipt of dues, etc., or to the treasurer at any other time ; but when not made at said stated meeting he shall pay interest (and installments of premium) up to the first regular meeting for loaning money after such payment. He may pay the loan in full, and thereby entitle him to have the shares borrowed upon released from liability for the loan, or he may have the withdrawal value of the shares applied as a part of the payment, and surrender his stock to the association, and have his bond (with any mortgage accompanying it) discharged. The board of directors shall direct the president and secretary to execute a proper discharge of any security held by the association, when for any cause it should be surrendered.

The blanks at the beginning of the section will be filled out with the words " weekly " or " monthly," according as the scheme requires weekly or monthly payments. The clause in the brackets will be omitted, except when the installment plan of premium is adopted, in which case the brackets will be removed. Under this section the borrower may pay the whole loan, or any share of the loan, at any time. If paid between the stated meetings for the sales of money, interest must be paid thereon up to such stated meeting after the payment. Under this section, no officer of the association will, on his own authority, have the right to discharge the securities; it must be authorized by the board of directors. We believe this to be the safest course; but as we have remarked in the section relating to the duties of president, some associations empower the president to discharge without authority from the board. The above section may be easily modified to adapt it to such a course.

Default on Securities.

SECTION 3. Whenever a borrower shall be ...... months in arrears in the payment of the dues upon the stock borrowed upon and interest upon the loan (or installments of premium bid) or either of them, the whole loan shall become due at the option of the board of directors, and they may proceed to enforce collection upon the securities held by the association. The withdrawal value, at the time of the commencement of the action, of all shares pledged as collateral security for the loan shall be applied upon the loan and arrearages of interest (installments of premium) and fines thereon, and the shares shall be deemed surrendered to the association.

The periods to be filled in the blanks left in the foregoing section as to the time the default shall extend will be influenced by the scheme of the association as to whether it calls for weekly or monthly installments. It is usual to give six months in cases where the installments are paid monthly, and three months where the installments are paid weekly.

Purchase of Real Estate.

SECTION 4. The board of directors may purchase at any public sale or at any private sale, when deemed advisable to secure the association from loss, any real estate upon which the association may hold a mortgage, judgment lien, or other incumbrance, or in which it may have any interest ; and may sell, convey, lease, or mortgage the same, or make improvements thereon, as shall seem for the best interest of the association. Upon the decease of a stockholder having received a loan, his heirs, legatees, or legal representatives, or the persons legally liable to pay the loan or the mortgage given to secure the loan, may, upon subscribing to the articles of association and by-laws, succeed to all the rights of the deceased in the association, subject to its rules and regulations.

ARTICLE SEVEN.

Fines.

SECTION 1. Whenever any stockholder shall make default in the payment of his dues or interest (or installments of premium) at any regular meeting or time for the payment of the same, when due, he shall pay a fine of ...... per cent on the sum defaulted, and shall continue to pay such fine for every said meeting or time while such default continues.

The provisions of this section are intended to be broad enough to apply to an association which adopts the plan of having dues paid to a single officer at stated times, as well as when the board of directors, or its finance committee, hold stated meetings, weekly or

monthly, for the receipt of dues, etc. It imposes the
fine for each default. To illustrate, suppose the
scheme be one requiring monthly dues, and the stockholder makes default in the payment of his dues, etc.,
for May, and makes no payment in June, he will be
fined for his June payments and also on his May payment still unpaid, and so on until he shall pay up. As
to the amount of the fine, there is much diversity in
the practice of associations. We believe in making it
10 per cent. It should be large enough to insure
prompt payment.

Forfeitures.

SECTION 2. In the event any stockholder holding free
shares shall be six months in arrears, at any time, for dues
thereon, the secretary shall serve upon him personally a notice showing said stockholder's arrearages upon said free
shares, and requiring him to pay said arrearages within sixty
days from the service of notice, or his said shares, and all
dues previously paid thereon, will be forfeited to said association ; and in the event a personal service of said notice
can not be made, a publication thereof in a daily or weekly
newspaper, published in the ...... of ......, once in each
week, for six successive weeks, shall be deemed equivalent
to a personal service, and the sixty days within which said
defaulting stockholder may pay up his arrearages in case of
service by publication, shall commence on the day of the last
publication; and in the event such defaulting stockholder
shall not pay up the arrearages aforesaid within the sixty
days aforesaid, the board of directors, at any regular meeting
thereof, by a majority vote, may declare such defaulting
stockholder's free shares forfeited to said association, and
all moneys previously paid thereon, and thereupon he shall
cease to be a member of said association for any purpose
whatever.

This section is framed to meet the requirements of section 4 of the act of 1851. In framing articles of association under any other act in the State of New York or elsewhere, it would be necessary for the incorporators to refer to the act under which they were incorporated, and determine whether there was any provision in the act limiting the power of forfeiture. If the general act contained no limitations upon the power of the association in declaring stock forfeited upon which default has been made in the payment of dues thereon, then a section might be drawn to take the place of the above, in language substantially as follows: "The board of directors shall have power, in the case of a stockholder .... months in arrears in payment of his dues, to declare his stock forfeited and all moneys due thereon from the association, in the event he shall not pay the same within .... days after a notice of the amount of his arrears has been duly served upon him personally, or left at his place of residence, as shown by the books of the association, with some person of suitable age and discretion by the secretary of the association; and if no person of suitable age and discretion can be found at said residence, then by affixing said notice to the front door thereof; but this section shall not apply in case default in payment has arisen by reason of the death of the defaulting stockholder."

ARTICLE EIGHT.

DISTRIBUTION OF PROFITS AND LOSSES.

SECTION 1. Profits and losses shall be distributed at least annually, and always before issuing a new series of stock. Profits shall be distributed in the form of a dividend added to the value of each share outstanding which has not matured. The dividend thus added to each share shall bear the same rate of percentage to the value of the share that the total net profits to be distributed bear to the total value of all the shares to which the distribution is made. In ascertaining the total net profits to be thus distributed, which have accrued since the last distribution, any losses sustained during that time shall be deducted from the gross profits. In the event the losses sustained shall exceed the profits, then the profits shall be deducted from the gross loss, and the net loss shall be assessed upon each share of stock outstanding upon the same principle above given for adding dividends, and the sum assessed upon each share shall be subtracted therefrom.

Matured stock shall not share in dividends or be liable for losses, but, instead thereof, each matured share, from the time of its maturity until paid off, shall draw interest at the rate of ...... per cent per annum, to be paid when the stock is paid.

This system of distributing profits and losses is simple, just, and equitable. It treats all stockholders as partners, and each partner receives profits in proportion to the capital which he has in the association, and treats as part of such capital all dividends made to him. We have, in Chapter III, discussed the manner of declaring the dividend. We give an illustration in Chapter IX. It should be clearly borne in mind that premiums not yet paid are not profits. Nothing should be counted as profits in declaring dividends which has not been actually paid in. In those associations that have already adopted, or should foolishly, as it seems to me, hereafter adopt the gross plan of premium with a system of rebates, whereby the borrower is allowed a rebate of one eighth or one ninth or one tenth upon the premium for each full year of the time remaining in which it is assumed it will take the stock to mature upon which the loan is made, in case he shall repay his loan, in ascertaining the amount of profits to distribute, loans should not be reckoned at their face value, but only at the sum the association would receive if paid off at that time—in fact, their *present value.* Upon this rock many associations have come to grief. While they had as a part of their scheme the rebate system, they have reckoned their loans outstanding in computing assets at their face value, or apparent value; whereas their real value was the sum which would pay them off at the time the dividend was declared. Matured stock should not be allowed dividends. They are awaiting payment, and the rate of interest allowed should be low. We suggest three per cent. Matured stock should be paid off as rapidly as the association has funds applicable to such purpose.

ARTICLE NINE.

WITHDRAWALS, AND HOW COMPUTED.

This is an important matter, and one in which in practice great diversity exists. It involves two distinct questions: 1. As to what percentage of the profits which have been added to the stock shall the association retain from the withdrawing stockholder? 2. Shall it be determined and fixed by the articles of association, or shall the power of determining the same from time to time be lodged in the board of directors? We will give a form of a proper article for either course; and first we give the form of an article which fixes definitely the share returned. It can be adapted to any rate per cent by simply changing the rate per cent we have used.

SECTION 1. Any stockholder owning free shares may withdraw the same, upon filing a written notice of his intention so to do with the secretary, and at the next meeting of the board of directors they shall direct orders upon the treasurer to be drawn to pay such stockholders desiring to withdraw, according to the priority in the filing of such notices, as soon as there are funds applicable to the payment of withdrawing stockholders under the provisions of these articles of association. Such withdrawing stockholder shall receive, less any fines he may owe, during the first six months the series has run in which the stock withdrawn was issued, the amount of dues paid thereon, and during the last six months of the first year he shall receive the dues paid thereon and interest at the rate of four per cent per annum ; and after the first year and until the close of the sixth year in the age of the series in which the stock withdrawn was issued, he shall receive the dues paid thereon, and seventy-five per cent of the profits which have been added to said shares in dividends up to and including the last distribution of profits and losses before such withdrawal, together with four per cent interest thereon from the last distribution, to which shall be added also dues paid since such distribution and four per cent interest thereon. During the seventh year of the series of stock, he shall receive eighty per cent of the profits, instead of seventy-five as above ; during the eighth year, eighty-five per cent ; during the ninth year, ninety per cent; and during the tenth year and until the series mature, ninety-five per cent.

We believe the rates given above are just and equitable. In the event, however, that a " guarantee fund " should be created and carried, then a larger percentage of the profits might be given to the withdrawing stockholder. The reasons for increasing the

12

percentage as the stock approaches maturity is to stimulate withdrawals, in order that when a series matures there shall not be a large number of free shares remaining. The following is a form in which the power of determining the withdrawal value is lodged with the board of directors within certain limitations. That portion of the foregoing form preceding the first period will be used with it:

The board of directors, at each meeting held for making and declaring a distribution of profits and losses, shall also determine the withdrawal value of the shares of stock until the next distribution of profits and losses. In determining such withdrawal value, they shall allow to all shares of stock over two years of age, in addition to the dues paid thereon, less any fines unpaid, seventy per cent of the profits which have accrued and been added to the value of the shares, and as much more as to them shall seem wise. They shall have discretionary power to make the percentage of profits withdrawn uniform upon all such shares, or increase the same as the shares increase in age. In the case of shares not over two years of age at the time of determining the withdrawal value, they shall allow, in lieu of a percentage of profits, interest upon the dues paid in at a rate of not less than four per cent per annum. Upon all withdrawals made until the next distribution of profits and losses, in addition to such withdrawal value, interest shall be paid upon such withdrawal value of the shares, and upon all dues paid subsequent to such declaration of withdrawal values, together with such dues, at the rate of four per cent per annum.

These sections assume the matured value of shares to be $200, and monthly dues $1. If the matured value is placed at a less sum, and dues at $1 a month, or twenty-five cents a week, the times specified, the sections should be shortened to correspond.

ARTICLE TEN.

THE DIVISION TO BE MADE IN THE APPLICATION OF THE FUNDS OF THE ASSOCIATION.

SECTION 1. The division of the moneys received by the association between the borrowers, withdrawing shareholders, and matured stock, shall be made as follows : When the association shall not have outstanding any matured stock, one half of the receipts from dues, interest, and fines at every stated meeting shall be offered to borrowers, and withdrawing shareholders shall be entitled to .the other half. In the event notices of withdrawals have not been filed sufficient to take said one half, the remainder thereof shall be also offered to borrowers. In case there should not be borrowers, and there should be a demand for more than one half by withdrawing stockholders, any sum remaining, after meeting the demands of borrowers, may be applied to withdrawals. And in the event of the association having matured stock unpaid, then one third shall be applicable to matured stock, one third to borrowers, and one third to withdrawals. In case there shall not be demand by borrowers for the one third set aside for them, the same shall be applied to the payment of matured stock, or such balance as remains after the applications of borrowers have been filled. Any moneys received by the association from the repayment of the principal of a loan shall be added to the share set aside for borrowers, if there be demand for the same. If not, they shall be applied in the same manner as provided above for dues, interest, and fines. If at any time there shall be an accumulation of the funds in the treasury of the association for which there is no demand by borrowers, matured stock, or withdrawals, and no prospect of a demand in the immediate future, the board of directors may, in their discretion, under rules made by them, compel the withdrawal of free shares in any series at any time after four years from the date of their issue, provided that the shareholders whose shares are to be thus withdrawn compulsorily shall be determined by lot, and that they shall be paid all dues paid thereon and all profits which have been added to their shares, less any fines and proportionate part of any loss sustained since the last distribution. Whenever a series of stock shall mature, the holders thereof shall respectively file with the secretary a notice asking for the payment of the same, and specifying the amount due, and such stock shall be paid in the order of the priority of the filing of such notices.

The foregoing article is intended to relieve all conflict that might arise between the three classes of persons, viz., holders of matured stock, borrowers, and stockholders desiring to withdraw, in relation to the application of the funds of the association. It also provides a regulation for the payment of matured stock. The stockholder, during the years that his stock is maturing, understands that at its maturity he can not receive his money, except as there are funds applicable to the payment of matured stock, and hence he will not be disappointed if his stock is not paid at once upon its arriving at maturity. The provision with reference to compelling withdrawals provides a safeguard against an accumulation of funds in the association which shall remain uninvested. An occasion will seldom arise for using this provision in the articles, but it is wise for such power to be given to the board of directors.

ARTICLE ELEVEN.

Compensation of Officers.

SECTION 1. No officer of this association shall receive compensation for services rendered, except the attorney, as before provided, and the treasurer and the secretary, unless the stockholders of the association, at an annual meeting, or a special meeting, shall authorize the payment of such compensation, and fix the amount thereof. The board of directors shall annually determine the compensation to be paid the secretary and the treasurer.

In nearly all associations of this character the only officers who receive compensation are the secretary and the treasurer, and the salaries paid to them are not large for the amount of services performed. Some associations allow compensation for president; some also provide for the payment of compensation to the committee which passes upon the sufficiency of loans, and charge the amount thereof to the borrowers. This section may be amended, as given above, to suit the incorporators of the association in that particular.

Incurring of Expenses.

SECTION 2. No officer of the association shall make or incur any expenses on behalf of the association unless duly authorized so to do by the board of directors.

By-Laws.

SECTION 3. The board of directors may enact by-laws for conducting the business of the association not in conflict with these articles of association or the laws of the State.

ARTICLE TWELVE.

AMENDMENTS TO THESE ARTICLES OF ASSOCIATION.

SECTION 1. These articles of association may be amended at any annual meeting of the stockholders, or at any special meeting called for that purpose, by a two-thirds vote of the stock represented at such meeting ; or they may be amended by a majority vote, provided the proposed amendments have been duly mailed to each stockholder one month preceding such meeting.

If the system adopted by the association is one vote for a stockholder, then the above section should read " stockholders " instead of " the stock represented."

It is impossible to frame articles of association that will answer the purpose of all associations that may be formed under the act of 1851; but, in framing the foregoing, we have attempted to adapt them to all the ordinary schemes upon which the true building and loan association may be conducted. We have no doubt that imperfections may be found in them, but we believe they will furnish a safe guide to all incorporators of associations of this class not only in the State of New York, but in every State in the Union, except as the powers of the corporation may be limited by the general act for the incorporation of this class of associations in the respective States, and that the changes to be made in them to adapt them to the laws of any State in the Union will be very few indeed.

Signing the Articles of Association.

After the articles of association have been adopted, they should be subscribed by all who have united in the formation of the society. In cases where a completed draft or printed copy of such articles of association have been presented to the meeting and have been adopted without material changes, such signing may be proceeded with at once; but in case changes have been made which will require a new copy to be made before they are in clean shape for signing, an adjournment of the meeting will be had to some future time to allow such draft to be prepared. Where an adjournment is had for the reason above stated, or for any other reason, two courses may be pursued. One is to have the articles of association ingrossed in a book which shall be known as the " Articles of Association Book," and at the adjourned meeting those who have united in forming the association can subscribe the articles of association in the book; and all other persons thereafter uniting with the association subscribe the same in the same book. All, in addition to their names, should give their post-office addresses.

The other course that may be pursued is to have the articles of association printed in form for distribution among the members, and to be bound in the pass - books which will be issued to each member when he commences paying dues upon his stock. This course will allow the printed copy to be pasted in the book for members to subscribe instead of the written copy. It will also provide for the copy which is to be filed in the county clerk's office as hereafter described.

Election of Officers.

In the event the articles of association adopted are in such condition that they may be subscribed at once, the election of officers should be proceeded with. If, however, the meeting adjourns to allow the articles of association to be ingrossed or to be printed, the election of officers should be delayed until the adjourned meeting. At such other time as they are elected, the proceedings for their election will be controlled by the provisions adopted in the articles of association except in the following particular : If the articles of association should provide that each shareholder shall be entitled to as many votes as he holds shares of stock, that provision will not be applicable at the first meeting for the election of officers, for the reason that no shares of stock have yet been issued; and each person uniting in the formation of the association, and who has subscribed the articles of association, will be simply entitled to one vote, the same as though the articles of association provided that in all meetings of the association each shareholder shall be entitled to one vote regardless of the number of shares owned by him.

Filing the Articles of Association.

As we have already seen by section 3 of the act of 1851, a copy of the articles of association, signed by the officers of the association, together with a statement showing when the association was formed; the place of the transaction of its business, and the names of its officers and directors at the time of making said statement, duly verified, must be filed in the office of the clerk of the county where the association is to transact its business. The following is the proper form for such statement:

To all whom it may concern:

We, the undersigned, do hereby state and certify that the foregoing is a true copy of the articles of association adopted by the ...... association of the ...... of the State of New York. That such association was organized and such articles of association adopted on the .... day of ......, 18.. That the place where said ...... association will conduct its business is the ...... in the county of ......, in the State of New York. That the following are the names of the officers and

directors or trustees of the said association at this time, to wit: ...., President ; ...., Vice-President ; ...., Treasurer ; ...., Secretary.
....
....
....
....
directors or trustees.

This statement should immediately follow the copy of the articles of association, and should be signed by each of the officers with their official titles. Immediately following the same should be an affidavit made by the president, or any other officer, as follows :

State of New York, }
County of ......, } *ss.*
......., President of the .... Association of the county of ......, in the State of New York, being duly sworn, says that he is the President of the .... Association of the county of ...., in the State of New York ; that the foregoing is a true copy of the articles of association of said association, and that the foregoing statement, in all respects, correctly states the date of the organization of the said association, the place where the business thereof is to be transacted, and the names of the officers, directors, or trustees thereof at this date, and that the names of the officers and trustees above signed to said copy of the articles of association and the statement of facts immediately following the same are the officers and directors or trustees of said association at this time, and that such statement is made and signed as above, in conformity to section 3 of the act of 1851, in Chapter 122, entitled " An act for the incorporation of Building, Mutual Loan, and Accumulating Fund Associations," for the purpose of effecting the incorporation of such association as by said section provided. Sworn to before me this ...... day of ......, 188..

When the instrument is completed it will contain, first, a true copy of the articles of association; next, the statement when the association was organized, the place where its business is to be transacted, and the names of its officers and directors or trustees; next, the signatures of the officers of the association; and lastly, the affidavit.

The copy used for making this instrument for filing may be a printed copy, in case the articles of association are printed. When completed, the same should be filed in the county clerk's office, where the association is located. With the filing of this instrument, the incorporation is completed.

CHAPTER IX.

THE keeping of accounts seems a very simple matter when an association is first organized; but after a few years' experience many vexatious difficulties will be met unless a proper system is adopted at the beginning. Begin right and the future is easy; start wrong, and the success of the association may be endangered. Under a wrong system there may appear to be a greater surplus to be distributed than in fact exists. Many associations in the past, working under the gross system with a system of rebates on the repayment of loans, have fallen into the error of treating as assets the face value of all securities held, without deducting the premium bid on the loan that would be deducted from the face value in case of repayment of the loan.

The system adopted should be as simple as possible and secure accuracy; but it will be found quite impossible to secure the desired accuracy unless the system involves double entry. There can be no excellence without labor. A set of account-books that will reveal at all times with unerring accuracy the actual condition of the association, is a source of pride to the secretary who has kept them, and inspires confidence in the shareholders in the wisdom of the management.

We can not enter upon an extended discussion of book-keeping, but the purpose we have in view in this work would be incomplete if we did not outline a suitable system of book-keeping. The system given in this chapter has been in actual operation for many years in one of the most successful associations in this country. The able secretary, James N. Ward, Esq., of Elmira, New York, a lawyer as well as an expert accountant, has written out for us the system in use by him, many features of which have been of his own origination, and whatever merit this system contains is due largely to him. We fully approve of it and assert that any secretary who adopts it will sooner or later thank us for outlining the system for him.

The outline given assumes the matured value of a share at $200; monthly dues of one dollar; interest at 6 per cent per annum; fines for default of payment of dues and interest, 10 per cent of amount defaulted each month; entrance fee twenty-five cents per share; transfer fee ten cents a share; stock issued in series. The plan of book-keeping given can be readily modified as to details, so as to adapt it to any changes from the typical scheme adopted. The remainder of this chapter is substantially in the language of Mr. Ward.

A treatise on book-keeping is not within the purview of a work of this kind; but for the assistance of the new secretary and treasurer, forms are here given which have been used for several years by the Chemung Valley Mutual Loan Association, of Elmira, New York, and have been fully proved by experience.

Specimen entries for each book are given in the forms. To keep a ledger-account with every member of an association, such as would show in dollars and cents the amount of dues paid by him and the dividends on his shares, would involve a vast amount of labor and consequent expense. The same information can be otherwise obtained with equal accuracy and much less labor and expense. Every share of stock is of precisely the same value in the same series. The main set of books will show the value of one share in each series; therefore, an auxiliary set of stock-books showing the series in which, and the number of shares in a series held by each member, gives all the necessary data with which to find the value of the shares of each individual member.

The simple multiplication of the value of one share by the number of shares in the series held by the individual member gives the desired information.

The secretary's main set of books consist of a dues, interest, and fines book; cash-received book; journal day-book; ledger and transfer book.

The secretary's auxiliary books consist of a stock journal day-book; stock ledger, with index giving the address of each member; stock trial-balance book; security register; and book containing by-laws, to be subscribed by members on joining the association; index and trial-balance book for main ledger; and inventory book.

For the purpose of these forms, it will be assumed that dues and interest are to be paid monthly. In associations where payments are to be made weekly or otherwise, the necessary modifications of the forms here given can readily be made. Notwithstanding the

DUES, INTEREST, AND FINES BOOK.

Shares.	Int.	NAME.	APRIL Due.	APRIL Paid.	MAY Due.	MAY Paid.	JUNE Due.	JUNE Paid.	JULY Due.	JULY Paid.	AUGUST Due.	AUGUST Paid.
20		Ward, James N..	$20 ¹⁸	$20	$20	$20	$20		$42 Pd. L.	$42	$20	$20
10		Wheeler, Samuel.	/15	15	15	15	15	$15	15	15	10	10
10	10	Williams, John D.	¹⁰/20	20	20	20	¹⁰/₁₀ 20	20	20	20	20	20
10	10	Williams, Lucy..	10	10	10	10	/20	20	20	20	20	20
5	5	Wood, Robert....	⁵/₅ /10 New.	10	10	10	10	10	21	21	10	10
10		Woods, Henry...	10 New.	12 50	10	10	10 New. 5	21 25	10 Sh. 10	10	10	10
10		Wright, George..	5	6 25	5	5	Drn.		5 New. 10	10	10	10
		Wright, Robert..	10	10	10 Trans. 5	10	5	5		5	5	5
5		Wright, John ...	10	10	5	5	5			42 50	10	10
10		Wrigley, Patrick.			Pd. Apl.		Pd. Apl.		Pd. Apl.		Pd. Apl.	
10		Wrigley, Joseph.	10	50								
				$163 75		$105		$91 25		$185 50		$115

first act of a new association after it is organized is to receive members and issue certificates of stock, yet it would seem that the most logical order in which to consider the books is to begin with the dues, interest, and fines book. This book is really a blotter for the main set of books, as will appear from examination of the accompanying form.

The foregoing is the " W " page of the dues, interest, and fines book, and gives all of the various entries which can properly come upon that book. The entries in this book are made by the secretary at the meeting as he stands beside the treasurer or member of committee when the money is paid in. The treasurer or other officer receives the money, announces the name of the member paying and the sum paid, and the secretary puts it down. The book contains a page or more for each letter of the alphabet, and is cut in at the margin and lettered like an index. The columns are so headed as to explain themselves, unless it be the left-hand columns. The column headed " Shares " contains the number of shares of non-matured stock which each member holds set opposite to the respective members' names.

The column headed "Int." gives the number of shares borrowed on, and, where the stock and interest and payments conform to the plan announced in the preceding remarks, the sum of the shares held and shares borrowed on, gives the sum in dollars which is to be paid monthly by the shareholder. It will be found convenient to minute under the month in which it occurs any change in the status of a member's shares. For example, in the beginning of the fiscal year " April " Samuel Wheeler has ten shares of stock, and has borrowed on five of them. This is shown in the April " due " column " $^{10}\!\!/\!_{15}$ "; in July he paid his loan which is minuted " Pd. L." Lucy Williams has ten shares; in June she borrows on ten shares; this is shown by the entry " $^{10}\!\!/\!_{20}$." In April Joseph Wrigley paid five months' dues—four months' in advance. This is shown by the entry " Pd. April " in the " due " columns of the four subsequent months. This form, when preparing such a book or blotter, should be enlarged so as to include the twelve months of a fiscal year, if series are issued yearly.

These memoranda are useful only in checking for errors and to prove accuracy.

The next book in rotation is shown by the following form, and may be properly styled the cash-received book.

The entries in the cash-received book are made from the dues, interest, and fines book, and also from the memorandum made by the secretary at the meeting of other payments received which do not properly belong in that book.

For the purpose of illustrating more fully, the July column of the dues, interest, and fines book, or blotter, before given, is carried into this book. By a comparison of the entries of the forms of the two books, the uses and purposes of the cash-received book will be apparent. The first money column shows the amount of dues paid, the second the amount of interest paid, the third the amount of fines paid, the fourth the amount of entrance fees paid (this column is used only when new shares have been issued to a member), and the fifth money column gives the

CASH-RECEIVED BOOK.

Cash received July 23, 1888.

L. F.		Dues.	Interest.	Fines.	Entrance fees.	Total.
	James N. Ward	$40		$2		$42
	Samuel Wheeler	10	$5			15
	John D. Williams	10	10			20
	Lucy Williams	10	10			20
	Robert Wood	10	10	1		21
	Henry Woods	10				10
	George Wright	10				10
	John Wright	5				5
	Patrick Wrigley	40			$2 50	42 50
	Dues	$145	$35	$3	$2 50	$185 50
	Interest....	35				
	Fines....	3				
	Entrance fees....	2 50				
		$185 50				
	Loans, Repayments by Samuel Wheeler..					1,000
	John D. Williams, advance payment.....					50
	Treasurer, charge him total receipts......					$1,235 50

13

total payment and is the sum of the entries in all of the other columns. The sum set down in the " total " column is also the same sum that is set down in the " paid " column of the same month of the dues, interest, and fines book opposite the name of the member. The totals of the first, second, third, and fourth columns added together must agree with the footing of the fifth or "total " column. After making and comparing the footings of the columns as shown in the form, the entries are made of the items on the memorandum before mentioned made by the secretary at the meeting. Referring to the preceding form, the first entry after the recapitulation shows that Samuel Wheeler, in addition to paying his dues and interest, paid $1,000, the amount of his loan. The next entry shows that John D. Williams, in addition to paying his dues and interest, paid $50 on account, to be accumulated with like payments, until combined, they will equal and cancel $200 (one share) of his loan, and thereby reduce his interest payment one dollar per month.

If the posting to the ledger is done directly from the cash-received book, without the intervention of the journal, " DUES " account is credited with the monthly total of the " dues " column, " INTEREST " account is credited with the monthly total of the "interest " column, " FINES " account is credited with the monthly total of the "fines" column, "ENTRANCE FEES " account is credited with the monthly total of the " entrance fees " column, " LOANS " account is credited with the monthly total of the loans repaid, any member is credited with the excess of his payment over the amount due from him for dues, interest and fines (no account is kept on the general ledger with members to show the amount of dues, interest, fines, or entrance fees paid), and the "TREASURER'S" account is charged with the sum total of the credits enumerated. In the event the scheme of the association as to premiums is the installment plan, there should be an additional column for premium paid. Under the gross plan, the premiums are paid in fact at the time the loan is perfected and the order given, the amount of the premium being deducted from the face of the loan. The entry for the premium may then be made in the journal day-book, according to the entry of the loan to John D. Williams, as shown in the third entry of the form of that book following.

The journal day-book is the next in order, and its form and use are familiar to all double-entry book-keepers. It is given here, however, perhaps unnecessarily, for the double purpose of making a complete and continuous set of forms, and to give a complete sample of the entries in loan association book-keeping.

Explanations so far as necessary will be placed under the entry in foot notes.

JOURNAL DAY–BOOK.

Elmira, N. Y., April 3, 1883.

The Elmira Mutual Loan Association, a corporation duly organized under and by virtue of the laws of the State of New York on the third day of April, 1883, with an authorized capital of not to exceed 10,000 shares, of the par value of $200 per share, outstanding at any one time, is now ready to begin business. Assets nothing. Liabilities for expenses of incorporation not yet audited.			
23.			
TREASURER, To SUNDRIES,* Receipts of 1st meeting for receiving dues:	$1,250		
To DUES on 1,000 shares issued,		$1,000	
To ENTRANCE FEES on 1,000 shares issued,		250	
24.			
EXPENSE, To TREASURER, Drew orders on the Treasurer for expenses of incorporation, as follows:	50	50	
No. 1. J. N. Ward for att'y's fees, $40			
No. 2. "Advertiser," association notices, 5			
No. 3. "Evening Star," association notices, 5			
$50			
27.			
LOANS, To SUNDRIES, Loaned to John D. Williams on his bond and mortgage of city property, 6 shares at $10 per share premium,	1,200		
To PREMIUM, on 6 shares at $10,		60	
To TREASURER, Order No. 4, drawn favor of John D. Williams for loan,		1,140	
28.			
FURNITURE and FIXTURES, To TREASURER, Drew order favor of H. S. Gilbert & Co. for fire-proof safe.	60	60	

* This entry is taken from and might be posted directly from the cash-received book, and omitted from this book entirely. The Dues a/c might also be omitted, and use the Capital Stock a/c.

TO KEEP ACCOUNTS.** 189

Elmira, N. Y., November 24, 1885.

SUNDRIES, To SUNDRIES,* J. N. Ward has withdrawn 5 shares series No. 1 Capital Stock, on which he has paid dues to and including the November meeting :		
CAPITAL STOCK, 1st series, 5 shares at $53.82,	266 60	
DUES, April to November meeting, 8 months at $5,	40	
INTEREST, April to November meeting, on 5 shares at $1.48,	7 40	
To LOSS and GAIN, Profits retained on 1st series, 5 shares at $0.63,		3 15
To TREASURER, Order No. 694, favor of J. N. Ward,		310 85
February 14, 1886. SUNDRIES, To SUNDRIES, The attorney of the association has this day paid over to the Treasurer the proceeds of the foreclosure of Richard Roe mortgage. The decree of foreclosure cancels 10 shares 2d series of stock, pledged by R. Roe to secure the loan, and applies the withdrawal value on Dec. 29, 1885, of said shares thereon. Withdrawal value, Dec. 29, 1885, of 2d series, 10 shares, at $35.34, $353 40 Less arrears of dues, $70 00 Less fines on arrears of dues, 24 86 ——— 94 86 Withdrawal value of said shares as applied, $258 54		
CAPITAL STOCK, 2d series, 10 shares at $25.61,	256 10	
DUES, 2 mos. paid in current year on 10 shares of stock, at $2,	20	
TREASURER, Amount paid to him by attorney,	1,853 92	
To LOANS, 10 shares loan to R. Roe, foreclosed,		2,000
To INTEREST, On loan and on judgment,		78 70
To FINES, On arrears of dues as above, $24 86 On arrears of interest, 24 86		49 72
To Loss and GAIN, Profits retained on canceled stock, 2d series, 10 shares, at $0.16,		1 60

* In case of withdrawal of stock, debit Capital Stock a/c with the holding value of the shares at the last annual meeting, and debit Dues account with the dues paid thereon during the current year, and credit Loss and Gain with the profits retained.

Elmira, N. Y., February 14, 1886.

SUNDRIES, To SUNDRIES,			
The attorney of the association reports the completion of the foreclosure of the mortgage to the association made by John Smith, and that on the 3d day of February, 1886, he bid off on behalf of the association the mortgaged property at $1,800, and that a judgment for deficiency of $334.82 has been entered in favor of the association against John Smith. The decree of foreclosure cancels 10 shares 3d series stock, pledged by John Smith to secure the loan, and applies the withdrawal value on Dec. 29, 1885, of said shares thereon.			
Withdrawal value on Dec. 29, 1885, of 3d series, 10 shares, at $21.86, $218 60			
Less arrears of dues, 7 mos., at $10, $70 00			
Less fines on arrears of dues, 24 86			
94 86			
Withdrawal value of said shares as applied, $123 74			
The attorney's bill of costs and expenses of the foreclosure is audited, and ordered paid, at $150.			
CAPITAL STOCK, 3d series, 10 shares, at $12.40,	124		
DUES, 2 months paid in current year on 10 shares of stock at $2 per share,	20		
REAL ESTATE, Smith property bid off at	1,800		
JUDGMENTS RECEIVABLE, For deficiency,	334 82		
To LOANS, 10 shares loan to J. Smith, foreclosed,		2,000	
To INTEREST, On loan and judgment,		78 70	
To FINES, On arrears of dues as above, $24 86			
On arrears of interest, 24 86		49 72	
To Loss and GAIN, Profits retained on canceled stock 3d series, 10 shares at $0.04,		40	
To TREASURER, Drew Order No. 701, favor J. N. Ward, for att'y's bill as audited as above,		150	

Elmira, N. Y., April 16, 1888.

The Elmira Mutual Loan Association, having reached the close of its fifth fiscal year, the following entries are made for the purpose of closing the books preparatory to making the annual report and statement of its condition.				
BALANCE, To SUNDRIES,* Accrued dues, interest, and fines unpaid at this date, as follows:			41	50

Name.	Dues.	Int.	Fines.
W. V. Calkins,	$10	..	....
C. W. Holmes,	10	$10	$1 00
H. S. Hudson,	10	..	50
	$30	$10	$1 50

To DUES, Accrued and unpaid as above,	30	
To INTEREST, Accrued and unpaid, as above,	10	
To FINES, Accrued and unpaid, as above,	1	50

SUNDRIES, To BALANCE,† Dues and interest paid in advance as follows:	60	

Name.	Dues.	Interest.
W. B. Coffin,	$5	..
J. E. Dohoney,	10	$5
G. D. Parsons,	20	20
	$35	$25

DUES, Paid in advance, as above,	35	
INTEREST, Paid in advance, as above,	25	

BALANCE,	1,308	
To INTEREST, Interest accrued on loans of 1,308 shares outstanding payable at April meeting.‡		1,308

* The items for this entry are obtained from the dues, interest, and fines book, by running through and finding those in arrears, and how much.

† The items for this entry are obtained from the dues, interest, and fines book by running through the book and finding those who have paid an even number of months in advance, and been marked paid. The page of dues, interest, and fines book heretofore given has an example in the entries following the name of Joseph Wrigley.

‡ This interest, it is evident, belongs to the profits of this year's business, although it is not payable until the first meeting of the next year.

Elmira, N. Y., April 16, 1888.

1	DUES, 　　　To CAPITAL STOCK, 12 months' dues on 7,000 shares of stock in all series now outstanding.*		84,000	84,000
	SUNDRIES,　　　To LOSS AND GAIN,† INTEREST, Net profit from this source, FINES,　　"　　　"　　　" ENTRANCE FEES, Net profit from this 　source, TRANSFER FEES, Net profits from this 　source, PREMIUM, Earned during year, REAL ESTATE, Net profit from this 　source, including rentals,		12,660 412 30 475 26 70 50 50	13,624
	LOSS AND GAIN, 　　　To EXPENSE, Expenses of conducting the business for the year,		732 48	732 48
1	LOSS AND GAIN, 　　　To CAPITAL STOCK,‡ The Board of Directors, on this 16th day of April, 1888, declared a divi- dend on the capital stock of 6 per cent *ad valorem*, as follows : Series No. 1, 1,200 shares at 　$3.59,　　　　　　　　$4,308 Series No. 2, 1,300 shares at $2.70, 3,510 Series No. 3, 1,400 shares at $1.92, 2,688 Series No. 4, 1,500 shares at $1.13, 1,695 Series No. 5, 1,600 shares at $0.39,　624 　　　　　　　　　　　　$12,825		12,825	12,825

* The capital stock has, or should have been, increased during the year by the full amount of twelve months' dues. If there are any arrears, they are collectible assets. If there are any advance payments, they are a liability.

† The items for this entry are taken from the ledger for all except the two at the foot, " Premium " and " Real Estate," and, with those exceptions, are the balances of the several accounts after posting the items from the dues, interest, and fines book before mentioned. The items of profit from " Premium " are ascertained by deducting from the balance of the ledger account the amount of premium which borrowers would be entitled to have returned to them in case all the loans were now repaid, the amount of premium liable to be returned to be ascertained from the record of each loan in the security register, on the basis prescribed by the by-laws.

‡ This entry is made up from the minutes of the directors' meeting at which the dividend is declared.

Elmira, N. Y., April 16, 1888.

BALANCE, To SUNDRIES,	$266,477 84		
To TREASURER, To close the account,		843 02	
To LOANS, " "		261,600	
To FURNITURE AND FIXTURES, To close the account,		150	
To W. H. PETERS's CONTRACT, To close the account,		1,750	
To REAL ESTATE, To close the account,		1,800	
To JUDGMENTS RECEIVABLE, To close the account,		334 82	
SUNDRIES, To BALANCE,		267,767 34	
PREMIUM, To close the account,	950		
LOSS AND GAIN, To close the account,	416 34		
1	CAPITAL STOCK, " "	265,326		
JOHN D. WILLIAMS, " "	75		
CLAY W. HOLMES, " "	1,000		

The Elmira Mutual Loan Association begins its sixth fiscal year with resources and liabilities as follows:

Resources.

SUNDRIES, To BALANCE,		267,827 34	
TREASURER, Cash in his hands,	843 02		
LOANS, Secured and outstanding,	261,600		
FURNITURE AND FIXTURES, As per inventory,	150		
W. H. PETERS's CONTRACT, Balance unpaid on his contract,	1,750		
REAL ESTATE, As per inventory or appraisal,	1,800		
JUDGMENTS RECEIVABLE, Unpaid judgment due association,	334 82		
FINES, Accrued and unpaid,	1 50		
DUES, " " "	30		
INTEREST, " " "	1,318		

Liabilities.

BALANCE, To SUNDRIES,	267,827 34		
To DUES, Paid in advance,		35	
To INTEREST, Paid in advance,		25	
To Loss and GAIN, Undivided profits held against judgment receivable considered doubtful,		416 34	
To JOHN D. WILLIAMS, Paym't by him toward cancellation of 1 share of loan,		75	
To CLAY W. HOLMES, Retained on loan until completion of house on the mortgaged premises,		1,000	
To PREMIUM, Unearned premiums on loans,		950	

Elmira, N. Y., April, 16, 1888.

1	To Capital Stock,		
	1st series, 1,200 shares, at $68.91,	$82,692	
	2d series, 1,300 shares, at $53.21,	69,173	
	3d series, 1,400 shares, at $39.53,	55,842	
	4th series, 1,500 shares, at $25.53,	38,295	
	5th series, 1,600 shares, at $12.39,	19,824	265,326

These last two entries seem to be self-explanatory. They are taken from the balance-sheet, if one is made up, or from the ledger, if not.

GENERAL LEDGER.

Dr.   *Capital Stock.*   Cr.

1889.				1889.				
April	16	To Balance,	21	$265,326	April	16	By Total credit,	$168,501
						16	By Dues,	18 84,000
						16	By Loss and Gain,	20 12,825
				$265,326				$265,326
					1888.			
					April	16	By balance,	28 $265,326

The form of this book and its use needs no explanation, as it is familiar to all book-keepers. The total credits and the closing entries only are given of the Capital Stock account.

Direction for making or preparing the Annual Report or Statement.

To begin with, an appraisal of all the real and personal property of the association should be made by a committee in the inventory book. The secretary should make a statement of the amount of premiums which (under the by-laws) would be returnable if all the loans outstanding should bo repaid at the next meeting. Also a statement of tho arrears of dues, interest, and fines separately (see entry in journal day-book). Also a statement of dues and interest paid in advance by any members (see entry in journal day-book). Trial balances must be taken to prove the correctness of the main ledger and stock ledger. As additional proof of the accuracy of the capital stock account in the main ledger, compare tho balance of the account with the holding value of all shares in all series shown in the last report (series now more than one year old), which the stock ledger shows to be still outstanding. For example, suppose the balance of the capital stock account in the main ledger to be $168,501, and the holding value at the commencement of the year of one share in each of the various series to be as follows : 1st series, $53.32 ; 2d series, $38.51 ; 3d series, $25.61 ; and 4th series, $12.40, and the stock ledger shows now outstanding as follows :

1st series	1,200 shares at	$53.32	as above	=	$63,984
2d "	1,300	"	38.51	"	50,063
3d "	1,400	"	25.61	"	35,854
4th "	1,500	"	12.40	"	18,600

And we have value of shares over one year old outstanding $168,501, proving that the capital stock account in the main ledger is correct. Additional proof of the correctness of the dues account in the main ledger is obtained by adding to the balance of the account all the arrears of dues, and deducting therefrom the dues paid in advance, and comparing tho results with the dues for the period on all the shares of all series outstanding. For example, suppose the main ledger shows the balance of the dues account to be $84,005, the arrears of dues are in all $30, and the dues paid in advance aggregate $35, we have $84,005 + $30 = $84,035 − $35 = $84,000.

. Numbers of shares outstanding as shown by stock ledger :

1st series	1,200 shares	
2d "	1,300 "	
3d "	1,400 "	
4th "	1,500 "	
5th "	1,600 "	
Total	7,000 "	at $12 = $84,000

(twelve months' dues at one dollar per month per share), which proves the dues account to be correct. Having thus proved and cross-checked the books, you know they are correct, and you can now proceed to close them. The closing entries are given in full in the form for the journal day-book, and need not be repeated here. The computations from which those entries are taken will now be given in detail. It will be found convenient to use a rough balance sheet, on which the results of the business can be kept before making the computation. No elaborate ruled sheet is necessary, and the whole can be made in pencil if preferred, so long as the figures are taken down accurately.

Following is the sheet from which the closing entries in the journal day-book were taken. It may as well be stated that the computation of profits are made as of the date of the next meeting for receiving dues (when a new series will be issued), and withdrawal values should bear interest from that date, and not the date of the annual meeting :

BALANCE-SHEET.

ACCOUNTS.	Trial balance. Dr.	Trial balance. Cr.	Inventory, or assets and liabilities not shown by ledger accounts. Assets.	Inventory... Liabilities.	Loss and Gain account. Loss.	Loss and Gain account. Gain.	Capital stock. Cr.	BALANCE. Resources.	BALANCE. Liabilities.
Treasurer	$943 02							$948 02	
Loans	261,600							261,600	
Furniture and fixtures	150		$150					150	
W. H. Peters's contract	1,750							1,750	
Premium		$1,000		$950		$50			$950
Judgments receivable	384 82		D'btful.					884 82	
Real estate	1,750		1,800					1,800	
John D. Williams		75							75
Clay W. Holmes		1,000				50			1,000
Fines		410 80	1 50			412 80		1 50	
Entrance fees		425 00				425			
Transfer fees		26 70		25		26 70			25
Interest		11,867	1,318			12,660		1,815	
Expense	782 43		80		$782 43			80	
Loss and gain		349 82		85		349 82			416 84
Dues		84,005					$84,000		85
Capital stock		168,501					168,501		265,825
Dividend					12,825		12,625		
Undivided profits (loss and gain account)					416 84				
	$267,160 82	$267,160 82			$18,978 82	$18,978 82	$265,826	$267,527 84	$267,527 84

The foregoing balance-sheet shows that the net profits for the year were $13,241.34, but for prudent management retain an amount equal to the amount of judgment receivable of doubtful value $334.82 as undivided profits, leaving for dividend $12,906.52. The capital stock account shows the capital as of the beginning of the year to be $168,501. Dues are also capital; but as they have been accumulating during the year, it must be ascertained what their equivalent for a year would be by equating the payments, by which we find the $84,000 dues to be equal to an investment for one year of $45,500; adding this to the capital stock account, balance gives capital invested for one year equal to $214,001. Divide the net profits, $12,906.52 by $214,001, and we find the dividend earned six per cent and a very small fraction. The fraction being so small, we leave the sum it represents to add to the undivided profits above mentioned.

It is necessary to get the dividend and holding value per share. The following method is recommended for its simplicity and accuracy: The dividend on one share of the last series issued is the same as the dividend on the dues or installments on one share of every other series for the year. Dues paid monthly during a year equal the investment of one dollar for seventy-eight* months, or $6.50 for the twelve months.

* The dollar paid for the first month's dues has been invested for twelve months; the dollar for the second month's dues has been invested for eleven months; the dollar paid for third month's dues has been invested ten months, and so on until the entire twelve months' dues are paid in. The twelfth months' dues being invested one month before the next series is issued, making as you will see by continuing the illustration, an investment equal to one dollar for seventy-eight months.

At six per cent rate of dividend earned gives dividend thirty-nine cents for the dues on one share of the last (fifth) series issued and of the dues portion of one share of every other series. The holding value of one share of first series at commencement of the year was $53.32 × .06 = $3.20, the dividend, plus thirty-nine cents dividend on the dues of one share as above equals $3.59, the total dividend on one share of first series.

Below is given the holding value of one share in each series, according to the above explanation, in the form in which the computation is made:

	First series.	Second series	Third series.	Fourth series.	Fifth series.
Holding value of 1 share at the beginning of the year.	$53 32	$38 51	$25 61	$12 40	
Dues paid during year	12 0J	12 00	12 00	12 00	$12 00
Dividend on holding value.	3 20	2 31	1 53	.74	
Dividend on dues paid in during the year.........	89	89	89	.89	.89
Total dividend one share ..	3 59	2 70	1 92	1 18	89
Present holding value of 1 share.................	$68 91	$53 21	$39 53	$25 53	$12 89

The balance-sheet and this computation are made up by the secretary and presented to the board of directors at a meeting held for the purpose of ascertaining and declaring the dividend, and when approved by them by a resolution entered in the minutes, are entered in the " journal day-book " (see closing entries) and the report for the members and for publication is made accordingly.

STOCK JOURNAL DAY-BOOK.

Reg. No. of loan.	L. F.		Certificate.	Series.	Shares.	Certificate.	Series.	Shares.
		Elmira, N. Y., April 23, 1883.						
	1	CAPITAL STOCK, SERIES No. 1,	1–5	1	45			
	72	To SUNDRIES,*				1	1	10
	72	To JAMES N. WARD,				2	1	10
	72	To SAMUEL WHEELER,				3	1	10
		To JOHN D. WILLIAMS,				4	1	10
		To LUCY WILLIAMS,				5	1	5
		To ROBERT WOOD,						
		27.						
1	2	Mem. Loan made at April meeting, John D. Williams, 6 shares.†						
		November 24, 1885.	1	1	5			
	72	JAMES N. WARD,				1	1	5
	1	To CAPITAL STOCK, SERIES 1,‡ Certificate No. 689, issued to J. N. Ward for five shares 1st series, retained by him.						
		SEYMOUR DEXTER,	203	2	5			
	72	To JAMES N. WARD,#				690	2	5
		February 14, 1886.						
		RICHARD ROE,	212	2	10			
		To CAPITAL STOCK, SERIES 2,				212	2	10
		JOHN SMITH,	408	3	10			
		To CAPITAL STOCK, SERIES 3,				408	3	10
		Mem. Loans foreclosed,‖						
		Richard Roe, 10 shares		2				
		John Smith, 10 "		3				
		20 shares						

* The above shows the form of entry in this book when shares are issued. The sum received for them appears in the cash-received book. They are in this department dealt with only in regard to the series and number of shares.

† This item is posted, in pencil, to the " Series and number of shares borrowed on " and the " Shares pledged " department of John D. Williams's account in the stock ledger.

‡ The above is the appropriate entry in case of a withdrawal of stock.

\# The above is the appropriate entry on a transfer of stock from one shareholder to another.

‖ The above are the appropriate entries in this book in case of the foreclosure of mortgages and the cancellation of shares according to the

STOCK LEDGER, PART I.

Dr.   *Capital Stock, Series One.*   *Cr.*

Date.	Remarks.	Fol.	Certificate No.	Stock Issued. S'ries	Stock Issued. Sh.	Date.	Remarks.	Fol.	Certificate No.	Stock redeemed. S'ries	Stock redeemed. Shar's
1888, April 23		1	1–5	1	45	1885 Nov. 24	By J. N. Ward	2	1	1	5

The entries in this book are taken from the stock journal day-book, and Part I shows the aggregate shares issued and redeemed in each series. The ruling is necessarily different from the individual accounts in the stock ledger shown on the next two pages, because the information desired is entirely different.

entries of the same date in the form of the journal day-book hereinbefore shown. The mem. entries are to be posted in pencil to the loans paid and shares released columns of Richard Roe and John Smith accounts in the stock ledger.

14

72   STOCK-LEDGER, PART II.

Dr.   *James N. Ward.*

Date.	Remarks.	Fol.	Cer-tifi-cate.	Se-ries.	Series and number of shares disposed of.										Shares borr'w'd			Shares paid.	
					1	2	3	4	5	6	7	8	9	10	Loan	Ser.	Sh.	Date.	Sh.
1885, Nov.	24 Withdrawn,	2	1	1	5														
1886, Apr.	25 Balance,	L.72	689 and 690	1 and 2	5	5													

Samuel Wheeler.

															27	1	5		

John D. Williams.

															1 78	1 1	6 5	1884 Jan. 28	1

This portion (Part II) of the stock-ledger is for keeping the accounts with the members to show how many shares of stock they have, how many have been borrowed on, and how many have been pledged. The credit side shows how many shares have been acquired, and the debtor side how many have been withdrawn. It is better to have twenty columns for " shares acquired " and " shares disposed of," instead of

STOCK-LEDGER, PART II. 72

James N. Ward. *Cr.*

Stock pledged.			Released.		Date.	Remarks.	Fol.	Certificate.	Series.	Series and number of shares acquired.									
Loan	Ser.	Sh.	Date.	Ed.						1	2	3	4	5	6	7	8	9	10
					1883. April 23	By Cap. Stock.	1	689 1	1	10									
					1885. Nov. 24	By Transfer,	2	690	2					5					
										10				5					
					1886. April 25	By Balance,	L.72	689 and 690	1 and 2	5	5								
					1887. April 22	By Cap. Stock,	41	715	5						10				

Samuel Wheeler.

27	1	10			1883. April 23	By Cap. Stock,	1	2	1	10									

John D. Williams.

1	1	6			1883. April 23	By Cap. Stock,	1	3	1	10									
73	1	5																	

ten, as shown. The columns for " shares borrowed " and " shares paid " amount to a single-entry ledger account, as do also the " shares pledged " and " released " columns, making really three ledger accounts with each member, all under the same heading. Reference to the stock journal day-book will supply the necessary information.

5   TRIAL BALANCE OF STOCK–LEDGER,

L. F.	NAME.	Dr.	Series and number of shares									
			1	2	3	4	5					
72	James N. Ward......		5	5			10					
72	Samuel Wheeler.....		10									
72	John D. Williams....		10									
1	Capital Stock, Series 1.	1200										
2	Capital Stock, Series 2.	1300										
3	Capital Stock, Series 3.	1400										
4	Capital Stock, Series 4.	1500										
5	Capital Stock, Series 5.	1600										
	Footings, page 1.....		275	275	250	325	315					
	Footings, page 2.....		325	300	300	375	375					
	Footings, page 3.....		300	325	350	375	425					
	Footings, page 4....		275	395	500	425	475					
		7000	1200	1300	1400	1500	1600					

INSURANCE EXPIRATION BOOK.

Reg. No.	NAME.	Location of property.	Amount.		Jan.	Feb.	Mch.	Apr.
1	John D. Williams..........	520 Lake St........	2000	00	1889			
278	Samuel Wheeler	921 Main St.......	1000	00				
301	Richard Roe	1206 Benton St....	2000	00				

This book has thirty-one pages, and is used for a single day to a page. A policy expiring on the twelfth day of any month in the year and any year would be entered on this page, the year being set down in the column headed for the proper month. Turn to the form of the security register, and you find loan No. 301, Richard Roe. His property is insured in the Ætna Insurance Co., and expires the last time on

TAKEN APRIL 16, 1888. 5

held.	Total Cr.	Series and number of shares borrowed on.															Total
		1	2	8	4	5											Total
	20 10 10	5 10															5 10
	1440 1675 1775 2070	60 75 65 85	45 55 85 90	85 45 85 65	25 65 80 55	38 45 68 92											208 285 898 407
	7000	800	275	250	225	258											1806

TWELFTH DAY OF THE MONTH.

May.	June	July.	Aug.	Sept.	Oct.	Nov.	Dec.	Company.	Agent.
1891			1887					Home, of New York...... Liberty, of New York..... Ætna, of Hartford.........	J. M. Sly & Co. J. M. Sly & Co. T. Perry & Co.

August 12, 1887. Above you find it on the page for the twelfth day of the month, and 1887 written in the August column. Entries are made from the policy when it is received, and in case of change of policies, so as to expire on a different day of the month, a new entry would be made as above under the new day of expiration.

61 SECURITY REGISTER FOR SECRETARY.

No.	Borrower.	Maker of bond and mortgage, and securities taken.	Shares borrowed on.			Date.	Amount.
			Certif.	Ser.	Sh.		
801	Richard Roe	1 bond executed by Richard Roe ... 1 mortgage executed by Richard Roe and Susan Roe, his wife. ... 1 assignment of stock executed by R. Roe				1884. April 30 1884. April 30 1884. April 30	2000 2000 2000
	Foreclosed.	1 certificate of stock, No. 212, for 2d series, 10 shares, pledged by Richard Roe. 1 abstract of title. 1 Ætna Ins. Co. policy, No. 7080. Received the above-named securities May 20, 1884. G. D. Parsons, Treasurer.	212	2	10		

When the loan is perfected and the mortgage is returned from the office for recording to the attorney of the association, the attorney should pass the papers over to the secretary, who will enter them on this register, and pass them over to the treasurer, taking the treasurer's receipt hereon for the papers passed over. This fixes the responsibility for the preservation of the papers, and if any are omitted, it is known at the time. It is convenient to make a brief minute in the column

SECURITY REGISTER FOR TREASURER.

No.	Borrower.	Maker of bond and mortgage, and securities taken.	Shares borrowed on.			Date.	Amount
			Certif.	Ser.	Sh.		
801	Richard Roe.	1 bond executed by Richard Roe ... 1 mortgage executed by Richard Roe and Susan Roe, his wife..... 1 assignment of stock executed by R. Roe......................				1884. April 30 1884. April 30 1884. April 30	2000 2000 2000
	Foreclosed.	1 certificate of stock, No. 212, for 2d series, 10 shares, pledged by Richard Roe. 1 abstract of title.	212	2	10		

SECURITY REGISTER. 61

Payments.		Amount of Insurance.	Insurance company.	Policy expires			Remarks.
Date.	Amount.			Month.	Day	Year.	
		2000	Ætna..........	Aug.	12	1884-'87	Mortgage recorded April 30, 1884, in book No. 71, page 68, of premises No. 1206 Benton St. February 14, 1886, this mortgage foreclosed and the proceeds paid over to the treasurer.

headed "Borrower" of the disposition of the loan as "foreclosed," "paid," while the fuller explanation appears in the "remarks" column.

The different policies of insurance on the property are to be entered here with date of expiration, to show the exact situation of the securities in each loan. The insurance expiration book is to give a handy minute of the expiration of all policies, to prevent failure to renew.

SECURITY REGISTER.

Payments.		Amount of insurance.	Insurance company.	Policy expires			Remarks.
Date.	Amount.			Month.	Day	Year.	
		£000	Ætna..........	Aug.	12	1884-'87	Mortgage recorded April 30, 1884, in book No. 71, page 68, of premises No. 1206 Benton St. February 14, 1886, this mortgage foreclosed and the proceeds received.

The treasurer's security register is ruled like the secretary's, the only variation in the make-up being that no receipt for the papers is provided. All of the remarks made in connection with the secretary's register apply to this, as the information desired is the same in both cases.

APPENDIX.

NEW YORK.

CHAPTER 556, LAWS OF 1887.

CO-OPERATIVE SAVINGS AND LOAN ASSOCIATION.

1. Corporators.—Corporate Name.

SECTION 1. Any fifteen or more persons, being of full age, may form an association as provided in this act. All associations formed under the provisions hereof shall be known as co-operative savings and loan associations; and the name of every association, so formed, shall contain, as a part thereof, the words Co-operative Savings and Loan Association.

2. Objects.

SEC. 2. The object and purpose of such associations shall be to encourage industry, frugality, home-building, and savings among its members; the accumulation of savings, the loaning of such accumulations to its members, and the repayment to each member of his savings when they have accumulated to a certain sum, or at any time when he shall desire the same, or the association shall desire to repay the same.

3. Certificate of Association.—Statements in.

SEC. 3. Said association shall become incorporated by the said fifteen or more persons making, signing, and acknowledging, in the manner and form prescribed for the acknowledgment of deeds in this State, a certificate, wherein shall be stated the name of said association; that the association is formed under and for the purposes prescribed in this act; the town, village, or city where the association is located within this State; and the limit of the number of shares of stock it shall have outstanding at any one time. When made as aforesaid, said certificate shall be filed and recorded in the office of the Secretary of State, and upon said certificate being so filed and recorded, the Secretary of State shall issue a certificate, in proper and suitable form, declaring the facts contained in said original certificate, and the filing and recording thereof in his office, and which latter certificate shall thereupon be recorded in the county clerk's office of the county where said association is located; and upon the same being so recorded, the persons named in the certificate first above mentioned, their associates and successors, shall become a corporate body.

4. Officers.—By-Laws.—Special Meetings, and voting thereat.— Holding over by Officers.

SEC. 4. The officers of the association shall consist of a president, vice-president, treasurer, and secretary, who shall be *ex-officio* members of the board of directors, which shall consist of nine members, exclusive of said *ex-officio* members. Other officers may be authorized by the by-laws. The duties and compensation of the officers, their terms of office, the time of their election, and time of periodical meetings of the officers and shareholders shall be determined by the by-laws; except that the board of directors shall determine each year the compensation of the treasurer and secretary.

Special meetings of the officers and shareholders shall be called and held as provided by the by-laws. Each shareholder shall be entitled to one vote, at all meetings of the shareholders, for each share owned by him or held by him as trustee not in arrears for dues. All officers shall hold office until their successors are duly elected and assume the duties of their office. No association shall expire from neglect on its part to elect officers at the time prescribed by the by-laws.

5. Capital of Association.—Limitation.—Shares, How Issued.— Unpledged Shares.—Limitation of Shares.

SEC. 5. The capital of said association shall consist of the accumulated savings of its members, which it holds, and shall not exceed at any time one million dollars, and shall be divided into shares of the matured value of two hundred dollars each. The total number of shares outstanding at any time shall not exceed ten thousand. The shares shall be issued in yearly or half-yearly series, in such amounts in each series, and at such times as shall be determined by the by-laws of the association. No share of a prior series shall be issued after the issuing of shares in a new series. Shares which have not been pledged as a collateral security for the repayment of a loan shall be called unpledged shares. Shares that have been so pledged, shall be called pledged shares. No person shall hold more than ten unpledged shares in any one series, nor more than twenty pledged shares in one series.

6. Dues.—Payment Thereof.—Fines for Arrears.—Entrance Fee.

SEC. 6. Savings paid to the association upon shares shall be called dues. At or before each stated monthly or semi-monthly meeting of the board of directors each shareholder shall pay to the board or a committee thereof, one dollar dues upon each share of stock held by him until the share reaches the value of two hundred dollars, or it is withdrawn, canceled or forfeited. Payment of dues on shares of each series shall commence from its issue. The association shall have power to impose and collect a fine, not exceeding ten per cent for each month in arrears, for every dollar of dues or interest which a shareholder shall refuse or neglect to pay at the time it is due. They shall also have power to charge an entrance fee of not exceeding twenty-five cents on every share of stock issued by the association.

7. Unpledged Shares, Withdrawal of Accumulations Upon.— Payment to Shareholders Withdrawing.—Proviso.—Retiring of Unpledged Shares.—Determination by Lot.

SEC. 7. The accumulations upon unpledged shares may be withdrawn, and the shares canceled after one month's written notice of such intention filed with the secretary at or before a stated monthly meeting of the board. If filed before such meeting, the one month's notice shall not be deemed to have commenced until the first regular meeting after the filing. The withdrawing shareholder shall be paid the amount of the withdrawal value of his accumulations as determined under the by-laws, at the last distribution of profits before the notice of withdrawal, together with all dues paid since such distribution, and such interest on the value of the shares at the time of the last distribution and on the dues thereafter paid, as the by-laws shall determine, less any fines unpaid and a proportionate share of any unadjusted loss; provided, that at no time shall more than one half the receipts of the association, and when the association is indebted upon matured shares, no more than one third, shall be applicable to the payment of withdrawing shareholders, without the consent of the board of directors; and when the demands of withdrawing shareholders exceed the moneys applicable to their payment, they shall be paid in the order in which their notices of withdrawal were filed with the secretary. The board of directors may at their discretion, under rules made by them, retire the unpledged shares of any series at any time after four years from the date of their issue, by enforcing withdrawals of the same; provided, that the shareholders whose shares are to be retired shall be determined by lot, and that they shall be paid the full value of their shares, less all fines and proportionate part of any unadjusted loss.

8. Payment of Dues, When to Cease.—Payment of Matured Shares.—Proportion of Receipts Applicable.

SEC. 8. When each unpledged share of a given series reaches the value of two hundred dollars, all payment of dues thereon shall cease, and the holder thereof shall be paid out of the funds of the association two hundred dollars therefor, with such rate of interest as shall be determined by the by-laws, from the time the board of directors shall declare such share to have matured, until paid; but at no time shall more than one third of the receipts of the association be applicable to the payment of matured shares, without the consent of the board of directors. The order of the payment of the matured shares shall be determined by the board of directors.

9. Loan of Accumulations to Members.—Open Bidding.—Persons Bidding Highest to Receive Loan.—Deduction of Premium.—Right to Borrow Restricted.

SEC. 9. At each monthly stated meeting, immediately following the receipt of dues and interest, the board of directors shall offer to members of the association desiring to borrow, all accumulations applicable to that purpose; the same shall be loaned in sums of two hundred dollars, the value of a matured share, or a multiple thereof, or the fractional parts of one fourth or one half thereof. If there shall be more than one member desiring to borrow, their right to a loan shall be determined by an open bidding of a premium per share ; the member bidding the highest premium shall be entitled to the loan, upon giving proper security. From the sum loaned shall be deducted at the time of loaning the amount of the premium bid. The receiving of such premium or interest paid on the loan shall not be deemed a violation of the usury laws. No member or members can borrow a larger sum than shall be equal to the matured value of the shares held by him or them. A borrowing member for each share or fractional part thereof borrowed upon, shall, in addition to the dues on his shares, pay monthly interest on his loan at the rate of six per cent per annum, or such lower rate as the by-laws shall name, until the shares borrowed upon reach the matured value of two hundred dollars each, or the loan is repaid; and when such matured value is reached, the share shall cancel the loan upon it, and the proper surrenders and acquittances be made.

10. Loans to be Secured by Bond and First Mortgage.—Transfer of Unpledged Shares to Secure Loan.—Forfeiture of Loan.—Conditions of Bond and Mortgage.—Repayment of Loans.

SEC. 10. For every loan made, a bond secured by a first mortgage upon unincumbered real estate shall be given, accompanied by a transfer and pledge to the association of the shares borrowed upon, and all accumulations that have or shall accrue thereon, as a collateral security for the repayment of the loan ; or, in lieu of the mortgage, the borrower, or another, may transfer and pledge to the association for the payment of the loan, unpledged shares, the withdrawal value of which under the by-laws, at the time of such borrowing, shall exceed the amount borrowed and interest thereon for six months. If the borrower neglects to offer security satisfactory to the board of directors, within the time provided by the by-laws, his right to the loan shall be forfeited, and he shall be charged with one month's interest, and all necessary expenses incurred, if any, under the by-laws, in reference to his proposed loan. All bonds and mortgages given to the association shall be deemed conditioned upon the performances of the provisions of this act relating to the repayment of loans and interest thereon, and the by-laws of the association, although the same may not be fully expressed therein. A borrower may repay a loan, and all arrears of interest and fines thereon, or one share thereof, that is, the sum of two hundred dollars, at any stated monthly meeting, or at any other time, but when not made at a stated meeting, he shall pay interest up to the first monthly meeting after such payment. He may repay his loan in full, thereby relieving his shares from liability upon the pledge thereof, made to the association, or he may, by a proper notice and direction as to the application, have the withdrawal value of the shares borrowed upon, applied in payment or part payment of his loan.

11. Arrearages of Members.—Notice to Pay Same.—Forfeiture in Certain Cases.— Withdrawal Value.

SEC. 11. Whenever any member shall be six months in arrears in the payment of his dues upon unpledged shares, the secretary shall give him notice thereof in writing and a statement of his arrearages, by mailing the same to him at the last post-office address given by him to the association, and if he shall not pay the same at the next or second stated monthly meeting thereafter, the board of directors may, at their option, declare his shares forfeited; and at the time of such forfeiture, the withdrawal value thereof shall be determined and stated, and the defaulting member shall be entitled to withdraw the same without interest, within one year upon such notice as shall be required of a withdrawing shareholder.

12. Loan to Become Due when Borrowing Member is Six Months in Arrears.—Effect Thereof.

SEC. 12. Whenever a borrowing member shall be six months in arrears in the payment of his dues and interest, or either, the whole loan shall become due at the option of the board of directors; and they may proceed to enforce collection upon the securities held by the association. The withdrawal value at the time of the commencement of the action, of all shares pledged as collateral security for the loan, shall be applied upon the loan and arrearages of interest and fines thereon, and the shares deemed surrendered to the association.

13. Purchase of Real Estate Held Under Mortgage.

SEC. 13. Any association may purchase at any sale, public or private, any real estate upon which it may have a mortgage, judgment, lien or other incumbrance, or in which it may have any interest; and may sell, convey, lease, or mortgage the same at pleasure to any person or persons.

14. Associations may Borrow Money for Paying Withdrawals, etc.—Loan of Surplus to other Associations.—Proceedings Therefor.

SEC. 14. Any association organized in pursuance of the provisions of this act, may borrow money for the purpose of making loans or paying withdrawals, not exceeding, however, two thousand dollars, so long as its accumulated capital does not exceed ten thousand dollars; and not exceeding six thousand dollars, so long as its accumulated capital shall be over ten thousand, and does not exceed sixty thousand dollars; and whenever its accumulated capital exceeds sixty thousand dollars, it may borrow money for the purposes aforesaid not exceeding ten per cent. of its accumulated capital. No money borrowed shall be for a longer term than one year. Any association having a surplus in its treasury, for which there is no demand for loans, withdrawing shareholders or matured stock, may loan the same to another association, organized under the provisions of this act, subject to the provisions of this section, on the part of the borrowing association. No association shall borrow or make loans herein authorized, except by a two-thirds vote of its board of directors. The vote to be recorded by ayes and nays in its regular minutes.

15. Profits and Losses, Distribution of.—Manner of Distribution.—Undistributed Profits.—Reservation of Guarantee Fund.

SEC. 15. Profits and losses shall be distributed at least annually, and always before issuing a new series of stock to the shares then outstanding. Profits and losses shall be distributed to all shares, in all series outstanding at the time of such distribution, in proportion to their holding value, as distinguished from their withdrawing value, except that, in addition thereto a distribution of not exceeding the amount of the entrance fee, in the discretion of the board of directors, may be made to each share outstanding in the last series issued prior to the distribution. At each periodical distribution of profits, the board of directors may reserve and carry as undistributed profits, in the nature of a guaranty fund, any sum from the net profits that in their discretion seems wise, to be applied upon any future losses that may occur from any cause whatsoever.

16. Transfer of Shares.—How made.—Transfer Fee.

SEC. 16. No transfers of shares shall be binding upon the association until the same have been made upon the books of the association; and the transferee thereof shall take the same, charged with all the liabilities and conditions attaching thereto in the hands of the one transferring the same. The association may require a "transfer fee" not exceeding twenty-five cents per share.

17. By-Laws, Adoption of.—Attorney for Association.

SEC. 17. The association as soon as duly incorporated shall possess power to adopt by-laws, not inconsistent with the provisions of this act, regulating the due conduct of the business of the association, defining the duties of officers and committees, times of meetings, mode of determining and declaring the withdrawing value of shares, and in relation to all other matters having reference to the conduct of the business, although not specifically mentioned in this act. The board of directors shall have power to appoint and remove at pleasure, an attorney for the association.

18. Eligibility to Membership in Association.—Accumulations, how far Exempt.—Associations Deemed Savings Institutions.

SEC. 18. Any person of full age and sound mind may become a member of the association by taking one or more shares therein, and subscribing the by-laws, and annexing to his signature his post-office address; and whenever he desires his post-office address changed, he shall give written notice thereof to the secretary of the association; and for the purpose of giving any member notice, by mail, the last post-office address given by him shall be deemed the proper one. A minor may hold shares in the name of a parent, guardian, or next friend as trustee for him. All accumulations upon shares in said association held by any person shall be exempt from execution and proceedings supplementary thereto, to the amount of six hundred dollars; and the association itself shall be deemed an institution for savings and not taxable under any corporation tax law which shall exempt savings-banks, or institutions for savings from taxation.

19. Annual Report to Bank Department.—Further Reports.

SEC. 19. Every association organized under the provisions of this act shall annually make a full report in writing of the affairs and condition of such corporation on the first day of January in each year to the Superintendent of the Bank Department in such form and by such officers of the corporation as the said superintendent may designate. Such report shall be verified by the oath of the officers making the same. Every association shall make any further reports which the said superintendent shall require, and in such form, and as to such matters relating to the condition and conducting of the business of the association as such superintendent shall designate. Any willful false swearing in making and verifying said reports shall be deemed perjury.

15

218 CO-OPERATIVE SAVINGS AND LOAN ASSOCIATIONS.

20. Forfeiture for Failure to Report.—Recovery of Penalty.

SEC. 20. If any such association shall fail to furnish to the Superintendent of the Bank Department any report required by this act, at the time so required, it shall forfeit the sum of ten dollars per day for every day such report shall be delayed or withheld; and the Superintendent may maintain an action in his name of office to recover such penalty, and the same shall be paid into the treasury of the State and applied to the expenses of the Bank Department.

21. Visitation by Bank Superintendent.

SEC. 21. All associations organized under the provisions of this act shall be subject to the visitation and examination at all times by the Superintendent of the Bank Department, his deputies or duly appointed agents, upon the application of three or more members of said association. If it shall appear to said superintendent, from the report of any said association, or from an examination made by him, his deputies or duly appointed agents, that any such association is violating the provisions of this act, or is conducting its business in an unsafe or unauthorized manner, he shall by an order under his hand and seal address to such association, direct the discontinuance of such illegal and unsafe practices; and whenever any association shall neglect or refuse to comply with such order, or make reports as required, he shall communicate such facts to the Attorney-General, who shall thereupon be authorized to institute proceedings against any such association as is now, or may hereafter be provided for by law in the case of an insolvent incorporation, or such other proceedings as the nature of the case may require.

22. Existing Loan and Accumulating Fund Associations, How Entitled to Benefits of this Act.

SEC. 22. Any association now existing and heretofore incorporated under the provisions of said chapter one hundred and twenty-two of the laws of eighteen hundred and fifty-one, may be entitled to the benefits of this act, on the majority vote of the shareholders of said association, directing the making and filing of the certificate mentioned in the third section of this act, and conforming the transaction of their business to the provisions of this act.

23. Exemption.

SEC. 23. Associations organized under this act shall not bo subject to the provisions of chapter one hundred and forty-three of the laws of eighteen hundred and eighty-six.

SEC. 24. This act shall take effect immediately.

CHAPTER 122, LAWS OF 1851.

An act for the incorporation of building, mutual loan, and accumulating fund associations.

Companies, How Formed.

SECTION 1. Any number of persons, not less than nine, may associate and form an incorporated company for the purpose of accumulating a fund for the purchase of real estate, the erection of buildings, or the making of other improvements on lands, or to pay off incumbrances thereon, or to aid its members in acquiring real estate, making improvements thereon, and removing incumbrances therefrom; and for the further purpose of accumulating a fund to be returned to its members who do not obtain advances as above mentioned, when the funds of such association shall amount to a certain sum per share, to be specified in the articles of association.

Articles of Association.

SEC. 2. Such persons shall severally subscribe articles of association, in which shall be set forth the name of the corporation, the time of its regular meetings, and how special meetings may be called, and what shall constitute a quorum to transact business at meetings; the qualifications of members and how constituted; what officers, trustees, and attorney there shall be, and how and when chosen, and their duties, and how removed or suspended from office; the entrance fee of new members and new shares, the monthly or weekly dues per share, the redemption fee on shares on which advances shall be made, and fees to be paid on the transfer of shares; the fines and penalties for the non-payment of dues or fees, or other violation of the articles of association; the manner of redemption of shares by advances made thereon, the mortgaged security to be taken on such advances, and how the same may be redeemed or changed; the manner of the transfer or withdrawal of shares; the manner of investing funds not required for advances on shares; the qualifications of voters at the meetings, and the mode of voting; the ultimate amount to be paid to the owners of unredeemed shares; the manner of altering or amending the articles of association, and such other provisions as shall be necessary for the convenient and effective transaction of the business thereof; provided that the same shall not in any respect contravene the Constitution or laws of this State.

Copy of Articles when to be Filed.—Powers and Limitations.

SEC. 3. A true copy of such articles, signed by the officers of the association, together with a statement showing when the association was organized, and the place of the transaction of its business, and the names of the officers and trustees at the time of the making of such statement, which shall be verified by oath or affirmation before any officer authorized to take affidavits, to be used in the courts of justice, shall be filed in the office of the clerk of the county in which such association shall transact its business; and thereupon the persons who have subscribed the articles of association as aforesaid, and such other persons as shall become members of such association, and their successors, shall be a body corporate by the name specified in such articles of association, and shall possess the powers and privileges and be subject to the provisions of title third of chapter eighteen of the first part of the Revised Statutes, so far as those provisions are consistent with the provisions of this act, and they shall, by their corporate name, be capable in law of purchasing, holding and conveying any real and personal estate whatever, which may be necessary to enable said company to carry on their operation named in such certificate.

Calls upon Stock.

SEC. 4. It shall be lawful for the trustees to call in and demand from the stockholders, respectively, all such sums of money by them subscribed, at such times and in such payments or installments as the articles of association shall prescribe, under the penalty of forfeiting the shares of stock subscribed for, and all previous payments made thereon, if payment shall not be made by the stockholder within sixty days after a personal demand or notice requiring such payment shall have been published for six successive weeks in the newspaper nearest to the place where the business of the company shall be carried on as aforesaid.

Borrowing Money.

SEC. 5. All corporations formed under this act shall have power to borrow money for temporary purposes not inconsistent with the objects of their organization; but no loan for such purposes shall have a longer duration than two years, nor shall such indebtedness exceed at any one time one fourth of the aggregate amount of the shares and parts of shares, and the income thereof, actually paid in and received.

Stock for Minors, etc.

SEC. 6. Parents and guardians may take and hold shares in such association in behalf and for the use of their minor children or wards, provided the cost of such shares be defrayed from the personal earnings of such minor children or wards, or by gifts from persons other than their male parents; married women may take and hold shares in such associations, provided the cost of such shares be defrayed from their personal earnings, the personal earnings of their children voluntarily bestowed for this purpose, or from property bequeathed or given to them by persons other than their husbands.

Dividends; Monthly Payments.

SEC. 7. The trustees of any association formed under the provisions of this act may, from time to time, declare dividends from the earnings of the association, payable in such manner as may be provided in the articles of association; but no dividend shall be declared, except from the earnings of the association, and if the trustees of any such association shall declare and pay any dividend when the company is insolvent, or any dividend, the payment of which would render it insolvent, they shall be jointly and severally liable to the extent of the dividend so declared and paid, for all the debts of the association then existing or that shall be thereafter contracted while they shall respectively continue in office; provided, that if any of the trustees shall object to the declaring of such dividend or to the payment of the same, and shall, at any time before the time fixed for the payment thereof, file a certificate of his objection in writing with the clerk of the company, and with the clerk of the county, he shall be exempt from the said liability. But no trustee who shall be present at any meeting when such dividend is declared, shall be exempt from such liability, unless he shall then and there object to the declaration or payment of such dividend, and shall also procure his objection to be noted in the book of minutes of such association. No holder of redeemed shares shall claim to be exempt from making the monthly or other stated payments provided in the articles of association, upon the ground that by reason of losses or otherwise, the association has continued longer than was originally anticipated, whereby the payments made on such shares may amount to more than the amount originally advanced, with legal interest thereon; nor shall the imposition of fines for the non-payment of dues or fees, or other violation of the articles of association, nor shall the making of any monthly payment required by the articles of association, or of any premium for loans made to members be deemed a violation of the provision of any statute against usury. (Thus amended by ch. 564 of the Laws of New York, 1875.)

Existing Associations, How Entitled to Benefit of this Act.

SEC. 8. Any existing association formed for the purposes mentioned in the first section of this act, may, on the vote of the majority of the voting shares, at any regular meeting after the passage of this act, become entitled to the benefit of this act, on complying with the second and third sections thereof, unless the second section has heretofore been complied with; in which case it shall be necessary to comply only with the said third section.

Embezzlement, How Punished.

SEC. 9. No officer, trustee, attorney, agent or servant of any association hereby incorporated, shall use or dispose of any part

of the funds of such association, or assign, transfer, cancel or
deliver up or acknowledge satisfaction of any bond, mortgage
or other written instrument belonging to such association, unless duly authorized, or be guilty of any fraud in the performance of his duties; and every person guilty of a violation of
this section shall be liable civilly to the party injured, to the
extent of the damage thereby incurred, and shall also be liable
to an indictment for a misdemeanor, punishable by fine or im-
prisonment, or both, in the discretion of the court by which he
shall be tried.

Annual Report to be Published.

SEC. 10. Each association formed under the provisions of
this act shall, at the close of the first year's operations, and annually at the same period in each year thereafter, publish in at
least two newspapers published in the same place where their
business may be located, or if no newspapers shall be published
in such place, then in any two newspapers published nearest
such place, a concise statement verified on the oaths of its president and secretary, showing the actual financial condition of
the association, and the amount of its property and liabilities,
specifying the same particularly.

Liability of Stockholders and Directors.

SEC. 11. All the shareholders of any association formed under this act, shall be individually liable to the creditors of said
association, to an amount equal to the amount of stock held by
them respectively, for all debts contracted by such association.
The directors or other officers of every association formed under
this act, shall be personally liable for any fraudulent use, disposition or investment of any moneys or property belonging to
such association, or for any loss which shall be incurred by any
investment made by such directors or other officers, other than
such as are mentioned in and authorized by this act; but no
director or other officer of any such association shall be liable as
aforesaid; except he authorized, sanctioned, approved or made
such fraudulent use, disposition or investment as aforesaid.

Liabilities of Trustees.

SEC. 12. No person holding stock in any such company, or executor, administrator, guardian or trustee, and no person holding such stock as collateral security, shall be personally subject to any liability as stockholder of such company; but the person pledging such stock shall be considered as holding the same, and shall be liable as a stockholder accordingly; and the estate and funds in the hands of such executor, administrator, guardian or trustee, shall be liable in like manner and to the same extent as the testator, or intestate or the ward or person interested in such trust fund would have been if he had been living and competent to act and hold the same stock in his own name.

Right of Voting.

SEC. 13. Every such executor, administrator, guardian or trustee, shall represent the share of stock in his hands at all meetings of the company, and may vote accordingly as a stockholder; and every person who shall pledge his stock as aforesaid may, nevertheless, represent the same at all such meetings and may vote accordingly as a stockholder.

Election of Officers.

SEC. 14. In case it shall happen at any time that an election of officers shall not be made on the date designated by the by-laws of said company, when it ought to have been made, the company for that reason shall not be dissolved; but it shall be lawful on any other day to hold an election for trustees in such manner as shall be provided for by the said by-laws; and all acts of trustees shall be valid and binding as against such company until their successors shall be elected.

Power to Repeal or Alter.

SEC. 15. The legislature may at any time alter, amend or repeal this act, or may annul or repeal any incorporation formed or created under this act; but such amendment or repeal shall not, nor shall the dissolution of any such company take away or impair any remedy given against any such corporation, its stockholders or officers, for any liability which shall have been previously incurred.

Capital Stock, how Increased or Diminished.

SEC. 16. Any company which may be formed under this act may increase or diminish its capital stock, by complying with the provisions of this act, to any amount which may be deemed sufficient and proper for the purposes of the corporation ; but before any corporation shall be entitled to diminish the amount of its capital stock, if the amount of its debts and liabilities shall exceed the amount of capital to which it is proposed to be reduced, such amount of debts and liabilities shall be satisfied and reduced so as not to exceed such diminished amount of capital.

Notice of Meeting.

SEC. 17. Whenever any company shall desire to call a meeting of the stockholders for the purpose of increasing or diminishing the amount of its capital stock, it shall be the duty of the trustees to publish a notice signed by at least a majority of them in a newspaper in the county, if any shall be published therein, at least three successive weeks, and to deposit a written or printed copy thereof in the post-office, addressed to each stockholder at his usual place of residence, at least three weeks previous to the day fixed upon for holding such meeting, specifying the object of the meeting, the time and place where and when such meeting shall be held, and the amount to which it shall be proposed to increase or diminish the capital, and a vote of at least two thirds of all the shares of stock shall be necessary to an increase or diminution of the amount of its capital stock.

Meeting, how Organized and Conducted.

SEC. 18. If at any time and place specified in the notice provided for in the preceding section of this act stockholders shall appear in person or by proxy, in numbers representing not less than two thirds of all the shares of stock of the corporation, they shall organize by choosing one of the trustees chairman of the meeting, and also a suitable person for secretary, and proceed to a vote of those present in person or by proxy ; and if on canvassing the votes it shall appear that a sufficient number of votes has been given in favor of increasing or diminishing the amount of capital, a certificate of the proceeding, showing a compliance with the provision of this act, the amount of the capital actually paid in, the whole amount of debts and liabilities of the company, and the amount to which the capital stock shall be increased or diminished, shall be made out, signed, and verified by the affidavit of the chairman and be countersigned by the secretary; and such certificate shall be acknowledged by the chairman and filed as required by the first section of this act, and when so filed the capital stock of such corporation shall be increased or diminished to the amount specified in such certificate.

Exemption.

SEC. 19. The shares held by the members of all associations incorporated under the provisions of this act shall be exempt from sale on execution for debt to an extent not exceeding six hundred dollars in such shares at their par value.

Loan to Members.

SEC. 20. No loan made by any such association to any of its members may exceed in amount the par value of the capital stock for which such member may have subscribed.

Certificate, how made Evidence.

SEC. 21. The copy of any certificate of incorporation, filed in pursuance of this act, certified by the county clerk or his deputy to be a true copy and of the whole of such certificate, shall be received in all courts and places as presumptive legal evidence of the facts therein stated.

CHAPTER 564, LAWS OF 1875.

An act to amend chapter one hundred and twenty-two of the laws of eighteen hundred and fifty-one, entitled "An act for the incorporation of building, mutual loan, and accumulating fund associations."

(SECTION 1 amends SEC. 7, ch. 122, of the Laws of 1851.)

To make Annual Reports.

SEC. 2. Every corporation organized under the provisions of this act, and every corporation heretofore organized under the laws of this State for purposes similar to those provided for in said act, shall annually make a full report in writing of the affairs and condition of such corporation, on the first day of January in each year, to the Superintendent of the Banking Department, in such form and by such officers of the corporation as the said Superintendent may designate, which report shall be in place of any report which any such corporation may now be required to make to the supreme court, the comptroller, or otherwise. Such report shall be verified by the oath or affirmation of the officers making such report; and any willful false swearing in regard to such report shall be deemed perjury and be subject to the prosecutions and punishments prescribed by law for that offense. Every such report shall be made within twenty days after the day to which it relates, and shall be in such form and contain such statements, returns, and information, as to the affairs, business, condition, obligations and resources of such corporation as the said Superintendent may from time to time prescribe and require; and the said Superintendent may, if he be of the opinion that it is desirable, require that a like report, either wholly or in part as to the particulars aforesaid, be made to him at any time by any such corporation aforesaid within such period as he may designate.

Examination of Affairs of Corporations.

SEC. 3. Whenever the stockholders of any corporation organized under the provisions of this act shall deem that a personal examination by said superintendent of the affairs of said corporation is desirable or necessary, it shall be the duty of said superintendent, on the request in writing, signed by not less than five of the stockholders of said corporation, that such examination be made either by himself or by some person duly appointed by him for that purpose, to make a full and careful examination of the affairs of said corporation, and make his report thereon, as herein provided. The person making such examination shall have power to administer oaths and take all testimony by him deemed necessary and proper and to compel the attendance of witnesses and the production of books and papers, by like process and in the same manner as now provided by law to procure the attendance of witnesses and the production of books and papers in the courts of record in this State. The expense of such examination shall be borne by said corporation, but no charge shall be made therefor, when the examination is made by said superintendent personally or by one of the salaried employés of his department, except for necessary traveling and other expenses; whenever said superintendent shall appoint any person other than a salaried officer in his department to make such examination, the amount charged therefor shall not exceed the sum of ten dollars per day for the time actually expended in making the same, and the actual and necessary expenses as hereinbefore provided. (Thus amended by ch. 96, Laws of 1878.)

Nature of Examination.

Sec. 4. On every such examination inquiry shall be made as to the condition and resources of the corporation generally, the mode of conducting and managing its affairs, the action of its directors or trustees, the investment of its funds, the safety and prudence of its management, the security afforded to those by whom its engagements are held, and whether the requirements of its charter and of law have been complied with in the administration of its affairs.

When found to be Violating Charter, Proceedings by Attorney-General.

Sec. 5. If it shall appear to the said Superintendent from the report of any such corporation, or from any examination made by him, or from the report of any examination made to him, that any corporation has committed a violation of its charter or of law, or is conducting business in an unsafe or unauthorized manner, he shall by an order under his hand and seal of office, addressed to such corporation, direct the discontinuance of such illegal or unsafe practices and conformity with the requirements of its charter and of law, and with safety and security in its transactions, and whenever any corporation shall refuse or neglect to make such report as is hereinbefore required, or to comply with any such order as aforesaid; or whenever it shall appear to the superintendent that it is unsafe or inexpedient for any corporation to continue to transact business, he shall communicate the facts to the attorney-general, who shall thereupon be authorized to institute such proceedings against any such corporation as are now, or may hereafter be provided for by law in the case of insolvent corporations, or such other proceedings as the nature of the case may require.

Penalty for Failure to Report.

SEC. 6. If any such corporation shall fail to furnish to the superintendent of the banking department any report or statement required by this act, at the time so required, it shall forfeit the sum of ten dollars per day for every day such report or statement shall be so delayed or withheld; and the said superintendent may maintain an action in his name of office to recover such penalty, and, when collected, the same shall be paid into the treasury of the State and be applied to the expenses of the bank department.

PENNSYLVANIA.

LAWS OF PENNSYLVANIA RELATING TO BUILDING AND LOAN ASSOCIATIONS.

Section one of the general law of Pennsylvania, relating to the incorporation of certain corporations, passed in 1874, provides: Sec. 1. " Be it enacted, etc., that corporations may be formed under the provisions of this act by the voluntary association of five or more persons for the purposes and in the manner mentioned herein." Then follows the classification of such corporations and the mode of their incorporation. Section 37 of said general act relates to building and loan associations, and provides as follows:

SECTION 37. Building and loan associations incorporated under the provisions of this act shall have the powers, and, from the date of the letters-patent creating the same, when not otherwise provided in this act, be governed, managed and controlled as follows:

CLAUSE 1. They shall have the power and franchise of loaning or advancing to the stockholders thereof the moneys accumulated, from time to time, and the power and right to secure the repayment of such moneys, and the performance of the other conditions upon which the loans are to be made, by bond and mortgage or other security, as well as the power and right to purchase or erect houses, and to sell, convey, lease or mortgage the same at pleasure to their stockholders, or others for the benefit of their stockholders, in such a manner also that the premiums taken by the said association, for the preference or priority of such loans, shall not be deemed usurious; and so also that in case of non-payment of the installments, premiums or interest by borrowing stockholders, for six months, payment of principal, premiums and interest, without deducting the premium paid, or interest thereon, may be enforced by proceeding on their securities according to law.

CLAUSE 2. The capital stock of any corporation created for such purposes, by virtue of this act, shall at no time consist in the aggregate of more than one million dollars, to be divided into shares of such denomination, not exceeding five hundred dollars each, and in such numbers as the corporators may, in the application for their charter, specify: *Provided*, That the capital stock may be issued in series, but no such series shall at any issue exceed in the aggregate five hundred thousand dollars, the installments on which stock are to be paid at such time and place as the by-laws shall appoint; no periodical payment of such installments to be made exceeding two dollars on each share, and said stock may be paid off and retired as the by-laws shall direct; every share of stock shall be subject to a lien for the payment of unpaid installments and other charges incurred thereon under the provisions of the charter and by-laws, and the by-laws may prescribe the form and manner of enforcing such lien; new shares of stock may be issued in lieu of the shares withdrawn or forfeited; the stock may be issued in one or in successive series, in such amount as the board of directors or the stockholders may determine; and any stockholder wishing to withdraw from the said corporation shall have power to do so, by giving thirty days' notice of his or her intention to withdraw, when he or she shall be entitled to receive the amount paid in by him or her, less all fines and other charges; but after the expiration of one year from the issuing of the series, such stockholder shall be entitled, in addition thereto, to legal interest thereon: *Provided*, That at no time shall more than one half of the funds in the treasury of the corporation be applicable to the demands.of withdrawing stockholders, without the consent of the board of directors, and that no stockholder shall be entitled to withdraw, whose stock is held in pledge for security. Upon the death of a stockholder, his or her legal representatives shall be entitled to receive the full amount paid in by him or her, and the legal interest thereon, first deducting all charges that may be due on the stock; no fines shall be charged to a deceased member's account, from and after his or her decease, unless his legal representatives of such decedent assume the future payments on the stock.

CLAUSE 3. The number, titles, function and compensation of the officers of any such corporation, their terms of office. the times of their elections, as well as the qualifications of electors, and the ratio and manner of voting, and the periodical meetings of the said corporation, shall be determined by the by-laws, when not provided by this act.

CLAUSE 4. The said officers shall hold stated meetings, at which the money in the treasury, if over the amount fixed by the charter as the full value of a share, shall be offered for loan, in open meeting, and the stockholder who shall bid the highest premium for the preference or priority of loan, shall be entitled to receive a loan of not more than the amount fixed by charter as the full value of a share, for each share of stock held by such stockholder: *Provided*, That a stockholder may borrow such fractional part of the amount fixed by charter as the full value of a share, as the by-laws may provide; good and ample security, as prescribed by the by-laws of the corporation, shall be given by the borrower, to secure the repayment of the loan, in case the borrower shall neglect to offer security, or shall offer security that is not approved by the directors, by such time as the by-laws may prescribe, he or she shall be charged with legal interest, together with any expenses incurred, and the loss in premium, if any, on a resale, and the money may be resold at the next stated meeting; in case of non-payment of install-ments or interest by borrowing stockholders, for the space of six months, payment of principal and interest, without deduct-ing the premium paid or interest thereon, may be enforced, by proceeding on their securities according to law.

CLAUSE 5. A borrower may repay a loan at any time, and in case of the repayment thereof, before the expiration of the eighth year, after the organization of the corporation, there shall be refunded to such borrower one eighth of the premium paid for every year of the said eight years then unexpired: *Provided,* When the stock is issued in separate series the time shall be computed from the date of the issuing the series of stock on which the loan was made.

CLAUSE 6. No premiums, fines, or interest on such premiums, that may accrue to the said corporation, according to the provisions of this act shall be deemed usurious; and the same may be collected as debts of like amount are now by law collected in this commonwealth.

CLAUSE 7. No corporation or association created under this act shall cease or expire from neglect on the part of the corporators to elect officers at the time mentioned in their charter or by-laws; and all officers elected by such corporation shall hold their offices until their successors are duly elected.

CLAUSE 8. Any loan or building association incorporated by or under this act, is hereby authorized and empowered to purchase, at any sheriff's or other judicial sale, or at any other sale, public or private, any real estate, upon which such association may have or hold any mortgage, judgment, lien, or other incumbrance, or ground-rent, or in which said association may have an interest, and the real estate so purchased, or any other that such association may hold or be entitled to at the passage of this act, to sell, convey, lease, or mortgage, at pleasure, to any person or persons whatsoever; and all sales of real estate heretofore made by such associations to any person or persons not members of the association so selling, are hereby confirmed and made valid.

CLAUSE 9. All such corporations shall have full power to purchase lands and to sell and convey the same, or any part thereof, to their stockholders or others in fee simple, with or without the reservation of ground-rents; but the quantity of land purchased by any one of said associations hereafter incorporated, shall not, in the whole, exceed fifty acres; and in all cases the land shall be disposed of within ten years from the date of the incorporation of such associations respectively.

CLAUSE 10. All land and building associations are hereby authorized to make sale of, and assign or extinguish, to any person or persons, the ground-rents created as aforesaid.

The foregoing general act was amended by No. 14 of the Laws of Pennsylvania, for the year 1870, which is as follows:

No. 14.

An act relating to mutual savings-fund, building, and loan associations, regulating the mode of charging premiums, bonus or interest in advance, of withdrawals, of repayment and collection of loans; also restricting the power to levy excessive fines, and defining the rights and liabilities of married women stockholders, and prescribing the non-application to these associations of the bonus tax and registry laws for corporations.

SECTION 1. *Be it enacted*, etc., That it shall be lawful for any mutual savings-fund, or building and loan association, now incorporated or hereafter to be incorporated, in addition to dues and interest, to charge and receive the premium or bonus bid by a stockholder for preference or priority of right to a loan in periodical installments; and such premium or bonus so paid in installments shall not be deemed usurious, but shall be taken to be a payment as it falls due, in contradistinction to a premium charged and paid in advance; and in so far as said premium or bonus so charged and paid, in addition to dues and interest, shall be in excess of two dollars for each periodical payment, the same shall be lawful, any law, usage, or custom to the contrary notwithstanding. It shall also be lawful for any mutual savings-fund or building and loan association to charge and deduct interest in advance, in lieu of premiums for preference or priority of right to a loan: *Provided*, That the certificate of incorporation of each association hereafter to be incorporated, and the certificate provided in section nine of this act for those incorporated, shall set forth whether the premium or bonus bid for the prior right to a loan shall be deducted therefrom in advance or paid in periodical installments, or whether interest in advance shall be deducted from the loan in lieu of‘ premium or bonus.

16

SEC. 2. Stockholders withdrawing voluntarily shall receive such proportion of the profits of the association or such rate of interest as may be prescribed by the by-laws, any law or usage to the contrary notwithstanding; but payment of the value of stock so withdrawn shall only be due when the funds now applicable by law to the demand of withdrawing stockholders are sufficient to meet and liquidate the same, and then only in the order of the respective times of presentation of the notices of such withdrawals, which must have been presented in writing at a previous stated meeting, and have been then and there indorsed as to times of presentation by the officer designated by the by-laws of the association.

SEC. 3. The by-laws may provide for the involuntary withdrawal and cancellation at or before the maturity of shares of stock not borrowed on: *Provided*, That such withdrawal and cancellation shall be *pro rata* among the shares of the same series of stock: *And provided further*, That not less than legal interest shall be credited and allowed to each share so withdrawn and canceled.

SEC. 4. A borrower may repay a loan at any time, and in case of the repayment thereof before the maturity of the shares pledged for said loan, there shall be refunded to such borrower (if the premiums, bonus, or interest shall have been deducted in advance), such proportions of the premiums, bonus, or advance interest bid, as the by-laws may determine: *Provided*, That in no case shall the association retain more than one one hundredth of said premiums or bonus for each calender month that has expired since the date of the meeting upon which the loan was made, or if the interest in advance, it shall retain only the interest due on the loan up to the time of settlement: *And further provided*, That such borrower shall receive the withdrawing value of the shares pledged for said loan, and the shares shall revert back to the association.

SEC. 5. In case of non-payment of installments of stock, premiums, dues, or interest, by borrowing stockholders, for the space of six months, payment of the same, together with the full principal of the loan, may be enforced by proceeding on their securities according to law; and the moneys so recovered shall be paid into the treasury of the association for such uses (loans or otherwise) as may be deemed proper by the association; and if the said moneys so recovered, together with the withdrawal value of the shares of such defaulting borrower, shall exceed the amount it would have required, according to the preceding section, to have voluntarily repaid the loan, together with all the expenses incurred by the association, such excess shall be repaid to such defaulting borrower.

SEC. 6. Fines or penalties for the non-payment of installments of dues, interest, and bonus or premium, shall not exceed two per centum per month on all arrearages.

SEC. 7. It shall be lawful for any married woman of full age to hold stock in any of said saving-funds, building, or loan associations; and, as such stockholder, she shall have all the rights and privileges of other members, including the right to borrow money from said associations and bid premiums therefor, and shall also have the right and power to secure such loan by transferring her said stock or other securities to said association from which the same was borrowed, or by executing bond and mortgage upon her separate real estate to secure said loan : *Provided, however,* that the husband of such married woman join in the execution of such bond and mortgage; and such married woman shall also have the right to sell, assign, and tranfer her said stock or withdraw the same, without joining the husband in such transfer or withdrawal; and it shall be lawful for any such savings-fund, building, or loan association to collect such loan made to such married woman, including the dues, interest, premium and fines, as loans are made by such associations to other members as are now by law collected, and such stock or interest in such stock shall not be liable for the debts of any husband of such married woman.

SEC. 8. The bonus or tax due to the commonwealth upon the capital stock of corporations, as provided for by the act of the first of May, one thousand eight hundred and sixty-eight, or by any other act, shall not apply to or be due from mutual savings-fund, or building and loan associations ; nor shall the registry for corporations, prescribed by the first section of the act of first of May, one thousand eight hundred and sixty-eight, the first section of the act of twenty-fourth of April, one thousand eight hundred and seventy-four, and the twenty-sixth section of the act of twenty-ninth of April, one thousand eight hundred and seventy-four, apply to or be required of mutual savings-fund, or building and loan associations.

Sec. 9. Mutual savings-fund, or building and loan associations, heretofore incorporated under the provisions of any law, shall be entitled to all the privileges, immunities, franchises, and powers conferred by this act, upon filing with the secretary of the commonwealth a certificate of their acceptance of the same in writing, under the duly authenticated seal of said association, which certificate also shall prescribe their mode or plan of charging premiums, bonus, or advance interest, as set forth in the first section of this act; and upon such acceptance and approval thereof by the governor, he shall issue letters patent to said corporation reciting the same.

Sec. 10. All laws or parts of laws inconsistent with the provisions of the act are hereby repealed.

MASSACHUSETTS.

The following is the law of this State, as reported by the Commissioners of Savings-Banks, December 31, 1887:

Section I. Twenty-five or more persons who associate themselves together by an agreement in writing, with the intention of forming a corporation for the purpose of accumulating the savings of its members paid into such corporation in fixed periodical installments, and lending to its members the funds so accumulated, shall be and remain a corporation upon complying with the provisions of the three following sections:

Sec. 2. The agreement shall set forth the fact that the subscribers thereto associated themselves with the intention of forming a corporation; the name by which the corporation shall be known; the purpose for which it is formed; the town or city, which shall be within this Commonwealth, in which it is located; and the limit of the capital to be accumulated.

Sec. 3. The name shall be one not previously in use by any existing corporation established under the laws of this Commonwealth, and shall be changed only by act of the General Court.

The words "co-operative savings-fund and loan association" shall form a part of the name.

Section three of chapter one hundred and seventeen of the Public Statutes, relative to the name of co-operative savings-fund and loan associations, is hereby amended by striking out the words "co-operative savings-fund and loan association," in the fourth line, and inserting in place thereof the words "co-operative bank."

The title of said chapter one hundred and seventeen of the Public Statutes is hereby amended by striking out the words "savings-fund and loan associations," and inserting in place thereof the word "banks."

The names of all co-operative savings-fund and loan associations heretofore organized are hereby changed by striking out in each the words "savings-fund and loan association," and inserting in place thereof the word "bank"; and they shall hereafter be known as "co-operative banks."

The first and second sections of this act shall take effect upon its passage, and the third section upon the first day of July, in the year eighteen hundred and eighty-three.

SEC. 4. The provisions of sections eighteen, twenty, and twenty-one of chapter one hundred and six shall apply to such corporations, except that, in the certificate signed by the Secretary of the Commonwealth, the limit of capital to be accumulated, as fixed in the agreement of association, shall be inserted, instead of the amount of the capital, that the certificate required by said section twenty-one to be filed and recorded may be signed and sworn to by the presiding and financial officers, and a majority at least of the officers possessing the powers of directors by whatever name they may be called, and that the fees to be paid for filing and recording the certificates required by said section twenty-one, including the issuing of the certificate of organization, shall be five dollars.

SEC. 5. The capital to be accumulated shall not exceed one million dollars, and shall be divided into shares of the ultimate value of two hundred dollars each. The limitation of capital to be accumulated in any co-operative bank now organized or hereafter formed under the provisions of chapter one hundred and seventeen of the Public Statutes shall be held to apply to capital actually paid in, and no such bank shall be restrained from issuing shares so long as the capital actually paid in on shares is not in excess of one million dollars. The shares may be issued in quarterly, half-yearly, or yearly series, in such amounts and at such times as the members may determine. No person shall hold more than twenty-five shares in the capital of any one such corporation. No shares of a prior series shall be issued after the issue of a new series.

SEC. 6. The number, title, duties, and compensation of the officers of the corporation, their terms of office, the time of their election, as well as the qualifications of electors and the time of each periodical meeting of the officers and members, shall be determined by the by-laws; but no member shall be entitled to more than one vote at any election. All officers shall continue in office until their successors are duly elected, and no corporation shall expire from neglect on its part to elect officers at the time prescribed by the by-laws.

In any co-operative bank now or hereafter formed under the provisions of chapter one hundred and seventeen of the Public Statutes, the offices of secretary and treasurer may be held by one and the same person.

SEC. 7. The officers shall hold stated monthly meetings. At or before each of these meetings every member shall pay to the corporation, as a contribution to its capital, one dollar as dues upon each share held by him until the share reaches the ultimate value of two hundred dollars or is withdrawn, canceled or forfeited. Payment of dues on each series shall commence from its issue.

SEC. 8. A member may withdraw his unpledged shares at any time by giving thirty days' notice of his intention so to do, written in a book held and provided by the corporation for that purpose. Upon such withdrawal the shareholder's account shall be settled as follows: From the amount then standing to the credit of the shares to be withdrawn there shall be deducted all fines, a proportionate part of any unadjusted loss, together with such proportion of the profits previously credited to the shares as the by-laws may provide, and such shareholders shall be paid the balance: *Provided*, that at no time shall more than one half of the funds in the treasury be applicable to the demands of withdrawing members without the consent of the directors. The directors may at their discretion, under rules made by them, retire the unpledged shares of any series at any time after four years from the date of their issue by enforcing the withdrawal of the same; but whenever there shall remain in any series, at the expiration of five years after the date of its issue, an excess above one hundred unpledged shares, then it shall be the duty of the directors to retire annually twenty-five per centum of such excess existing at said expiration of five years after the date of its issue, so that not more than one hundred unpledged shares shall remain in such series at the expiration of nine years from the date of its issue, and thereafter the directors may in their discretion retire such other unpledged shares as they consider the best interests of the bank to require : *Provided*, that whenever under the provisions of this section the withdrawal of shares is to be enforced the shares to be retired shall be determined by lot, and the holders thereof shall be paid the full value of their shares, less all fines and a proportionate part of any unadjusted loss : *Provided, also*, that shares pledged for share loans shall be treated as unpledged shares.

Shares may be issued in the name of a minor, and if so issued may, at the discretion of the directors, be withdrawn, in manner as provided in section two of this act, by such minor, the parent or guardian of such minor, and in either case the payments made on such withdrawals of shares shall be valid. When a share or shares are held by any one in trust for another, the name and residence of the person for whom such share or shares are held shall be disclosed, and the account shall be kept in the name of such holder as trustee for such person ; and, if no other notice of the existence and terms of such trust has been given in writing to the corporation, in the event of the death of the trustee such shares may be withdrawn by the person for whom such deposit was made or by his legal representatives.

Sec. 9. When each unpledged share of a given series reaches the value of two hundred dollars all payments of dues thereon shall cease, and the holder thereof shall be paid out of the funds of the corporation two hundred dollars thereof with interest at the rate of six per cent a year from the time of such maturity to the time of such payment: *Provided,* that at no time shall more than one half of the funds in the treasury be applicable to the payment of such matured shares without the consent of the directors: *Provided, further*, that when any series of shares, either pledged or unpledged, reaches maturity between the dates of adjustment of profits or whenever shares are retired between such dates, the holders of such shares shall, in addition to the value thereof, be entitled to interest at the rate of six per cent per annum for all full months from the date of the preceding adjustment.

Chapter one hundred and seventeen of the Public Statutes is amended as follows by adding to section nine the following words: " And that before paying matured shares all arrears and fines shall be deducted."

SEC. 10. The moneys accumulated, after due allowance made for all necessary and proper expenses and for the withdrawal of shares, shall at each stated monthly meeting be offered to the members according to the premiums bid by them for priority of right to a loan. Every member whose bid is accepted shall be entitled, upon giving proper security, to receive a loan of two hundred dollars for each share held by him or such fractional part of two hundred dollars as the by-laws may allow. If a balance of money remains unsold after a monthly sale, the directors may invest the same in any of the securities named in the second clause of section twenty of chapter one hundred and sixteen.

SEC. 11. Premiums for loans shall consist of a percentage charged on the amount lent in addition to interest, and shall be deemed to be a consideration paid by the borrower for the present use and possession of the future or ultimate value of his shares, and shall, together with interest and fines, be received by the corporation as a profit on the capital invested in the loan, and shall be distributed to the various shares and series of said capital as hereinafter provided.

SEC. 12. A borrowing member, for each share borrowed upon, shall, in addition to his dues and monthly premium, pay monthly interest on his loan at the rate of six per cent per annum until his shares reach the ultimate value of two hundred dollars each, or the loan has been repaid; and when said ultimate value is reached, said shares and loan shall be declared canceled and satisfied, and the balance, if any, due upon the shares shall be paid to the member.

Any corporation organized under said chapter one hundred and seventeen may provide in its by-laws that the bid for loans at its stated monthly meeting shall, instead of a premium, be a rate of annual interest upon the sum desired, payable in monthly installments. Such bids shall include the whole interest to be paid, and may be at any rate not less than five per centum per annum.

SEC. 13. For every loan made, a note secured by first mortgage of real estate shall be given, accompanied by a transfer and pledge of the shares of the borrower. The shares so pledged shall be held by the corporation as collateral security for the performance of the conditions of said note and mortgage. Said note and mortgage shall recite the number of shares pledged and the amount of money advanced thereon, and shall be conditioned for the payment, at the stated meetings of the corporation, of the monthly dues on said shares, and the interest and premium on the loan, together with all fines on payments in arrears until said shares reach the ultimate value of two hundred dollars each, or said loan is otherwise canceled and discharged: *Provided*, that the shares, without other security, may, in the discretion of the directors, be pledged as security for loans, to an amount not exceeding their value as adjusted at the last adjustment and valuation of shares before the time of the loan.

If the borrower neglects to offer security satisfactory to the directors within the time prescribed by the by-laws, his right to the loan shall be forfeited, and he shall be charged with one month's interest and one month's premium at the rate bid by him, together with all expenses, if any, incurred ; and the money appropriated for such loan may be reloaned at the next or any subsequent meeting.

SEC. 14. A borrower may repay a loan at any time, upon application to the corporation, whereupon, on settlement of his account, he shall be charged with the full amount of the original loan, together with all monthly installments of interest, premium and fines in arrears, and shall be given credit for the withdrawing value of his shares pledged and transferred as security; and the balance shall be received by the corporation in full satisfaction and discharge of said loan: *Provided*, that all settlements made at periods intervening between stated meetings of the directors shall be made as of the date of the stated meeting next succeeding such settlement; and, *Provided*, that a borrower desiring to retain his shares and membership may at his option repay his loan without claiming credit for said shares, whereupon said shares shall be retransferred to him, and shall be free from any claim by reason of said canceled loan. Partial payment of loans on real estate made by any co-operative bank may be received in sums of fifty dollars or any multiple thereof; and for each two hundred dollars so repaid one share of stock shall be released from pledge.

SEC. 15. Members who make default in the payment of their monthly dues, interest, and premiums, shall be charged a fine not exceeding two per cent. a month on each dollar in arrears. No fines shall be charged after the expiration of six months from the first lapse in any such payment, nor upon a fine in arrears. The shares of a member who continues in arrears more than six months shall, at the option of the directors, if the member fails to pay the arrears within thirty days after notice, be declared forfeited, and the withdrawing value of the shares at the time of the first default shall be ascertained, and, after deducting all fines and other legal charges, the balance remaining shall be transferred to an account to be designated the "Forfeited Share Account," to the credit of the defaulting member. Said member, if not a borrower, shall be entitled, upon thirty days' notice, to receive the balance so transferred without interest from the time of the transfer, in the order of his turn, out of the funds appropriated to the payment of withdrawals. All shares so forfeited or transferred shall cease to participate in any profits of the corporation accruing after the last adjustment and valuation of said shares before said first default.

SEC. 16. If a borrowing member is in arrears for dues, interest, premium or fines, for more than six months, the directors may, at their discretion, declare the shares forfeited, after one month's notice, if the arrears continue unpaid. The account of such borrowing member shall then be debited with the arrears

of interest "premium," and fines of date of forfeiture, and the
shares shall be credited upon the loan at their withdrawing
value. The balance of the account may, and after six months
shall, be enforced against the security, and be recovered as secured debts are recovered at law.

SEC. 17. The general accounts of every such corporation
shall be kept by double entry. All moneys received by the corporation from each member shall be receipted for by persons
designated by the directors, in a pass-book provided for by the
corporation for the use of, and to be held by, the member; and
said pass-book shall be plainly marked with the name and residence of the holder thereof, the number of shares held by him,
and the number or designation of the series or issue to which
said shares respectively belong, and the date of the issue of
such series. All moneys so received shall be originally entered
by the proper officer in a book to be called the "cash-book," to
be provided by the corporation for the purpose, and the entries
therein shall be so made as to show the name of the payer, the
number of shares, the number or designation of the series or
issue of the particular share or shares so entered, together with
the amount of dues, interest, premiums, and fines paid thereon,
as the case may be. Each payment shall be classified and entered into a column devoted to its kind. Said cash-book shall
be closed after the termination of each stated meeting, and
shall be an exhibit of the receipts of all moneys paid at said
meeting. All payments made by the corporation for any purpose whatsoever shall be by order, check, or draft upon the
treasurer, signed by the president and secretary, and indorsed
by the persons in whose favor the same are drawn. The name
of the payee, the amount paid, and the purpose, object, or thing
for which the payment is made, together with its date, shall be
entered on the margin of said order, check, or draft. The treasurer shall dispose of and secure the safe keeping of all moneys,
securities, and property of the corporation, in the manner designated by the by-laws, and the treasurer and secretary shall
give such security for the faithful performance of their respective duties as the by-laws may direct.

SEC. 18. The profits and losses may be distributed annually,
semi-annualy, or quarterly, to the shares then existing, but shall

be distributed at least once in each year, and whenever a new series of shares is to be issued. Profits and losses shall be distributed to the various shares existing at the time of such distribution, in proportion to their value at that time, and shall be computed upon the basis of a single share fully paid to the date of distribution. Losses shall be apportioned immediately after their occurrence.

At each periodical distribution of profits the directors shall reserve as a guarantee fund a sum not less than one nor more than five per cent of the net profits accruing since the next preceding adjustment, until such fund amounts to five per cent of the dues capital, which fund shall thereafter be maintained and held; and said fund shall be at all times available to meet losses in the business of the corporation from depreciation of its securities or otherwise.

SEC. 19. Any such corporation may purchase at any sale, public or private, any real estate upon which it may have a mortgage, judgment, lien, or other incumbrance, or in which it may have an interest; and may sell, lease, convey, or mortgage, at pleasure, the real estate so purchased to any person or persons whatsoever. All real estate so acquired shall be sold within five years from the acquisition of the title thereto.

SEC. 20. The commissioners of savings-banks shall perform in reference to every such corporation, the same duties, and shall have the same powers, as are required of or given to them in reference to savings-banks, and shall annually make a report to the General Court of such facts and statements respecting such associations, and in such forms as they deem that the public interest requires. Every officer of such corporation shall answer truly all inquiries made, and shall make all returns required by the commissioners.

OHIO.

LAWS OF OHIO RELATING TO BUILDING ASSOCIATIONS.

SECTION 3833. A corporation organized for the purpose of raising money to be loaned among its members for use in buying lots or in building and repairing. or other purposes, may levy, assess, and collect from its members such sums of money, by rates of stated dues, fines, interest and premiums on loans, or may otherwise raise money as the corporation by its constitution and by-laws shall provide; and it may acquire, hold, incumber and convey all such real estate and personal property as may be legitimately pledged to it on such loans, or may otherwise be transferred to it in the due course of its business; but the dues, fines and premiums so paid by its members, although in addition to the legal rate of interest on loans taken by it, shall not be construed to make the loans so taken usurious; and no person shall hold more than twenty shares in any such corporation in his own right.

SEC. 3834. Such corporation may receive on deposit all sums of money offered for that purpose, on such terms, and at such rates of interest, not exceeding the legal rate, as may be prescribed by the board of directors, and loan the same pursuant to the preceding section.

SEC. 3835a. So much of the earnings as may be necessary shall be set apart to defray the current expenses of the corporation, and a portion of the earnings, to be determined by the board of directors, shall be reserved annually or semi-annually for the payment of contingent losses, and the residue of such earnings or dividends shall be transferred to the credit of all members, to be paid to them at such times, and in such manner, and in such proportions as the corporation by its constitution and by-laws in conformity with this act may provide; and upon the cancellation of any share or shares that have been fully paid, the corporation shall pay to such member or members their *pro rata* share of so much of the reserve fund as has been accumulated during the membership and remains therein at the time of the termination of the membership of such member or members.

SEC. 3835b. Such corporation shall be authorized to provide in its constitution and by-laws, rules and regulations, for the terms of membership; for the annual subscribing shares of stock therein; for an annual or semi-annual division of the earnings of the dividends or earnings among the members; for a rebate of interest at the end of each year on the amount of dues paid on loans; for the sale of money; for the time and amount of the payment of dues, interest, premiums, fines, and other assessments; for the withdrawal of non-borrowing members, and also for the withdrawal of non-borrowing members of part payments on their shares of stock; for the cancellation of the securities of borrowing members upon demand being made by them or their legal representatives.

SEC. 3835c. All adjustments of loans between such corporation and its borrowing members shall be upon the following terms, to wit: After the premium for one year has been paid, and also the interest and premium on such loans up to the day of settlement, the borrowing member shall pay to the corporation an amount which, added to the dues and dividends credited, will equal the sum actually borrowed; and also such fines and other assessments as are provided for by the constitution and by-laws of such corporation.

SEC. 3835d. The stock or shares of individual members or depositors of such corporation shall be considered and held as credits, and the said members and depositors, individually, shall list for taxation the number of shares held by them, and the true value thereof in money, on the day preceding the second Monday in April in each year, and the same shall be assessed at such valuation and taxes as other property.

SEC. 3835e. Any building association, after at least three fourths of its capital stock is fully subscribed and taken, may increase its capital stock by a vote of its board of directors, a majority of the members of such board of directors voting in favor thereof; and a certificate of such action of the board of directors shall be filed with the Secretary of State.

SEC. 3836. All shares of stock held in such corporations by or in the name of a minor, shall, upon application therefor, be paid to such minor or persons who hold such shares of stock for the minor, and the same shall be valid payment.

Passed May 8, 1886.

(Ohio Laws V, pp. 116, 117.)

FORMS.

No. 1.

We submit the following as a form for suitable by-laws for an association incorporated under the New York act of 1887. They are, in fact, the by-laws of the Elmira Co-operative Savings and Loan Association, organized in 1888, and were drawn by us with much care; and supplement the act of 1887 in those matters left to the discretion of the association by the act, according to our conception of the true co-operative savings and loan association. They can be readily modified to meet the wishes of those who may differ with us on minor details.

The certificate of incorporation (see form in Chapter VII) fixes the name and place of doing business, hence they are not given in the by-laws.

BY-LAWS OF THE ... . CO-OPERATIVE SAVINGS AND LOAN ASSOCIATION.

Officers.

SECTION 1. The officers of this association shall be a President, Vice-President, Treasurer, Secretary, a Board of Directors, and an Attorney.

SEC. 2. The Board of Directors shall consist of thirteen members of whom nine shall be elected, and the President, Vice-President, Treasurer and Secretary shall be *ex-officio* members.

SEC. 3. The Attorney shall be appointed and removed at pleasure by the Board of Directors; all other officers shall be elected annually by ballot by the stockholders. In case of vacancies, the Board of Directors may fill the same until the next annual election.

SEC. 4. The *President* shall preside at all meetings of the stockholders and of the Board of Directors; sign all certificates of stock, and all orders upon the Treasurer for the payment or appropriation of moneys, and perform all other duties usually appertaining to such office.

SEC. 5. The *Vice-President*, in the absence or disability of the President, shall perform the duties of President.

SEC. 6. The *Treasurer* shall be the custodian of all funds, securities, contracts and deeds belonging to the association, subject however to the direction of the Board of Directors. He shall receipt for all moneys paid to him, and pay all orders or drafts upon him, ordered by the Board of Directors and signed by the President and attested by the Secretary. He shall keep suitable and accurate books of account of all his transactions, and make a report of the finances of the association at each stated meeting of the Board of Directors, which report shall be filed by the Secretary and entered in the minutes of the meeting. His books of accounts shall be subject to the call and inspection of the Board of Directors at any time and shall be subject to the inspection of any stockholder at all reasonable hours. He shall give a bond with at least two sureties, one or more of whom shall not be connected with the bank where he deposits the funds of the association, in an amount prescribed by the Board of Directors, and in form, and with sureties and the sufficiency thereof, subject to their approval. At the expiration of his term of office, he shall deliver to his successor in office, within five days after the qualification of such successor, all moneys, books and papers of the association in his possession.

SEC. 7. The *Secretary* shall be present at all meetings of the stockholders and Board of Directors in person, or shall have a proxy from the Board of Directors, and keep correct minutes of the proceedings, which shall be transcribed into a suitable minute-book and read at the next meeting for the approval of the Board. He shall also keep a stock ledger wherein shall appear a minute of every certificate of stock issued and all transfers until surrendered ; also an order-book, showing date, the amount, what given for, and the payee of all orders attested by him ; also a security-book, wherein shall appear a minute of all securities taken by the association; also a dues, interest and fine book, wherein shall appear the amount due from and paid by each shareholder at each meeting for the receipt of dues. He shall make a monthly report of the number of shares outstanding, and such other facts as the Board of Directors may require. He shall make a detailed report of the business of the association at each annual meeting, and at all meetings when required by the Board of Directors or President. His books shall be open for inspection by any stockholder at all reasonable hours. He shall have charge of the publications and the correspondence of the association, and shall deliver to his successor in office, within five days after the qualification of such successor, all books and papers in his possession belonging to the association.

SEC. 8. A *Finance Committee* of three members shall be appointed by the President from the nine elected members of the Board, who shall serve for four months; a second and a third committee shall be appointed in the same manner during the year; such committees shall be so arranged that each of said nine directors shall serve upon a committee for four months during the year. The President and Vice-President shall at all times be members *ex officio* of this committee.

SEC. 9. The *Attorney* shall examine the abstracts of title, procured from the County Clerk, to all real estate which has been offered to the association as security for loans and approved by the Finance Committee, and, if found satisfactory, he shall indorse his approval thereon. He shall prepare all securities given to the association and cause all mortgages to be recorded as soon as delivered. His charges for such services shall be reasonable and paid by the borrower, unless the Board otherwise direct. He shall meet with the Board of Directors when requested, but shall have no vote.

SEC. 10. No officer, other than the Treasurer, Secretary, and Attorney, shall receive compensation for any services rendered by him. The salaries of the Treasurer and Secretary shall be fixed by the Board of Directors. The Attorney shall not be entitled to compensation for his attendance upon the ordinary stated meetings of the Board of Directors, stockholders, or Finance Committee. All officers and committees shall be entitled to all expenses necessarily incurred by them in the proper discharge of their duties.

SEC. 11. The Board of Directors, by a two-thirds vote, shall have power to suspend any officer of the association, for cause, which shall be stated in writing and served upon him at the time of such suspension; whereupon a special meeting of the stockholders shall be called to consider such suspension, and at

17

such special meeting, or a meeting adjourned therefrom, the offending officer shall be reinstated or removed by a majority vote of the stock represented at such meeting.

Meetings.

SEC. 12. The annual meetings of the shareholders of the association shall be held on the *first Monday evening* in the month of *February* in each year for the election of officers and the transaction of the business of the association.

SEC. 13. Special meetings of the shareholders shall be convened by the President, at the written request of ten shareholders. A notice of such meeting, stating the time, place, and business to be brought before the meeting, shall be mailed by the Secretary, postage prepaid, to each shareholder, at his post-office address as it appears upon the books of the association, at least five days before the date of such meeting. In event such special meeting is desired to consider the suspension of the President, such special meeting shall be called by the Secretary.

SEC. 14. The stated monthly meeting of the Board of Directors shall be held on the *second Monday evening* in each month. The Finance Committee of the Board shall meet the same evening, from seven to nine o'clock, to receive dues and any other moneys due or payable to the association. The whole Board shall convene immediately following the receipt of dues, etc., and bidding for loans.

SEC. 15. Special meetings of the Board of Directors may be called at any time by the President, and shall be called by him on the written request of three directors. At least twenty-four hours' notice of a special meeting of the Board shall be given orally by the Secretary, or by leaving a written notice of such meeting at the business place or the residence of each director.

SEC. 16. Five members of the Board shall constitute a quorum for the transaction of all business, except the suspension of an officer, the loaning of money to another association, and the borrowing of money by the association.

SEC. 17. The Finance Committee shall meet at seven and one-half o'clock on each *Friday* evening following the monthly meeting of the Board of Directors, for the purpose of passing upon the sufficiency of the securities offered for the loans bid off at such monthly meeting. The Secretary and Attorney shall meet with the Committee, but shall have no vote.

Stock, Entrance Fee, and Transfer Fee.

SEC. 18. The stock of the association shall be issued in yearly series, and each shareholder shall be entitled to a certificate of the shares of stock held by him or her, issued in the name and under the seal of the association, and signed by the President and Secretary. The series, beginning with the first issued, shall be numbered in regular order—one, two, three, and so on—and the certificate shall plainly state the number of the series in which the shares are issued. An entrance fee of twenty-five cents shall be charged for each share of stock issued. A certificate of unpledged shares of stock may be transferred by assignment, in person or by attorney, in the presence of the President or Secretary, and the assignment shall be minuted upon the stock-book of the association and indorsed upon the certificate, and the assignee, by signing the by-laws and paying a transfer fee of *ten* cents a share, shall become a member of the association.

SEC. 19. A certificate of stock upon which a loan has been made, may be transferred in the same manner as in the last section described, subject to the rights of the association in the following case: First, where the assignee, in case of a real-estate loan, has purchased the mortgaged property and assumed the payment of the mortgage; second, where the loan is secured by the stock transferred and the assignee assumes the payment of the loan and makes his bond to the association for such payment.

Payment of Dues, etc.

SEC. 20. At the request of the Finance Committee, the Secretary and Treasurer shall aid them in the receipt of dues, etc. One member of the Committee at the time the dues and other payments are made shall receipt for the same in a pass-book, which shall be given to the shareholder with his certificate of stock; while another member of the Committee shall check off the amount paid from the dues, interest and fine book which the Secretary shall have at such meeting. At the close of the meeting for the receipt of dues, etc., the Committee shall turn over the funds received to the Treasurer and take his receipt therefor.

SEC. 21. The Finance Committee or any other officer shall not receive dues or other payments due the association at any other time than at the stated meetings, except the Treasurer may receive payments of loans under the provisions of section ten of the act under which this association is formed and incorporated.

SEC. 22. Whenever a shareholder shall be in arrears for dues, interest and fines, and a payment shall be made insufficient to square them all, the payment shall first be applied to the payment of the fines, and second to dues and interest in equal parts.

Fines.

SEC. 23. For every dollar of dues, interest and fines which a shareholder neglects or refuses to pay, he shall pay a fine of ten cents for each month in arrears. In the case of the death of the shareholder his estate shall not be chargeable with fines for non-payment of dues at the stated monthly meeting of the Board immediately following such death, nor shall any fines be imposed in such case at any subsequent meeting for the receiving of dues unless the personal representatives of such deceased shareholder or their assigns shall elect to carry the shares of stock of the deceased shareholder; but such shares shall be withdrawn and their withdrawal value computed, as prescribed in section twenty-six hereof, to the date of such death, shall be due and payable to his personal representatives at the first stated monthly meeting of the Board following the service of a written demand therefor upon the Secretary or as soon thereafter as the association shall have funds applicable to the payment of withdrawing stock.

SEC. 24. The successful bidder for a loan at the stated meetings shall immediately furnish to the Board a written description of the security which he proposes for his loan. The same shall pass without a motion to the Finance Committee unless the Board of Directors shall by a unanimous vote decide to pass upon the sufficiency of the security offered forthwith. The Board may also direct that the Finance Committee report to the Board for their determination upon the sufficiency of the security. In all other cases the Finance Committee shall personally examine the real estate offered as security and appraise the value thereof before the time fixed for their meeting to pass upon its sufficiency as a security; and if at their meeting they approve of the security as to its value and the Attorney shall approve of the title, the loan shall be made without further action by the Board of Directors; and when the mortgage has been placed in the Clerk's office for record, the President shall sign and the Secretary shall attest and deliver an order upon the Treasurer for the amount going to the borrower upon his loan. All the securities for the loan shall thereupon be delivered to the Secretary, who shall enter the same at once in the security-book, and the Secretary shall thereupon deliver the same with all assignments and abstracts of title and insurance papers to the Treasurer.

SEC. 25. Action upon security offered for loans shall not be had by the Finance Committee or by the Board of Directors in the presence of the borrower. If a borrower shall fail to offer satisfactory security for his proposed loan before the next stated meeting, his right to a loan upon his bid shall be forfeited unless the Board otherwise direct.

Dividends.

SEC. 26. The Board of Directors, at a meeting held subsequent to the last stated monthly meeting in the fiscal year and before the annual meeting, shall declare a dividend distributing the profits since the last dividend, under the provisions of section fifteen of the said act under which the association is incorporated. They shall also at said meeting, or a meeting adjourned therefrom and held before the annual meeting, determine the withdrawal value of the shares of stock until the next distribution of profits. In determining such withdrawal value they shall allow to all shares over two years of age at least seventy-five per cent of the profits which have accrued and have been added to the value of the shares and as much more as to them shall seem wise. They shall have discretionary power to make the percentage of profits withdrawn uniform upon all such shares or increase the same as the shares increase in age. In the case of shares not over two years of age at the time of determining the withdrawal value, they shall allow, in lieu of a percentage of profits, interest upon the dues paid in at a rate of not less than four and a half per cent per annum. Such withdrawal value shall be reported at the annual meeting, and take effect on the date of the first monthly meeting thereafter; and upon all withdrawals made until the next annual meeting, in addition to such withdrawal value, interest shall be paid upon the withdrawal value of the shares and upon all dues paid subsequent to said annual meeting, together with such dues, at the rate of four per cent per annum.

SEC. 27. The President at the last monthly meeting in the fiscal year shall appoint an auditing committee of three shareholders, who are not officers, to examine the accounts of the Treasurer and Secretary and report thereon to the annual meeting. He shall also appoint a committee of three stockholders, not officers, to make an examination of their accounts at any time during the year when so required in writing by ten shareholders; and he may appoint such committee at any time upon his own motion.

SEC. 28. No officer shall have power to make an expenditure or incur any liability on behalf of the association without authority given therefor by the Board of Directors.

SEC. 29. Every order drawn upon the Treasurer shall be dated when made and state the payee and the purpose for which it is drawn, and a stub from which the order shall be detached shall contain a statement of the same facts.

SEC. 30. These by-laws may be altered or amended at any annual or special meeting of the shareholders by a two-thirds vote of the shareholders present.

No. 2.

The following is a copy of the by-laws of the Guardian Co-operative Bank of Boston, Massachusetts. D. Eldridge, Esq., its Secretary and Treasurer, and one of the most conspicuous men in Massachusetts at this time, in extending this form of co-operation and insisting upon correct methods in the transaction of their business, recommends these by-laws as proper in form and matter under the Massachusetts law:

ARTICLE I.
NAME AND OBJECT.

This corporation shall be known by the name of "The Guardian Co-operative Bank," and its object shall be the accumulation of a capital in money, to be derived from savings and accumulations of the members thereof, to be paid into said corporation in fixed periodical installments, and the lending of such funds so accumulated to its members, in accordance with the provisions of chapter one hundred and seventeen of the Public Statutes of the year eighteen hundred and eighty-one of the Legislature of Massachusetts.

ARTICLE II.
CAPITAL STOCK.

The capital stock of the corporation (to be accumulated) shall be one million dollars, and shall be divided into shares of the ultimate value of two hundred dollars each, which shall be issued in quarterly, half-yearly, or yearly series, as the members may determine.

ARTICLE III.
LOCATION.

This corporation shall be located in the city of Boston, Massachusetts, and the office or place of business or meeting shall be determined by the Board of Directors.

ARTICLE IV.
OFFICERS AND THEIR DUTIES.

SECTION 1. The officers of this corporation shall consist of a President, a Vice-President, a Secretary, who shall be Clerk of the Corporation, a Treasurer, and fifteen Directors, all of whom shall constitute a Board of Directors, and each of whom must be a shareholder. The offices of Secretary and Treasurer may be held by one and the same person. After the first election they shall be elected by the shareholders at the annual meeting, and shall continue in office and perform their respective duties until their successors are duly elected. In case of vacancy in the office of President, Vice-President, Secretary, or Treasurer by death, resignation or otherwise, the remaining members of the Board of Directors shall make such temporary appointment as may be absolutely necessary to carry on the business of the corporation, and immediately call a special meeting of the shareholders for the purpose of electing such new officer or officers as may be necessary to fill the aforesaid vacancy or vacancies for the unexpired term. All other vacancies may be filled by the remaining members of the Board.

SEC. 2. The Board of Directors shall have the general management of the business of the corporation. They shall make an annual report at the annual meeting of the affairs of the corporation.

SEC. 3. The President shall preside at all regular and special meetings of the corporation and of the Board of Directors. The Vice-President shall, in the absence of the President, perform all his duties. In the absence of the President and Vice-President, the Board of Directors may elect a presiding officer *pro tempore*. The President shall, immediately after the annual meeting, nominate from the Board of Directors, subject to confirmation separately by the Board, for a term of one year, two competent persons who shall constitute a Finance Committee, and the first named of whom shall be chairman. The duties of the Finance Committee shall be to examine the general expense bills of the corporation, and, if necessary, to assist the Secretary in receiving the money paid at the regular monthly meetings, with such other duties as the President may designate. The President shall also, immediately after the annual meeting, nominate from the Board of Directors, subject to confirmation separately by the Board, for a term of one year, five competent persons who shall constitute a Security Committee, and the first named of whom shall be chairman. The duties of the Security Committee shall be to examine the real estate offered as security for loans, and to report in writing as to its value, and whether, in their opinion, the corporation can safely loan the amount applied for. The actual expenses of the Security Committee shall be borne by the corporation, provided that, in case of more than ordinary expenses, the borrower shall pay a portion thereof, if the Board of Directors grant the loan conditioned upon such partial payment of expenses. The personal examination by the Security Committee, of any parcel of real estate offered as security for loans, may be omitted by special vote of the Board of Directors.

No member of the Security Committee shall make official report upon any property, offered as security for a loan, in which he has a personal interest.

SEC. 4. The Secretary shall keep correct records of the meetings of the corporation and of the Board of Directors. He shall receive all moneys due the corporation, and pay the same promptly to the Treasurer.

He shall be the corporation's book-keeper, and have charge of all books and papers necessary to the performance of his duties, and shall turn over to his successor in office all such books and papers within two weeks after the election of such successor. He shall notify the directors of all special meetings of the Board, and all shareholders of the regular and special meetings of the corporation. Notice of all regular and of every special meeting of the corporation shall be published by the Secretary not less than three times, one being a Saturday, in one or more daily newspapers published in Boston, the first publication thereof to be not less than one week previous to such meeting Such notice shall state the day, hour, place, and business of such meeting. He shall prepare the annual report for the Directors.

He shall perform such other duties as the Board of Directors may determine. He shall receive such compensation for his services as the Board of Directors may determine, and shall be paid the same in monthly installments. He shall furnish security satisfactory to the Board of Directors, for the faithful performance of his duties. In the absence of the Secretary from a monthly meeting, the President shall appoint a Secretary *pro tempore.*

SEC. 5. The Treasurer shall receive from the Secretary all moneys paid to the corporation, and give his receipt therefor. He shall pay all drafts of the Secretary, when signed by the proper officers. He shall be the custodian of all deeds, mortgages, mortgage-notes, policies of insurance, or other securities of the corporation, except his own bond, which shall be in the custody of the President. He shall keep a correct account of all moneys received and paid, and shall make a written report of the same at each monthly meeting of the Directors. His books shall at all times be open to the inspection of the Directors.

· He shall furnish security, satisfactory to the Board of Directors, for the faithful performance of his duties. He shall receive such compensation for his services as the Board of Directors may determine.

Upon the expiration of his term of office, or in the event of his death, or his resignation, or removal from office, he, or his legal representatives, shall deliver to his successor all books, moneys, papers, and other property of the corporation.

SEC. 6. The Board of Directors shall appoint an attorney, who shall examine all titles to property offered as security for loans, and shall prepare all papers of a legal nature required by the corporation. In case of loans, the member offering security therefor shall pay the attorney's fees, whether the security is accepted or rejected, subject to decision by the Board of Directors in case of dispute as to the amount of the attorney's charges.

ARTICLE V.

REGULAR MEETINGS.

The annual meeting of the shareholders shall be held on the first Friday in June, in each and every year, at half-past seven o'clock, P. M. Monthly meetings of the Board of Directors shall be held on the first Friday in each and every month, at half-past seven o'clock, P. M., for the purpose of transacting any business that may be necessary. If either of said Fridays shall be a legal holiday, or observed as such, the meeting may be held on such other evening of the same week as the Board of Directors may designate, *provided* that notice of the change shall be given at the next preceding monthly meeting.

The shareholders shall meet on the first Friday in May, in each and every year, at half-past seven o'clock, P. M., for the purpose of making nominations for officers and Auditors for the ensuing fiscal year. In case of failure on the part of the shareholders to nominate a sufficient number to fill the various offices (including Auditors), it shall then become the duty of the Board of Directors to complete the list. The Secretary shall cause the list of nominees to be printed for use as ballots at the annual meeting, none being eligible except the nominees.

All elections shall be by ballot, and no member shall be entitled to vote at any election who has not been a member one month, nor shall the namo of any person not a member bo placed upon the list of nominees. At all elections a check list shall be used, and the polls shall be open from half-past seven o'clock, P. M., to nine o'clock, P. M., and be in charge of two or more members appointed by the presiding officer. No shareholder shall vote by proxy.

ARTICLE VI.
SPECIAL MEETINGS.

A special meeting of the shareholders shall be called by the Secretary upon the written petition of ten shareholders, addressed to the Board of Directors, setting forth the cause for such special meeting, *provided* that none of said ten members are in arrears on any account, and *provided further*, that each of them shall have been a shareholder one month, and *provided*, that at said special meeting, if called, no business shall be transacted except that for which the meeting was called as set forth in the petition. In the absence of the President and Vice-President from such special meeting, the shareholders present may appoint a presiding officer *pro tempore.*

Special meetings of the shareholders may be called by the President, or by the Board of Directors.

ARTICLE VII.
QUORUM.

Twenty-five shareholders, or a majority of the actual number of shareholders shall constitute a quorum in special or regular meetings of the corporation.

Nine members or a majority of those actually in office, shall constitute a quorum of the Board of Directors, *provided*, that moneys may be received and loaned at the monthly meetings without a quorum of the Directors.

ARTICLE VIII.
AUDITORS.

There shall be three Auditors elected annually at the annual meeting, to serve one year. Their duties shall be to examine and audit the books, accounts and vouchers of the Secretary and Treasurer, and certify as to the correctness of the same at or before the annual meeting next following their election. They shall have power to make partial or special reports at any regular monthly meeting. Vacancies occurring from any cause shall be filled for the unexpired term by the Board of Directors, No person shall serve as an Auditor and Director at the same time. The Directors shall appoint Auditors to serve until the first annual meeting.

ARTICLE IX.
SEAL.

The corporate seal shall consist of the *name* and *location* of the corporation, and the *date* of its charter, the whole to be surrounded by an ornamental circular border. It shall be produced by a single impression of an embossing press. It shall be in the custody of the Treasurer, and he shall see that it is affixed to all official papers that require it.

ARTICLE X.
FINES.

In default of the monthly payment of dues, interest or premiums, the shareholder shall be subject to a fine of two cents per month upon each and every dollar, or fractional part thereof not less than fifty cents, in arrears.

ARTICLE XI.
TRANSFER FEES.

One or more shares held in the name of one person in any one series of stock, may be transferred to another person upon payment of a fee of twenty-five cents for each transfer.

ARTICLE XII.
LOANS ON REAL ESTATE.

Each and every shareholder is entitled to a loan of two hundred dollars upon each share held by him unpledged, and not in arrears on any account. All money subject to loan shall be offered at competitive sale by the President or some person designated by him, at each regular monthly meeting of the Directors. All loans shall be in sums of fifty dollars or its multiple and all interest and premiums shall be payable monthly in advance. Any person shall forfeit his right to a loan if, after successfully bidding for the money, he shall fail to furnish satisfactory security before the next succeeding monthly meeting, *provided* that the right to said loan may be continued while the interest and premium are actually paid in advance.

ARTICLE XIII.
SECURITY FOR REAL-ESTATE LOANS.

No single parcel of real estate shall be taken as security for loans to two or more members. Two or more parcels of real estate may be taken as security from one borrower.

All real estate taken as security for loans, must be located in the State of Massachusetts. No borrower shall pledge more than one series of shares for any one loan.

ARTICLE XIV.
LOANS ON SHARES.

Loans on shares are made under the following statutory provision: "The shares, without other security, may in the discretion of the directors be pledged as security for loans, to an amount not exceeding their value as adjusted at the last adjustment and valuation of shares before the time of the loan."

ARTICLE XV.
BIDS FOR LOANS.

The bids for loans shall be in sums of five cents or its multiple, per share per month.

No sum greater than $2,000 shall be taken upon one bid.

No more than one loan shall be claimed upon one bid.

ARTICLE XVI.
INSURANCE.

All buildings upon real estate taken as security for loans shall be insured against fire for the benefit of the corporation at the expense of the borrower. All policies shall be in the custody of the Treasurer, and he shall see that no policy is suffered to lapse.

ARTICLE XVII.
WITHDRAWALS.

Shares may be withdrawn upon one month's notice, when the shareholder's account shall be settled as follows: From the amount then standing to the credit of the shares to be with-drawn, there shall be deducted all fines, a proportionate part of any unadjusted loss, and one fourth of all the profits which have been placed to the credit of said shares, and he shall be paid the balance. A notice to withdraw shall become null and void if not acted upon within two months.

ARTICLE XVIII.
RETIRING OF SHARES.

When in the discretion of the Board of Directors it is deemed expedient to retire the unpledged shares of any series, (as pro-vided by statute) notice of their intention to do so shall be sent by mail to each holder of such shares one month prior to the retirement, and such shareholders shall be notified by mail of the result of the drawing.

ARTICLE XIX.
LOST OR STOLEN PASS-BOOKS.

In case a pass-book is lost or stolen, immediate information of the same must be given to the Secretary. As the officers of this corporation may be unable to identify every shareholder, the corporation will not be responsible for loss sustained, when the shareholder fails to notify the officers that his pass-book has been lost or stolen, if his shares shall be fraudulently with-drawn by another, *provided*, that in case of the alleged loss or theft of a pass-book, the Finance Committee may at their dis-cretion authorize the issue of a duplicate, or may authorize the payment of the shares without the pass-book if withdrawn in full, but may in either case require a bond to indemnify the cor-poration for any loss it may sustain on account of the lost or stolen pass-book.

ARTICLE XX.
PRICE OF SHARES.

The price of the shares of this corporation shall be as fol-lows: On the date of issue, $1.00; on the second month, $2.02; on the third month, $3.06; on the fourth month, $4.12; on the fifth month, $5.20; on the sixth month, $6.30; provided that shares issued to qualify a borrower, the price shall be $1.00, $2.00, $3.00, $4.00, $5.00 and $6.00 respectively.

ARTICLE XXI.

DISCHARGES OF MORTGAGES.

Any mortgage held by this corporation may be discharged by the Secretary or the Treasurer upon the receipt of the amount due thereon, provided that the discharge shall be approved in writing by one Director.

ARTICLE XXII.

AMENDMENTS.

These by-laws may be amended by a two-thirds vote of the members present and voting at a regular or special meeting, *provided*, that the proposed amendments shall have been submitted to the corporation in writing at a meeting held at least four weeks previous to action on the same.

No. 3.

The following are the articles of association or constitution of The People's Building and Loan Association of the town of Harrison in New Jersey.

This is one of the most successful associations in that State. It was organized in 1873, and adopted the serial plan of issuing its stock in August, 1874. It is a model constitution for the scheme which it embodies.

CONSTITUTION.

ARTICLE I.

TITLE AND OBJECT.

This association shall be denominated "THE PEOPLE'S BUILDING AND LOAN ASSOCIATION OF THE TOWN OF HARRISON." Its object is to provide a means for the regular, safe and profitable investment of the savings of its members; and, by these savings, to accumulate a fund for the purpose of making loans to stockholders, whereby they may be enabled to build or provide for themselves dwelling-houses, or to purchase building-lots or other real property.

ARTICLE II.

SECTION 1. The members of this association shall be residents of the United States. Minors may hold stock in this association by guardians. A parent procuring stock for a minor child may, during the minority of such child, represent him or her in all the rights of membership except that of holding office. When such child shall have attained the age of twenty-one years, he or she shall be dealt with as the absolute owner of the stock and be considered a member.

SEC. 2. A payment by any stockholder, trustee, guardian or representative for a minor, of one or more installments of one dollar on a share of stock shall constitute such stockholder, trustee, guardian or representative for a minor, a member of this association, and as such shall be subject to all fines and penalties imposed by this constitution, and entitled to all the privileges of membership.

SEC. 3. Each and every stockholder, trustee, guardian or representative for a minor, for each and every share of stock held by him or her in this association shall pay the sum of one dollar, as installments, on the third Tuesday of each and every month; these payments shall be made to the Treasurer, or such other person or persons as shall from time to time by the laws or regulations of this association be authorized to receive the same, at such hour as provided for in this constitution, and at such place as the Board of Directors shall provide, the said payments to continue until it shall be ascertained that the value of the whole stock of their respective series be sufficient to divide to each share of stock in such respective series the sum of two hundred dollars. The time for payments for each month shall terminate as soon as the Secretary shall have waited on all present and left the place of meeting.

SEC. 4. In case any stockholder, trustee, guardian or representative for a minor shall neglect or refuse to pay his or her monthly dues, each and every such person so neglecting or refusing shall incur a monthly fine of five per cent, which shall be charged on all sums remaining unpaid.

SEC. 5. In case any stockholder (not having taken a loan) shall neglect or refuse to pay his or her monthly installments or fines for the space of six months each and every stockholder so neglecting or refusing shall be tendered by the Treasurer the amount of installments actually paid by him or her, without any allowance for interest, first deducting all fines and forfeitures that may be charged against him or her, and from that time he or he shall cease to be a member of this association. Provided, that such action shall not be taken against a defaulting stockholder, unless he or she shall have been notified by the Secretary one month previously.

SEC. 6. Any non-borrowing stockholder wishing to withdraw from this association may do so by giving a written notice to the Secretary five days prior to the meeting of the Board of Directors, which shall be held on the evening of the third Tuesday of each month, of such intention to withdraw, etc. During the first year of his or her respective series of stock, he or she shall be entitled to receive the actual amount of installments paid in, less any fines he or she may owe. After the expiration of the first year, he or she shall receive the actual amount of installments paid in, less any fines he or she may owe, with interest at the rate of four per cent per annum ; after the expiration of the second year, five per cent per annum ; after the expiration of the third year, six per cent per annum ; after the expiration of the fourth year, such percentage for the average time of investment as shall be shown by the last annual report to be the net earnings of the association, less the following percentage of discount off said net earnings, according to the age of the respective series of stock, to wit: after the fourth year, thirty-five per cent; after the fifth year, thirty per cent ; after the sixth year, twenty-five per cent; after the seventh year, twenty per cent; after the eighth year, fifteen per cent ; after the ninth year, ten per cent; and after the tenth year, and until the respective series mature, five per cent. It is provided, however, that at any time not more than one half of the monthly receipts shall be appropriated to such redemption of stock without the consent of the Board of Directors.

SEC. 7. Upon the death of a stockholder who has not received a loan or loans, his or her legal representatives shall be entitled to receive from this association the actual amount of installments paid in on his or her stock, less any fines he or she

18

may owe, with interest added to the same, at rates in accordance with section six of this article; then his or her interest in this association shall terminate, unless the legal representatives of such deceased shall continue the payments of installments on such stock for three months after his or her decease, thereby assuming the future payments on the stock.

SEC. 8. When it shall be ascertained through the Auditors that the value of each share of stock in any series amounts to two hundred dollars, a meeting of the stockholders in such series shall be convened, at which time a division shall take place; every stockholder of the matured series shall receive the sum of two hundred dollars for each share of stock held by him or her in such series, or his or her securities of that amount with the same fully satisfied and canceled off record, and then that series shall cease and determine.

ARTICLE III.
SERIES OF STOCK AND DISTRIBUTION OF EARNINGS.

SECTION 1. A new series of stock may be commenced on and at the annual meeting of the association, held on the third Tuesday of September in every year; provided the same be determined on by the Board of Directors at least one month prior to the annual meeting of the association, and public notice given thereof.

SEC. 2. It shall be the duty of the Secretary to assist the Auditors in settling and adjusting the accounts of the association, and determining the value of the shares in each respective series prior to the annual meeting, or at any other time, as occasion may require; and, in order that no series of stock may be given a greater percentage of the earnings of the association than is due thereto, they shall distribute the net earnings of the association and determine the value of the shares in accordance with the following rules: Each series' investment to be multiplied by the average time invested, the results to be added together for a sum of results, each result to be multiplied by the total net earnings of the association, the product divided by the sum of results, the quotient in each case showing each series' share of the net earnings. Divide each series' share of the net earnings by the number of shares in that series and the result will be the net gain per share.

ARTICLE IV.
CERTIFICATES OF STOCK.

Each stockholder shall be entitled to a certificate of stock issued in the name of the association under the corporate seal thereof, signed by the President and attested by the Secretary; which certificate may be transferred by assignment in person or by attorney in presence of the Secretary, and shall be recorded in the proper book kept by the Secretary for that purpose, and indorsed on the certificate, which shall be surrendered and a new one issued therefor to the party to whom transferred. It is provided, however, that no stock shall be transferred while any fines, installments, or other liens remain charged against the same, nor until the tranferree shall have assumed all the obligations of the original stockholders.

ARTICLE V.
OFFICERS.

The officers of this association shall be a President, Vice-President, Treasurer, Secretary, eleven Directors, and three Auditors, all of whom must be stockholders.

ARTICLE VI.
PRESIDENT.

The President shall be elected by the stockholders at the annual meeting. It shall be his duty to preside at all meetings of this association, and of the Board of Directors, to preserve order therein, to sign all orders on the Treasurer for the payment of money when ordered by the Board of Directors, and to perform all other duties usually appertaining to the office of President. It shall be his duty, when so ordered by the Board of Directors, to give releases and acquittances for all moneys which shall be paid to the association upon any bond, bill, note, mortgage, or other security, and, if necessary, acknowledge satisfaction of the same on record.

ARTICLE VII.
VICE-PRESIDENT.

The Vice-President shall be elected by the stockholders at the annual meeting. It shall be his duty, in the absence of the

President, to preside at all meetings of the stockholders and of the Board of Directors, and discharge all duties appertaining to the office of President. It shall be his duty, in the event of the death or resignation of the President, to perform all the duties of that office until the next succeeding annual meeting.

It shall also be his duty to keep a book in which he shall record the names of all persons who pay money into the treasury, and the amount which each person paid.

ARTICLE VIII.
TREASURER.

The Treasurer shall be elected by the Board of Directors. His duty shall be to receive all money paid into the association from all sources whatsoever; to deposit the same to the account of the association in a regular bank of deposit designated by the Board of Directors, and to pay all orders drawn upon the Treasurer by order of the Board of Directors, when signed by the President and attested by the Secretary, the said orders to be paid by checks drawn on the said bank, and the said checks to be signed by himself, together with the President and Secretary, with the seal of the association stamped thereon. It shall also be his duty to receive and hold in trust for the association all bonds, mortgages, and other securities on which money may be loaned by the association. He shall give bond with such security and for such sum as the Board of Directors may direct, for the faithful performance of his duties, and at the expiration of his office he shall deliver all money, bonds, mortgages, bills, notes, books, papers, and all other property belonging to the association in his possession, or under his control, to his successor in office.

ARTICLE IX.
SECRETARY.

The Secretary shall be elected by the Board of Directors. It shall be his duty to keep accurate minutes of the proceedings of this association and of the Board of Directors, to record the same in books to be kept for that purpose. He shall keep accurate accounts with all the stockholders, and attest all orders drawn on the Treasurer for the payment of money when so ordered by the Board of Directors, and also keep all policies of insurance transferred to the association as collateral, and see that they are kept renewed. He shall (at the expense of the association) notify the stockholders of the annual meetings by public notice conspicuously placed and advertisement in a newspaper published in the town. He shall be prepared at all times to inform the stockholders of the state of the financial concerns of the association, and at the yearly meetings furnish a detailed statement of the finances. He shall receive such salary as the Board of Directors may direct. At the expiration of his term of office, he shall deliver all books, papers, and property belonging to the association in his possession to his successor in office. It shall be his duty at each regular meeting of the Board of Directors to present to said Board a list of all premiums on policies of insurance held as collateral security by this association, that may be coming due during the subsequent month, and it shall be the duty of the Board of Directors to order a draft issued on the Treasurer for a sum of money sufficient to pay such premiums, unless the same shall have been paid by the owners, or agents of such owners; and the renewals of such policies as shall be so paid by the Secretary shall be his vouchers for the amount paid by him, and the balance, if any, he shall pay into the treasury of this association.

ARTICLE X.
DIRECTORS.

SECTION 1. The Directors, together with the President and Vice-President, shall constitute the Board of Directors. The Directors shall be elected by the stockholders at the annual meeting of the association. Immediately after the first election they shall meet and divide themselves into three classes, and draw lots for one, two and three years. Those drawing one year shall have their places supplied at the next annual election; those drawing two years, shall have their places supplied at the second annual election thereafter; and those drawing three years, shall have their places supplied at the third annual election thereafter. At each succeeding election, Directors shall be chosen to supply the places of those whose terms expire.

SEC. 2. The Board of Directors shall meet regularly on the third Tuesday in each and every month at such place as they,

or a majority of them, shall appoint, to receive from the stockholders their monthly installments, interest and fines, and pay
the same into the treasury; to loan out the funds and see to
their safe investment, and to attend to the financial concerns of
the association generally. But if there be no quorum present,
then any three or more of the Directors in attendance shall be
authorized to receive the aforesaid monthly installments, interest
and fines, and offer the money for loan as specified in Article
XIII, section one.—The Board of Directors shall also meet on
the evening of the second Monday following the regular meeting, for the purpose of transacting such other business of the
association as may be necessary.

Sec. 3. The time of the meetings of the Board of Directors
from the first of May to the first of September, inclusive, in
each and every year, shall be 8 o'clock, P. M., and during the
other months of the year, 7.30 o'clock, P. M.

Sec. 4. A quorum shall consist of not less than seven. The
President or any Director being absent without sufficient excuse
for three monthly meetings successively, his office as President
or Director shall be declared vacant.—The Board shall have
power to fill all vacancies that may occur until the next annual
meeting. In case of the absence of the President and Vice-
President, the Directors shall have power to elect a President
pro tempore. Officers of their own appointment may be *removed*
by them at pleasure.

Sec. 5. It shall be the duty of the Board of Directors to purchase at foreclosures any property mortgaged to the association, if such action shall be considered by them, or a majority
of them, for the benefit of the association.

ARTICLE XI.
AUDITORS.

The Auditors shall be elected by the stockholders at the
annual meeting of the association. Immediately after the first
election they shall meet and draw lots for their terms of office,
viz., for one, two and three years, respectively. The one drawing for one year shall have his place supplied at the next annual
election; the one drawing for two years shall have his place
supplied at the second annual election; and the one drawing for

three years shall have his place supplied at the third annual election. At each succeeding annual election Auditors shall be chosen by the stockholders to supply the places of those whose terms expire, or of a vacancy in an unexpired term.

Their duty shall be to settle and adjust the accounts of the association prior to the annual meeting, and to report to the stockholders with a faithful and ample exhibit of the financial affairs of the association, the state of the treasury and the value of the shares; which exhibit they shall have printed at the expense of the association.

In the event of their neglect or refusal to furnish to the stockholders at their annual meeting a detailed exhibit of the finances, as hereinbefore provided, they shall be fined five dollars each.

They shall have power at any time to inspect the accounts of the Treasurer and Secretary, and upon five days' due notice call a meeting of the stockholders.

They shall have power to fill any vacancy that may occur in their number, until the next annual election; but in the event of their inability to agree upon a choice, the vacancy shall be filled by the Board of Directors.

They shall superintend all elections but theirs, (which shall be conducted by a committee from the Board of Directors).

ARTICLE XII.
SOLICITOR.

The Board of Directors shall appoint a solicitor for the association who shall examine all title deeds, and make the necessary searches for ascertaining the title to all property offered to this association as mortgage security, and give his written opinion thereon. He shall prepare all bonds, mortgages, agreements and all other writings to be taken or given by this association in the course of its business, and also transact all other law business of this Association whenever required by the Board of Directors, for which he shall receive a fair compensation.

His charges for fees and disbursements in making searches, recording and proving papers, for preparing all mortgages and other written instruments, and for examining papers, titles and other matters, shall be borne by the party applying for the loan.

He is required to give such security for the faithful performance of his duties as the Board of Directors shall determine. In
all disputes as to the amount of his charges, the same shall be
determined by the Board of Directors.

ARTICLE XIII.
LOANS.

SECTION 1. Whenever and as often as the sum of two hundred
dollars may be in the treasury, it shall be loaned out in open
meeting, at auction, to the highest bidder; providing, however,
the said money shall not be sold at less than one per cent premium. Every stockholder who is not in arrears with his or her
monthly installments, interest and fines, shall be entitled to receive a loan of two hundred dollars, less the premium bid by
him or her, for each share of stock held by him or her in this
association.

SEC. 2. In addition to the premium bid for a loan (which
must be paid or deducted from the amount of the loan at or
before receiving the same), every stockholder shall be held as
contracting to pay all taxes that may be assessed at any time
upon said loan.

SEC. 3. Whenever a stockholder shall be declared to be entitled to a loan or loans, and before receiving the same, he or
she shall secure the payment thereof to the association by a
bond and mortgage for the full amount of the sum loaned,
and for the payment of such fines as may be imposed for the
failure of paying installments and interest when due, and by the
deposit of the policy of fire insurance, and for every loan of two
hundred dollars made to a stockholder at least one share of
stock, of the series in which he or she shall borrow, shall be
assigned as collateral security to said bond and mortgage. In
case of failure to give satisfactory security for each loan within
one month, the month's interest shall be charged to the borrower
and the loan revert to the association. No money shall be
loaned on any property already incumbered. Each stockholder
shall be entitled to borrow to the full amount of his or her
shares actually held by him or her at that time; and in case
there should not be a sufficient amount in the hands of the
Treasurer, he or she will be entitled to the balance of their

loans at the same rate from the first money that comes into the treasury.

SEC. 4. It shall be the duty of the President to sell the money in the treasury, in the manner aforesaid in section one of this article, at a regular monthly meeting. Loans shall be granted to such stockholders as shall offer or bid the highest premiums therefor.

SEC. 5. Each stockholder of this association on receiving a loan or loans therefrom, shall be entitled to a deduction on the premium bid, of one tenth for each and every full year that has expired since the series of stock in which he or she borrows was issued.

SEC. 6. Stockholders taking loans from this association shall pay interest monthly to the Treasurer at the rate of one half of one per cent per month. Borrowers refusing or neglecting to pay the interest on their loans shall incur a monthly fine of five per cent for each monthly neglect on each loan of two hundred dollars by them held. If the interest is suffered to remain unpaid more than six months, the Board of Directors may compel payment of principal and interest by ordering proceedings on the bond and mortgage according to law.

SEC. 7. Stockholders shall be entitled to borrow to the amount of their installments actually paid in, after the series in which they shall borrow shall have been issued at least one year, on their bond with interest for the same, and on transferring their stock to the association as security; and in case any stockholders borrowing upon their bond shall neglect or refuse to pay their installments, interest and fines for the space of six months, then the stock transferred to the association shall be forfeited.

SEC. 8. No security for a loan or loans shall be deemed sufficient unless approved of by at least two thirds of the directors present at a meeting of the Board.

SEC. 9. Any borrower who is not in arrears to the association may repay a loan at any time, and, in case of the repayment thereof before the expiration of the eighth year after the series in which his or her stock was issued, such borrowers shall be allowed the following credit, viz., the amount of installments actually paid into the association on the respective series, and one eighth of the premium paid for said loan for every full year of the said eight years unexpired, together with whatever interest he or she may be entitled to receive, as provided in Article II, section six. Provided, that notice of such repayment shall be given in like manner as provided for stockholders withdrawing.

SEC. 10. This association shall have power to insure all buildings upon which loans are made, and also to renew the same and collect the amount paid therefor, in the same manner and with like fines as installments and interest are collected unless the mortgageors shall give policies thereon and keep the same renewed in good and responsible insurance companies.

ARTICLE XIV.
REDEMPTION OF STOCK.

In the event of the money in the treasury of the association not selling at or over one per cent premium, in accordance with Article XIII, section one, the Board of Directors shall retain the same in the treasury until the next regular monthly meeting, when it shall be applied to the redemption of stock in the oldest series and in the following manner: They shall authorize the Secretary to notify the stockholders in the said series of their intention of redeeming such number of shares as the money in the treasury will permit and of the time and place of meeting.

At the meeting so held, the present value of the shares in said series shall be announced by the Secretary, whereupon the President shall proceed to receive from the stockholders present, by auction, bids of premium on the announced value of the stock; and the stockholder bidding the highest premium shall be entitled to receive the announced value of his or her shares of stock redeemed, less the rate of premium bid. For each share of stock so redeemed, the stockholder selling the same shall surrender to the association his or her certificate of stock.

ARTICLE XV.
MEETINGS.

Meetings of the stockholders shall be held on the third Tuesday in September in each and every year. Twenty members shall constitute a quorum. Special meetings shall be called by the Secretary when requested by ten members, but the object of such meeting so called must be inserted in the notice.

ARTICLE XVI.
ELECTIONS.

The annual election for officers shall be held on the third Tuesday of September of every year, and one week's notice of the place, object and time of meeting shall be given by the Secretary as hereinbefore provided. Each member present at an election shall be entitled to one vote. No stockholder shall be eligible to office nor entitled to vote until he or she shall have been at least three months a member.

ARTICLE XVII.
FINES.

All officers neglecting to attend any annual meeting shall be fined one dollar each.

The Treasurer (or deputy) for non-attendance at any monthly meeting shall be fined fifty cents.

The Secretary forfeits five dollars for neglecting to pay premiums on any insurance policy which is not paid by the owner.

The Secretary, for neglecting to attend any meetings of the Board of Directors or of the stockholders, shall be fined one dollar. All fines shall be charged by the Secretary with the monthly dues or deducted from the salary or compensation of such officers as receive any at the time of receiving the same.

ARTICLE XVIII.
BY-LAWS.

The Board of Directors may enact by-laws for their own government not repugnant with this Constitution.

ARTICLE XIX.
PLACE OF MEETING.

The Board of Directors, or a majority, are to select a place of meeting for themselves and the association.

ARTICLE XX.

This constitution shall not be altered or amended except at an annual or special meeting, of which due notice shall have been given, and by a vote of two thirds of the stockholders present.

ARTICLE XXI.
SALARIES AND EXPENSES.

The salaries and fees of officers of this association shall be fixed by the Board of Directors. All other expenses incurred for books, printing, etc., must be sanctioned by the Board of Directors.

No. 4.
NEW YORK. MORTGAGE.

Form of Mortgage to be taken by an Association organized under the Act of 1887.

This INDENTURE made this ...... day of ......, in the year of our Lord one thousand eight hundred and ......, between ......, of the ...... of ......, and State of ......, part ..... of the first part, and "THE ...... CO-OPERATIVE SAVINGS AND LOAN ASSOCIATION of the ...... of ......, in the county of ...... and State of New York, a corporation duly organized under the provisions of Chapter 556 of the laws of 1887 of the said State of New York, party of the second part, WITNESSETH that the said part.. of the first part, in consideration of the sum of ...... dollars duly paid, the receipt whereof is hereby duly acknowledged, ha.. sold and by these presents do.. grant and convey to the said party of the second part, its successors and assigns, all that tract or parcel of land situate in the ...... of ...... county of ......, and State of New York ....

....

....

[Here insert description of mortgaged premises.]

....

....

This grant is intended as a security for the payment of the sum of ...... dollars, together with interest thereon at the rate of six per cent per annum, in the manner and at the times provided in and required by the by-laws of the said party of the second part and the said act under the provisions of which the said party of the second part is incorporated, special reference

being had to such portions of said act and the said by-laws as relate particularly to loans made to borrowers and the payment of
such loans and the interest thereon and the payment of fines in
case of defaulted payments thereby required, and the said provisions shall be deemed a part of this instrument as fully and completely as though set forth at length herein, according to the
conditions of a bond this day executed and delivered by the
said ...... to the said party of the second part; and this
conveyance shall be void if such payment be made as herein
specified. But in case default shall be made in the payment of
the principal sum hereby intended to be secured, or in the payment of the interest thereon, or of any part of said principal or
interest as above specified, it shall be lawful for the party of the
second part, its successors or assigns, at any time thereafter, to
sell the premises hereby granted, or any part thereof, in the
manner prescribed by law, and retain the amount then due for
principal, interest and fines, together with the costs and charges
of making such sale, and the overplus, if any there be, shall be
paid by the party making such sale, on demand, to the said
......, ... heirs or assigns.

AND IT IS HEREBY FURTHER EXPRESSLY AGREED that should
any default be made in the payment of said principal sum or
the interest thereon, or any part of said principal and interest,
as hereinbefore provided to be paid, and the same remain unpaid and in arrears for the time of six months, or should any
tax or assessment levied or imposed upon the premises hereinbefore described, become due and payable and remain unpaid
by the part.. of the first part for the time of six months,
then and from thenceforth, that is to say, after the lapse of the
said six months, in either of the aforesaid events, the aforesaid
principal sum or any and all sums then unpaid, with all arrearages of interest and fines thereon, shall, at the option of the
said party of the second part, its successors or assigns, become
and be due and payable immediately thereafter, although the
period first above limited for the payment thereof may not then
have expired, anything hereinbefore contained to the contrary
thereof in any wise notwithstanding.

AND IT IS FURTHER ALSO HEREBY EXPRESSLY AGREED by and
between the parties to this instrument that the said part.. of

the first part shall keep the buildings erected and to be erected upon the lands hereinbefore described insured against loss and damage by fire and pay the premiums therefor and assign the policy and certificate thereof to the said party of the second part as a collateral security hereto, and in default thereof it shall be lawful for the said party of the second part to effect such insurance, and the premium or premiums paid for securing such insurance and continuing the same, shall be a lien on such mortgaged premises added to the amount secured by these presents, and payable on demand with interest at the rate of six per cent per annum.

IN WITNESS WHEREOF, the part.. of the first part ha.. hereunto set ...... hand.. and seal.. the day and year first above written.

Sealed and delivered
    in the presence of   .... (L. S.)

State of New York, }
    County of ...... } *ss.*

On this ...... day of ......, in the year of our Lord one thousand eight hundred and ......, before me, the subscriber, personally appeared ....
....
to me known to be the same person.. described in and who executed the within instrument and ...... and acknowledged that ..he.. executed the same.

                  ....
                  ....

No. 5.
NEW YORK. BOND.

Form of a Bond when the Association is incorporated under the Act of 1887.

KNOW ALL MEN BY THESE PRESENTS that 1, ..., of the ...... of ......, in the County of ......, and State of New York, am firmly held and bound unto THE ...... CO-OPERATIVE SAVINGS AND LOAN ASSOCIATION of the ...... of ...... in the County of ...... and State of New York, a corporation duly organized under the provisions of Chapter 556 of the laws of 1887 of the State of New York, in the sum of ...... dollars, lawful money of the United States of America, to be paid to the said THE ...... CO-OPERATIVE SAVINGS AND LOAN ASSOCIATION, its successors or assigns. For which payment, well and truly to be made, I hereby bind myself, my heirs, executors, and administrators, jointly and severally, firmly by · these presents. Sealed with my seal and dated this ...... day of ......, one thousand eight hundred and ......

THE CONDITION OF THE ABOVE OBLIGATION IS SUCH, that if the above bounden ......, his heirs, executors, or administrators shall well and truly pay or cause to be paid unto the above-named THE ...... CO-OPERATIVE SAVINGS AND LOAN ASSOCIATION, its successors or assigns, the sum of ...... dollars, together with interest thereon at the rate of six per cent per annum, in the manner and at the times provided in and required by the by-laws of the said THE ...... CO-OPERATIVE SAVINGS AND LOAN ASSOCIATION and the said act under the provisions of which the same is incorporated, special reference being had to such portions of each thereof as relate particularly to loans made to borrowers and the repayment of such loans and the interest thereon, and the payment of fines in case of defaulted payments thereby required, and the said provisions shall be deemed a part of this obligation as fully and completely as though set forth at length herein, without fraud or delay, then the preceding obligation to be void, otherwise to remain in full force and virtue.

AND IT IS HEREBY EXPRESSLY AGREED that should any default be made in the payments upon said principal and interest or either of them or any part thereof, as hereinbefore agreed to be made, and the same shall remain unpaid and in arrears for the time of six months, (or should any tax or assessment levied or imposed upon the premises described in the mortgage accompanying this bond, become due and payable, and remain unpaid by the obligor herein for the time of six months *), then and from

* In the event the bond is secured in full by a pledge of stock, the clauses relating to taxes, assessments, and insurance will be omitted. An association, in the preparation of its blanks, should, as a matter of

thenceforth, that is to say, after the lapse of said six months, the aforesaid principal sum or any and all sums thereof then remaining unpaid, with all arrearages of interest and fines thereon, shall, at the option of the said THE CO-OPERATIVE SAVINGS AND LOAN ASSOCIATION, its successors or assigns, become due and payable immediately thereafter, although the period first above specified for the payment thereof may not have expired, anything hereinbefore contained to the contrary notwithstanding.

AND IT IS FURTHER HEREBY EXPRESSLY AGREED by and between the parties to these presents that the said obligor shall keep the buildings erected and to be erected upon the lands described in the mortgage accompanying this bond insured against loss and damage by fire, in an amount and by insurers approved by the said obligee, its successors or assigns, and pay the premiums therefor, and assign the policy and certificate thereof to the said obligee as a collateral security hereto, and in default thereof it shall be lawful for the said obligee to effect such insurance, and the premium or premiums paid for securing such insurance shall be added to the principal sum hereby secured to be paid, and shall be payable on demand with interest at the rate of six per cent per annum.*

Sealed and delivered
in the presence of .... (L. S.)

State of New York, } ss.
County of ......

On this ...... day of ......, in the year of our Lord one thousand eight hundred and ......, before me, the subscriber, personally appeared ......, to me known to be the same person described in and who executed the foregoing instrument, and duly acknowledged that ..he.. executed the same.

....

convenience, have them printed in both ways, one for a " stock loan " and one for a " mortgage loan."

* Ibid.

No. 6.
NEW YORK. MORTGAGE.

Form of Mortgage to be taken by an Association incorporated under the Act of 1851.

This INDENTURE made this ...... day of ......, in the year of our Lord one thousand eight hundred and ......, between ...... of the ...... of ......, county of ......, and State of ......, part .. of the first part, and the ...... association of the ...... of ......, in the county of ......, and State of New York, party of the second part, WITNESSETH that the said part.. of the first part, in consideration of the sum of ...... dollars duly paid, the receipt whereof is hereby acknowledged, ha.. sold and by these presents do.. grant and convey to the said party of the second part, its successors or assigns, all that tract or parcel of land situate in the ...... of ......, county of ......, and State of New York, ...
....
....

[Here insert description of mortgaged premises.]
....
....

This grant is intended as a security for the payment of the sum of ...... dollars, with interest thereon at the rate of six per cent per annum, in the manner and at the times provided in and required by the articles of association and by-laws of the party of the second part hereto, special reference being had to such portions of each thereof as relate particularly to loans made to borrowers, and the payment of such loans and interest thereon, and fines upon defaulted payments, to which said articles of association and by-laws reference is hereby made for the times and the manner of the payment of said sum, with interest thereon, and the same are hereby deemed to be a part of this instrument as fully and completely as though fully set forth at length herein, according to the condition of a bond this day executed and delivered by the said ......, to the said party of the second part; and this conveyance shall be void if payments be made as herein specified.

But in case default be made in the payment of the principal

19

sum hereby intended to be secured or in the payment of the interest thereon, or in any part of such principal or interest or fines upon defaulted payments as above provided, it shall be lawful for the party of the second part, its successors or assigns, at any time thereafter, to sell the said premises hereby granted, or any part thereof, in the manner prescribed by law, and out of the moneys arising from said sale to retain the amount then due for principal, interest, and fines, together with the costs and charges for making such sale, and the overplus, if any there be, shall be paid by the party making such sale, on demand, to the said ......, ... heirs, executors, and assigns.

AND IT IS FURTHER HEREBY EXPRESSLY AGREED that should any default be made in the payment of said principal and interest, or of any part thereof, at any time when the same is made payable as hereinbefore provided, and the same shall remain unpaid and in arrears for the time of six months, or should any tax or assessment levied or imposed upon the premises hereinbefore described become due and payable and remain unpaid by the part.. of the first part for the time of six months, then and from thenceforth, that is to say, after the lapse of the said six months, the aforesaid principal sum or any and all sums then unpaid, with all arrearages of interest and fines thereon, shall, at the option of the said party of the second part, its successors or assigns, become and be due and payable immediately thereafter, although the period hereinbefore provided for the payment thereof may not then have expired, anything hereinbefore contained to the contrary thereof in any wise notwithstanding.

[Here insert the clause relating to insurance as found in the preceding form of mortgage under the act of 1887. Also the attestation clause and acknowledgment as there found.]

No. 7.

NEW YORK. BOND.

Form of Bond to be taken by an Association incorporated under the Act of 1851.

KNOW ALL MEN BY THESE PRESENTS that I, ..., of the ...... of ......, in the county of ......, and State

of New York, am held and firmly bound unto THE ......
ASSOCIATION OF THE ...... of ......, in the county of
......, and State of New York, in the sum of ......
dollars, lawful money of the United States, to be paid to the
said ...... association, or to its successors or assigns, for
which payment well and truly to be made ...... bind ......
and ...... heirs, executors or administrators, jointly and severally, firmly by these presents.

Sealed this ...... day of ...... in the year of our Lord one
thousand eight hundred and ......

THE CONDITION OF THIS OBLIGATION IS SUCH THAT, if the
above bounden ......, ... heirs, executors, or administrators,
shall and do well and truly pay or cause to be paid unto the
above-named ...... association, its successors or assigns, the
sum of ...... dollars, with interest thereon at the rate of six per
cent. per annum, in the manner and at the times provided in
and required by the articles of association and by-laws of the
obligee herein, special reference being had to such portions of
each thereof as relate particularly to loans made to borrowers
and the payment of such loans, principal, interest, and fines
upon defaulted payments, and to which said articles of association and by-laws reference is hereby made for the times and
conditions of the payment of said sum, with interest thereon,
and fines in case of defaulted payments, and which portions of
said articles of association and by-laws shall be deemed a part
of this obligation as fully and completely as though stated at
length herein, without fraud or delay, then the preceding obligation to be void; otherwise to remain in full force and
virtue.

AND IT IS FURTHER HEREBY EXPRESSLY AGREED, that should
any default be made in the payment of the said principal or
interest or any part thereof as the same are hereinbefore provided to be paid, and the same shall remain unpaid and in
arrears for the time of six months (or should any tax or assessment be levied or imposed upon the premises described in the
mortgage accompanying this bond, become due and payable,
and remain unpaid by the obligor herein for the time of six
months), then and from thenceforth, that is to say, after the
lapse of the said six months in either of the preceding events,

the aforesaid principal sum, or any and all sums then unpaid, with arrearages of interest and fines thereon, shall, at the option of the said ...... association, its successors or assigns, become and be due and payable immediately thereafter, although the period first above provided for the payment thereof may not then have expired, anything hereinbefore contained to the contrary notwithstanding.*

No. 8.

TREASURER'S BOND.

KNOW ALL MEN BY THESE PRESENTS that we, ...
....
are held and firmly bound unto The ...... Co-operative Savings and Loan Association of ......, in the county of ......, and State of ......, in the sum of ...... thousand dollars, lawful money of the United States, to be paid to the said ...... Co-operative Savings and Loan Association, its successor or assigns, for which payment well and truly to be made, we do hereby bind ourselves, our heirs, executors, and administrators jointly and severally, firmly by these presents.

Sealed with our seals and dated the ...... day of ......, 18...

Whereas the above bounden ...... has been duly elected Treasurer of The ...... Co-operative Savings and Loan Association,

Now, THEREFORE, the condition of the above obligation is such, that if the said ...... shall well, faithfully, and honestly in all things perform the duties of said office during his continuance in office, and shall, at the expiration of his said

---

* In the event the bond is accompanied by a mortgage, add the clause found in the preceding form of bond under the act of 1887, in reference to insurance; and in the event the bond is not accompanied by a mortgage, omit from the foregoing form the clause relating to taxes and assessments. The suggestions in the note to the preceding form for the bond under the act of 1887 are also applicable to the preparation of blanks under the act of 1851. For acknowledgment to this bond, see preceding forms.

office, or whenever and as often as required, make and render
unto said ...... Co-operative Savings and Loan Association, or
the Board of Directors thereof, a just and true account of all
moneys, securities, property, and other things which shall come
into his possession, custody, control, or charge as such officer,
and shall pay and deliver over to his successor in office, or any
other person duly authorized to receive the same, all sums of
money, securities, property, and other things belonging to said
...... Co-operative Savings and Loan Association, and in
his possession, control, or charge as Treasurer, then this obligation to be void, otherwise to remain in full force and effect.

.... (L. S.)
.... (L. S.)
.... (L. S.)

[The acknowledgment same as in form No. 5.]

No. 9.

ASSIGNMENT OF STOCK TO SECURE A LOAN.

KNOW ALL MEN BY THESE PRESENTS that I, ..., of the
...... of. ....., in the county of ......, and State of ......, in
consideration of a loan made to me by The ...... Co-operative
Savings and Loan Association of $......, have agreed to assign
and transfer and do hereby assign and transfer unto the said
association, its successors and assigns, all my right, title, and
interest in and to ...... shares of series No. ......, also ......
shares of series No. ......, of the capital stock of the said association now belonging to me and standing in my name, as a
security, collateral to my bond this day given to said association
for the payment of said loan and interest thereon at the time
and times and in the manner therein mentioned. And I hereby
authorize said association, in case I should make default in the
payment of said loan and interest thereon or any part thereof
as required by said bond, and shall so remain in default for six
months, to cancel said shares of stock above described and apply
the withdrawal value thereof at such time upon my said loan,
and in the event any surplus remains after the full payment of
said loan and interest thereon and fines, the same shall be paid

to me, my executors, administrators, or assigns, and I hereby covenant and agree with said association to continue to pay dues upon said shares of stock until said loan shall be wholly paid.

In witness whereof I have hereunto set my hand this ...... day of ......, 18...

....

[Acknowledgment same as in form No. 5.]

No. 10.

NOTICE OF REPAYMENT OF LOAN AND WITH-DRAWAL OF STOCK.

To the Board of Directors of the ...... Co-operative Savings and Loan Association.

GENTLEMEN: Please take notice that I have repaid my loan of ...... shares, less the withdrawal value of the following shares of stock which the association holds as security for the payment of said loan, viz., ... shares in series No. ...... and ...... shares in series No. ......

I further also hereby give notice of my desire to withdraw said shares of stock and have the withdrawal value thereof applied upon said loan, thereby completing the payment of the same; and for such purpose I hereby authorize you to direct that the order issued to pay such withdrawal value be made payable to the Treasurer of said association.

I request that you duly authorize the proper officers to execute a discharge of my mortgage to the association.

....

No. 11.

WITHDRAWAL NOTICE.

To the Board of Directors of the ...... Co-operative Savings and Loan Association.

GENTLEMEN: I hereby give notice of my desire to withdraw the following shares of stock owned by me and standing in my name on the books of your association, viz., ... shares, series ......; ...... shares, series ......

I hereby direct that the order issued for such withdrawal value be made payable to the order of myself.

Dated, ... 18...

....

─────────

No. 12.

STOCK PROXY.

KNOW ALL MEN BY THESE PRESENTS that I, ..., a stockholder in The ...... Co-operative Savings and Loan Association, have appointed and do hereby appoint ...., my true and lawful attorney, with power of substitution and revocation for me and in my name to vote, as fully as I might do if personally present, at the annual (or special) meeting of the stockholders of said association, to be held on the ...... day of ......, 18...

Witness my hand this ...... day of ......, 18...

....

State of ...... }
County of .. } ss.

On this ...... day of ......, 18.., before me, the subscriber, personally appeared ...., to me known to be the same person named in and who signed the foregoing proxy, and duly acknowledged that ..he.. executed the same.

....

─────────

No. 13.

DESCRIPTION OF SECURITIES OFFERED BY BORROWER AND REPORT OF FINANCE COMMITTEE THEREON.

To the Board of Directors of the ...... Co-operative Savings and Loan Association:

GENTLEMEN: For the purpose of securing the repayment of the loan of ...... shares, amounting to $......, which you have awarded to me, in addition to the usual bond required and as collateral thereto, I offer you the securities following: 1st., ... shares of series No. ...... of your association, now

standing in my name and upon which such loan is made. ......
shares of series No. ......, ... shares of series No. ...... ;
2d., a first mortgage on real estate known as No. ...... on
...... Street. The lot is ...... feet front and rear, and ......
deep. There is situate on said lot a ...... dwelling-house
facing ...... Street, having ...... stories. The first story
contains ...... rooms ...... finished; the second story contains ...... rooms ...... finished........................
....
....
There is also on the lot ....
....
The buildings are in ...... repair and insured as follows :
Dwelling-house at $. ......; barn at $. ....
....
The premises are assessed for taxation at $...................
    Dated ...., 18......

                                ....

The undersigned Finance Committee hereby report that they
have personally examined the real estate described in the foregoing application and find such description substantially correct, except..
....
....
We appraise the value thereof at $...... and approve of the
same for a loan of $......, provided the mortgage is accom-
panied by an abstract of title approved by the attorney of the
association and contains suitable provisions for insurance upon
the buildings against loss by fire or lightning for the benefit of
the association.
    Dated ...., 188...
                ....⎫
                ....⎬ *Finance Com.*
                ....⎭

No. 14.

CERTIFICATE OF STOCK.

Series No. ......   Issue of 18...

THE ...... CO-OPERATIVE
SAVINGS AND LOAN ASSOCIATION,
......, N. Y.

...... shares.   No. ......

This is to certify that ...... is entitled to ...... shares, series No. ...... of the capital stock of The .... Co-operative Savings and Loan Association, transferable only on the books of the said association in person or by attorney, in the presence of the President or Secretary, upon surrender of this certificate.

(L. S.)   Given under the seal of the association at ......,
       N. Y., ..., 18...

.............., *President.*
.............., *Secretary.*

....

No. 15.

FORM OF ASSIGNMENT OF SHARES OF STOCK.

(to be printed on the back of the certificate).

For value received I do hereby sell, assign, transfer, and set over unto ...... all my right, title, and interest in and to ...... shares, series No. ...... of the capital stock of The ...... Savings and Loan Association, and I do hereby constitute and appoint ...... my true and lawful attorney, irrevocable, for me and in my name and behalf to assign and transfer to ...... the said shares of capital stock hereby sold and for that purpose to do all acts and execute all papers necessary to perfect such sale and transfer upon the books of said association.

Witness my hand and seal this ...... day of ......, 18...

.... (L. S.)

[Acknowledgment clause same as in form No. 5.]

No. 16.

SHAREHOLDER'S PASS-BOOK.

18...	Dollars.	Cents.	
March.........			
April..........			
May...........			
June..........			
July...........			
August........			
September.....			
October........			
November.....			
December......			
January.......			
February......			

The above is a convenient form for the pass-book. The front cover has written upon it the name of the shareholder. One page, as above given, covers a year of time, in an association, of monthly dues. The officer receipting for the money fills in the amount paid opposite the month and signs his name to the right. The book can be made up to cover any length of time desired. Between each leaf should be bound in a thin blotting-paper, so that the receipting officer can close the book at once on making the entries, as a matter of saving time.

No. 17.   ANNUAL REPORT.

The ...... annual Report of the ...... Co-operative Savings and Loan Association from ......, 18.., to ......, 18..

RECEIPTS.		DISBURSEMENTS.	
Cash at last report...	$——	Mortgage loans......	$——
Dues...............	——	Stock loans.........	——
Interest............	——	Stock withdrawn.....	——
Fines..............	——	Matured stock.......	——
Entrance fees.......	——	Salary of secretary...	——
Transfer fees.......	——	Salary of treasurer...	——
Premiums..........	——	Rent..............	——
Loans repaid.......	——	Account-books......	——
Dues paid in advance.	——	Printing...........	——
Borrowed money.....	——	Paid borrowed money.	——
		Balance cash........	——
Total........	$——	Total........	$——

PROFITS.		LOSS.	
Undivided profits at last report.......	$——	Salaries............	$——
Interest............	——	Rent..............	——
Premiums..........	——	Account-books......	——
Fines..............	——	Printing...........	——
Entrance fees.......	——	Incidental expenses..	——
Transfer fees.......	——	Amount dividends declared.........	——
Profits on withdrawals	——	Balance undivided profits.........	——
Total........	$——	Total........	$——

ASSETS.

Loans secured by first mortgage on real estate........	$——
Loans secured by pledge of stock of the association...	——
Dues, interest, and fines in arrears...	——
Cash in the treasury.............................	——
Other personal property..........................	——
Total..................................	$——

LIABILITIES.

Capital stock, ... series, ... shares at $——, $———
" " .... " .... " ——, ————
" " .... " .... " ——, ————
" " .... " .... " ——, ————
Dues and interest paid in advance............. ———
Undivided profits......................... ———
Borrowed money........................... ———

Total............................. $———

STATISTICS.

Total number of shares outstanding................ ———
Total number of shareholders..................... ———
Greatest number of shares held by one shareholder.... ———
Total number of shares borrowed upon............. ———
Total number of borrowers........................ ———
Largest loan.................................... $———

NUMBER OF SHARES BORROWED UPON IN EACH SERIES.

.... series .... series .... series .... series.
.... shares .... shares .... shares .... shares.

AMOUNT DUES PAID, AMOUNT OF PROFITS, HOLDING VALUE, AND WITHDRAWAL VALUE OF ONE SHARE IN EACH SERIES.

Amount dues paid ..... series ..... series ..... series .....
Amount of profits ....
Holding value ....
Withdrawal value ....

Dated ...., 18..

................., *Secretary.*

The undersigned, auditing committee of the stockholders, hereby report that they have carefully examined the books of the Secretary, and verified the entries therein, and find the foregoing report correct in all respects.

Dated ...., 18..

.... ⎫
.... ⎬ *Auditing Committee.*
.... ⎭

No. 18.

SECRETARY'S MONTHLY REPORT.

YEAR.	Total shares outstanding.	Dues paid.	Total shares borrowed upon.	Interest paid.	Fines paid.	Entrance fees paid.	Transfer fees paid.	Premiums paid.	Total receipts exclusive of loans repaid.
Jan...									
Feb...									
March									
April..									

Stock withdrawn.				Loans repaid.				
Series No.	No. of shares.	Amount paid.	Profits retained by association.	Series No.	No. of shares.	Amount	Expenses paid.	Remarks.

NOTE.—The lower part of the above form belongs on the right of the upper part. In preparing a blank for use it should be so placed, and the rulings across the page extended to include a year. If the association has become the owner of real estate, and receives rents, a proper heading and ruling should be inserted to enter them.

.

GENERAL INDEX.

THE END.

ORIGINS OF THE ENGLISH PEOPLE AND OF THE ENGLISH LANGUAGE. COMPILED FROM THE BEST AND LATEST AUTHORITIES.

By JEAN ROEMER, LL. D., Professor of the French Language and Literature and Vice-President of the College of the City of New York. With Chart and Lithographic Fac-similes of Anglo-Saxon and Early French Writings. 1 vol., 8vo, pages xxiii + 658, cloth. Price, $3.50.

This work is essentially an introduction to the study of early English literature. Founded on the latest works of specialists, who have explored the many branches of the subject, it traces the sources of Modern English among the various races of men—Celts, Romans, Saxons, Danes, and Normans—who, at various epochs, have found their way into the British Isles ; and, by inquiring into the origin and national characteristics of these races, their customs, wants, and forms of religion, their social and political differences, their relative progress in the arts of civilized life, it enables the student to draw his own conclusions as to the various influences tending to a corresponding fusion of their various idioms and dialects, resulting in the formation of that great and wonderful language which, from a mere jargon, as it was at first, has grown into the national speech of England.

THE INTERNATIONAL EDUCATION SERIES. Edited by W. T. HARRIS, LL. D.

THE PHILOSOPHY OF EDUCATION. By JOHANN KARL FRIEDRICH ROSENKRANZ. 12mo, cloth. Price, $1.50.

A HISTORY OF EDUCATION. By Professor F. V. N. PAINTER, of Roanoke College, Virginia. 12mo, cloth. Price, $1.50.

THE RISE AND EARLY CONSTITUTION OF UNIVERSITIES. With a Survey of Mediæval Education. By S. S. LAURIE, LL. D. 12mo, cloth. Price, $1.50.

THE VENTILATION AND WARMING OF SCHOOL BUILDINGS. By GILBERT B. MORRISON. 12mo, cloth. Price, 75 cents.

ELEMENTARY PSYCHOLOGY AND EDUCATION. By Dr. J. BALDWIN. 12mo, cloth. Price, $1.50.

THE EDUCATION OF MAN. By FRIEDRICH FROEBEL. Translated from the German and Annotated by W. N. HAILMANN, A. M., Superintendent of Public Schools at La Porte, Indiana. 12mo, cloth. Price, $1.50.

(Other volumes to follow.)

THE COLLEGE AND THE CHURCH: THE "HOW I WAS EDUCATED" PAPERS, AND THE DENOMINATIONAL "CONFESSIONS," from "The Forum Magazine."

Crown 8vo, cloth, gilt top. Price, $1.50.

The two series of articles, "How I was Educated" and "Confessions," attracted great attention as they appeared in "The Forum," and are now published in one volume in obedience to numerous requests. The "Confessions" are printed anonymously, but the "How I was Educated" papers are signed, the authors being some of the most distinguished of American scholars.

New York: D. APPLETON & CO., 1, 3, & 5 Bond Street.

APPLETONS' PHYSICAL GEOGRAPHY. Illustrated with engravings, diagrams and maps in color, and including a separate chapter on the geological history and the physical features of the United States. By JOHN D. QUACKENBOS, A. M., M. D., Adjunct Professor of the English Language and Literature, Columbia College, New York, *Literary Editor ;* JOHN S. NEWBERRY, M. D., LL. D., Professor of Geology and Paleontology, Columbia College; CHARLES H. HITCHCOCK, Ph. D., Professor of Geology and Mineralogy, Dartmouth College ; W. LE CONTE STEVENS, Ph. D., Professor of Physics, Packer Collegiate Institute; HENRY GANNETT, E. M., Chief Geographer of the United States Geological Survey; WILLIAM H. DALL, of the United States National Museum; C. HART MERRIAM, M. D., Ornithologist of the Department of Agriculture; NATHANIEL L. BRITTON, E. M., Ph. D., Lecturer in Botany, Columbia College ; GEORGE F. KUNZ, Gem Expert and Mineralogist with Messrs. Tiffany & Co., New York; Lieutenant GEORGE M. STONEY, Naval Department, Washington. Large 4to. Cloth, $1.90.

APPLETONS' ATLAS OF THE UNITED STATES. Consisting of General Maps of the United States and Territories, and a County Map of each of the States, all printed in Colors, together with Railway Maps and Descriptive Text Outlining the History, Geography, and Political and Educational Organization of the States, with latest Statistics of their Resources and Industries. Imperial 8vo, cloth. $1.50.

THE EARTH AND ITS INHABITANTS. By ELISÉE RECLUS. Translated and edited by E. G. Ravenstein. With numerous Illustrations, Maps, and Charts.

M. Reclus the distinguished French Geographer has given in this work the most thorough and comprehensive treatise on the countries of the world yet produced. Maps, plans, and illustrations are lavish. It is subdivided as follows :

EUROPE, in 5 volumes. Imperial 8vo.

ASIA, in 4 volumes. Imperial 8vo.

AFRICA, in 3 volumes. Imperial 8vo.

AMERICA. (*In preparation.*)

Price, $6.00 per volume in library binding. Sold only by subscription.

A NEW PHYSICAL GEOGRAPHY. By ELISÉE RECLUS. In two volumes. Vol. I. The Earth. Vol. II. The Ocean, Atmosphere, and Life. With Maps and Illustrations. Price, $6.00 per volume, library binding. Sold only by subscription.

New York: D. APPLETON & CO., 1, 3, & 5 Bond Street.

THE HISTORY OF BIMETALLISM IN THE UNITED STATES. By J. Laurence Laughlin, Ph. D., Assistant Professor of Political Economy in Harvard University ; author of "The Study of Political Economy," etc. With Sixteen Charts and numerous Tables. One volume. 8vo. Cloth, $2.25.

"Although the plan of this book was conceived with the view of presenting simply a history of bimetallism in the United States, it has been necessary, in the nature of the subject, to make it something more than that. And yet it was my hope that the effect of an historical inquiry in suppressing some of the theoretical vagaries of the day might be realized by showing what our actual experience with bimetallism has been in contrast with the assertions of some writers as to what it may be."—*From Preface.*

THE STUDY OF POLITICAL ECONOMY. HINTS TO STUDENTS AND TEACHERS. By J. Laurence Laughlin, Ph. D., Assistant Professor of Political Economy in Harvard University. 16mo. Cloth, $1.00.

"The existence of this little book is due to an attempt to convey, by lectures to students, an understanding of the position which political economy holds in regard, not merely to its actual usefulness for every citizen, but to its disciplinary power. . . . The interest which the public now manifests in economic studies led me to put the material of my lectures into a general form, in order that they might assist inquirers in any part of the country."—*From Preface.*

MILL'S PRINCIPLES OF POLITICAL ECONOMY: ABRIDGED WITH CRITICAL, BIBLIOGRAPHICAL, AND EXPLANATORY NOTES, AND A SKETCH OF THE HISTORY OF POLITICAL ECONOMY. By J. Laurence Laughlin, Ph. D., Assistant Professor of Political Economy in Harvard University With Twenty-four Maps and Charts. A Text-book for Colleges. 8vo. 658 pages. Cloth, $3.50.

"An experience of five years with Mr. Mill's treatise in the class-room convinced me, not only of the great usefulness of what still remains one of the most lucid and systematic books yet published which cover the whole range of the study, but I have also been convinced of the need of such additions as should give the results of later thinking, without militating against the general tenor of Mr. Mill's system; of such illustrations as should fit it better for American students, by turning their attention to the application of principles in the facts around us ; of a bibliography which should make it easier to get at the writers of other schools who offer opposing views on controverted questions; and of some attempts to lighten those parts of his work in which Mr. Mill frightened away the reader by an appearance of too great abstractness, and to render them, if possible, more easy of comprehension to the student who first approaches Political Economy through this author."—*From Preface.*

POLITICAL ECONOMY. By W. Stanley Jevons, Professor of Logic and Political Economy in Owens College, Manchester. 18mo. Flexible cloth, 45 cents.

MONEY AND THE MECHANISM OF EXCHANGE. By W. Stanley Jevons. 12mo. Cloth, $1.75.

D. APPLETON & CO.'S PUBLICATIONS.

ALEXANDER BAIN'S WORKS.

THE SENSES AND THE INTELLECT. By ALEXANDER BAIN. LL. D., Professor of Logic in the University of Aberdeen. 8vo. Cloth, $5.00.

The object of this treatise is to give a full and systematic account of two principal divisions of the science of mind—the senses and the intellect. The value of the third edition of the work is greatly enhanced by an account of the psychology of Aristotle, which has been contributed by Mr. Grote.

THE EMOTIONS AND THE WILL. By ALEXANDER BAIN, LL. D. 8vo. Cloth, $5.00.

The present publication is a sequel to the former one on "The Senses and the Intellect," and completes a systematic exposition of the human mind.

MENTAL SCIENCE. A Compendium of Psychology and the History of Philosophy. Designed as a Text-book for High-Schools and Colleges. By ALEXANDER BAIN, LL. D. 12mo. Cloth, leather back, $1.50.

The present volume is an abstract of two voluminous works, "The Senses and the Intellect" and "The Emotions and the Will," and presents in a compressed and lucid form the views which are there more extensively elaborated.

MORAL SCIENCE. A Compendium of Ethics. By ALEXANDER BAIN, LL. D. 12mo. Cloth, leather back, $1.50.

The present dissertation falls under two divisions. The first division, entitled The Theory of Ethics, gives an account of the questions or points brought into discussion, and handles at length the two of greatest prominence, the Ethical Standard and the Moral Faculty. The second division—on the Ethical Systems—is a full detail of all the systems, ancient and modern.

MIND AND BODY. Theories of their Relations. By ALEXANDER BAIN, LL. D. 12mo. Cloth, $1.50.

"A forcible statement of the connection between mind and body, studying their subtile interworkings by the light of the most recent physiological investigations."—*Christian Register.*

LOGIC, DEDUCTIVE AND INDUCTIVE. By ALEXANDER BAIN, LL. D. Revised edition. 12mo. Cloth, leather back, $2.00.

EDUCATION AS A SCIENCE. By ALEXANDER BAIN, LL. D. 12mo. Cloth, $1.75.

ENGLISH COMPOSITION AND RHETORIC. Enlarged edition. Part I. Intellectual Elements of Style. By ALEXANDER BAIN, LL. D., Emeritus Professor of Logic in the University of Aberdeen. 12mo. Cloth, leather back, $1.50.

ON TEACHING ENGLISH. With Detailed Examples and an Inquiry into the Definition of Poetry. By ALEXANDER BAIN, LL. D. 12mo. Cloth, $1.25.

PRACTICAL ESSAYS. By ALEXANDER BAIN, LL. D. 12mo. Cloth, $1.50.

New York: D. APPLETON & CO., 1, 3, & 5 Bond Street.

BOOKS FOR EVERY HOUSEHOLD.

Cooley's Cyclopædia of Practical Receipts,

And Collateral Information in the Arts, Manufactures, Professions, and Trades, including Medicine, Pharmacy, and Domestic Economy. Designed as a Comprehensive Supplement to the Pharmacopœia, and General Book of Reference for the Manufacturer, Tradesman, Amateur, and Heads of Families. *Sixth edition.* Revised and partly rewritten by RICHARD V. TUSON, Professor of Chemistry and Toxicology in the Royal Veterinary College. Complete in two volumes, 8vo, 1,796 pages. With Illustrations. Price, $9.00.

"The great characteristic of this work is its general usefulness. In covering such diverse subjects, the very best and most recent research seems to have been sought for, and the work is remarkable for intelligent industry. This very complete work can, then, be highly recommended as fulfilling to the letter what it purports to be—a cyclopædia of practical receipts."—*New York Times.*

"It is a well-edited special work, compiled with excellent judgment for special purposes, which are kept constantly in mind. If it is more comprehensive than its title suggests, it is only because it is impossible to define the limits of its purpose with exactitude, or to describe its contents upon a title-page. Illustrations of the text are freely used, and the mechanical execution of the work is excellent."—*New York Evening Post.*

The Chemistry of Common Life.

By the late Professor JAMES F. W. JOHNSTON. A new edition, revised and enlarged, and brought down to the Present Time, by ARTHUR HERBERT CHURCH, M. A., Oxon., author of "Food: its Sources, Constituents, and Uses." Illustrated with Maps and numerous Engravings on Wood. In one vol., 12mo, 592 pages. Cloth. Price, $2.00.

SUMMARY OF CONTENTS.—The Air we Breathe; the Water we Drink; the Soil we Cultivate; the Plant we Rear; the Bread we Eat; the Beef we Cook; the Beverages we Infuse; the Sweets we Extract; the Liquors we Ferment; the Narcotics we Indulge in; the Poisons we Select; the Odors we Enjoy; the Smells we Dislike; the Colors we Admire; What we Breathe and Breathe for; What, How, and Why we Digest; the Body we Cherish; the Circulation of Matter.

In the number and variety of striking illustrations, in the simplicity of its style, and in the closeness and cogency of its arguments, Professor Johnston's "Chemistry of Common Life" has as yet found no equal among the many books of a similar character which its success originated, and it steadily maintains its pre-eminence in the popular scientific literature of the day. In preparing this edition for the press, the editor had the opportunity of consulting Professor Johnston's private and corrected copy of "The Chemistry of Common Life," who had, before his death, gleaned very many fresh details, so that he was able not only to incorporate with his revision some really valuable matter, but to learn the kind of addition which the author contemplated.

New York: D. APPLETON & CO., 1, 3, & 5 Bond Street.

THE

HISTORICAL REFERENCE - BOOK,

COMPRISING :

*A Chronological Table of Universal History, a Chronological Diction-
ary of Universal History, a Biographical Dictionary.*

WITH GEOGRAPHICAL NOTES.

FOR THE USE OF STUDENTS, TEACHERS, AND READERS.

By LOUIS HEILPRIN.

New edition. Crown 8vo. Half leather, $3.00.

"A second revised edition of Mr. Louis Heilprin's 'Historical Reference-Book' has just appeared, marking the well-earned success of this admirable work—a dictionary of dates, a dictionary of events (with a special gazetteer for the places mentioned), and a concise biographical dictionary, all in one, and all in the highest degree trustworthy. Mr. Heilprin's revision is as thorough as his original work. Any one can test it by running over the list of persons deceased since this manual first appeared. Corrections, too, have been made, as we can testify in one instance at least."—*New York Evening Post.*

"One of the most complete, compact, and valuable works of reference yet produced."—*Troy Daily Times.*

"Unequaled in its field."—*Boston Courier.*

"A small library in itself."—*Chicago Dial.*

"An invaluable book of reference, useful alike to the student and the general reader. The arrangement could scarcely be better or more convenient."—*New York Herald.*

"The conspectus of the world's history presented in the first part of the book is as full as the wisest terseness could put within the space."—*Philadelphia American.*

"We miss hardly anything that we should consider desirable, and we have not been able to detect a single mistake or misprint."—*New York Nation.*

"So far as we have tested the accuracy of the present work we have found it without flaw."—*Christian Union.*

"The conspicuous merits of the work are condensation and accuracy. These points alone should suffice to give the 'Historical Reference-Book' a place in every public and private library."—*Boston Beacon.*

"The method of the tabulation is admirable for ready reference."—*New York Home Journal.*

"This cyclopædia of condensed knowledge is a work that will speedily become a necessity to the general reader, as well as to the student."—*Detroit Free Press.*

"For clearness, correctness, and the readiness with which the reader can find the information of which he is in search, the volume is far in advance of any work of its kind with which we are acquainted."—*Boston Saturday Evening Gazette.*

"The latest dates have been given. *The geographical notes which accompany the historical incidents are a novel addition, and exceedingly helpful.* The size also commends it, making it convenient for constant reference, while the three divisions and careful elimination of minor and uninteresting incidents make it much easier to find dates and events about which accuracy is necessary. Sir William Hamilton avers that too retentive a memory tends to hinder the development of the judgment by presenting too much for decision. A work like this is thus better than memory. It is a 'mental larder' which needs no care, and whose contents are ever available."—*New York University Quarterly.*

New York: D. APPLETON & CO., 1, 3, & 5 Bond Street.

VALUABLE HAND-BOOKS.

ERRORS IN THE USE OF ENGLISH. By the late WILLIAM B. HODGSON, LL. D., Professor of Political Economy in the University of Edinburgh. American revised edition. 12mo, cloth, $1.50.

" This posthumous work of Dr. Hodgson deserves a hearty welcome, for it is sure to do good service for the object it has in view—improved accuracy in the use of the English language. . . . Perhaps its chief use will be in very distinctly proving with what wonderful carelessness or incompetency the English language is generally written. For the examples of error here brought together are not picked from obscure or inferior writings. Among the grammatical sinners whose trespasses are here recorded appear many of our best-known authors and publications."—*The Academy.*

GRAMMAR WITHOUT A MASTER.

THE ENGLISH GRAMMAR OF WILLIAM COBBETT. Carefully revised and annotated by ALFRED AYRES. With Index. 18mo, cloth, extra, $1.00.

" I know it well, and have read it with great admiration."—RICHARD GRANT WHITE.

" Cobbett's Grammar is probably the most readable grammar ever written. For the purposes of self-education it is unrivaled."—*From the Editor's Preface.*

THE ORTHOEPIST: A Pronouncing Manual, containing about Three Thousand Five Hundred Words, including a Considerable Number of the Names of Foreign Authors, Artists, etc., that are often mispronounced. By ALFRED AYRES. 18mo, cloth, extra, $1.00.

" It gives us pleasure to say that we think the author, in the treatment of this very difficult and intricate subject, English pronunciation, gives proof of not only an unusual degree of orthoëpical knowledge, but also, for the most part, of rare judgment and taste."—JOSEPH THOMAS, LL. D., *in Literary World.*

THE VERBALIST: A Manual devoted to Brief Discussions of the Right and the Wrong Use of Words, and to some other matters of Interest to those who would Speak and Write with Propriety, including a Treatise on Punctuation. By ALFRED AYRES. 18mo, cloth, extra, $1.00.

" This is the best kind of an English grammar. It teaches the right use of our mother-tongue by giving instances of the wrong use of it, and showing why they are wrong."—*The Churchman.*

" Every one can learn something from this volume, and most of us a great deal."—*Springfield Republican.*

New York: D. APPLETON & CO., 1, 3, & 5 Bond Street.

more authoritative than ever before. This last revision will be without doubt, both from its desirable form and accurate text, the standard one."— *Boston Traveller.*

" Our examination of the first volume leads us to believe that the thought of the historian loses nothing by the abbreviation of the text. A closer and later approximation to the best results of scholarship and criticism is reached. The public gains by its more compact brevity and in amount of matter, and in economy of time and money."—*The Independent* (New York).

" There is nothing to be said at this day of the value of ' Bancroft.' Its authority is no longer in dispute, and as a piece of vivid and realistic historical writing it stands among the best works of its class. It may be taken for granted that this new edition will greatly extend its usefulness."—*Philadelphia North American.*

" While it is not quite true that the marks of Mr. Bancroft's revision of his great history of the United States are visible on every page, a careful comparison of the earlier editions and this shows that the claim to improvement is by no means ill-founded. Sometimes whole paragraphs have been cut out; still oftener the extravagances of a youthful style have been carefully pruned, and the gain has been manifest in sobriety and effect."— *Philadelphia Press.*

" The work is much improved in its new dress and revised form, and will be welcomed by all, for Bancroft's history of our country is still *facile princeps* among histories of our land."—*Chicago Tribune.*

" Thus far he has removed many of the objections which stood against his history as a work of permanent value; and there is a certain solid, thorough, substantial character to his great history which gives it a permanent weight in the world of letters. The work now takes rank with the best histories of the school of philosophical narrative to which the author belongs."—*Boston Herald.*

" The edition of 1876 exhibited no little pruning and correction; but the author has again gone over the entire field, and, with a care and devotion worthy of the theme and of his reputation, has wrought what he says must be *his last revision.* This latest edition will be sought by many who have for years been familiar with its predecessors."—*Utica* (N. Y.) *Herald.*

For sale by all booksellers; or sent by mail, post-paid, on receipt of price.

New York: D. APPLETON & CO., Publishers, 1, 3, & 5 Bond Street.

THE
REAR-GUARD OF THE REVOLUTION.
WITH PORTRAIT OF JOHN SEVIER, AND MAP.

JOHN SEVIER AS A COMMONWEALTH-BUILDER.
WITH MAP.

THE ADVANCE-GUARD OF WESTERN CIVILIZATION.
WITH PORTRAIT OF JAMES ROBERTSON, AND MAP.

By JAMES R. GILMORE
(*Edmund Kirke*).

Each work 12mo, cloth - - - - - - - - - **Price, $1.50.**

These three volumes are narratives of the adventures of the pioneers that first crossed the Alleghanies and settled in what is now Tennessee, under the leadership of two remarkable men, James Robertson and John Sevier.

"They cover a neglected period of American history, and they disclose facts well worthy the attention of historians—namely, that these Western men turned the tide of the American Revolution, and subsequently saved the newly-formed Union from disruption, and thereby made possible our present great republic. This should be enough to secure for their story an attentive hearing, had it not the added charm of presenting to view three characters—John Sevier, James Robertson, and Isaac Shelby—who are as worthy of the imitation of our American youth as any in their country's history."

From a paper adopted by the Tennessee Historical Society.

"Mr. Edmund Kirke sojourned for several years in Western North Carolina and in East Tennessee, and, being fascinated with our previous history, he became diligent in the collection of facts, which are here embodied in a most interesting volume. The matter does not consist of mere sketches or recitals, but relates a history, and in a style elegant in expression and suited to the dignity of the subject."

From JOHN SEVIER, of Tennessee, a great-grandson of Governor Sevier.

"Your book ('John Sevier') came to me by accident. I read it, and found the facts all related just as they have been told to me by father and grandfather, but clothed in a style and language that must make the work as entertaining as a romance."

From Hon. JOHN M. LEA, *President of the Tennessee Historical Society, Nashville.*

"The 'Rear-Guard' has given a fresh interest in the name of Governor Sevier, and, in common with all the people of Tennessee, we are under obligations to you for the faithful and fascinating manner in which you have related our pioneer history."

"These episodes are as fascinating as the legends of the Scottish Highlands, or middle-age chivalry."—*The Eclectic Magazine.*

"The story of a patriot like John Sevier, told as well as Mr. Gilmore tells it, must make the ideals of the young citizen—and the old one, too, for that matter —higher and purer."—*The North American Review.*

"John Sevier was a man with as strong and marked a personality as Mr. Gilmore could have desired. He was commanding, original, and picturesque." —*The New York Independent.*

D. APPLETON & CO., PUBLISHERS, NEW YORK.

www.ingramcontent.com/pod-product-compliance
Lightning Source LLC
Chambersburg PA
CBHW021216270326
41929CB00010B/1149